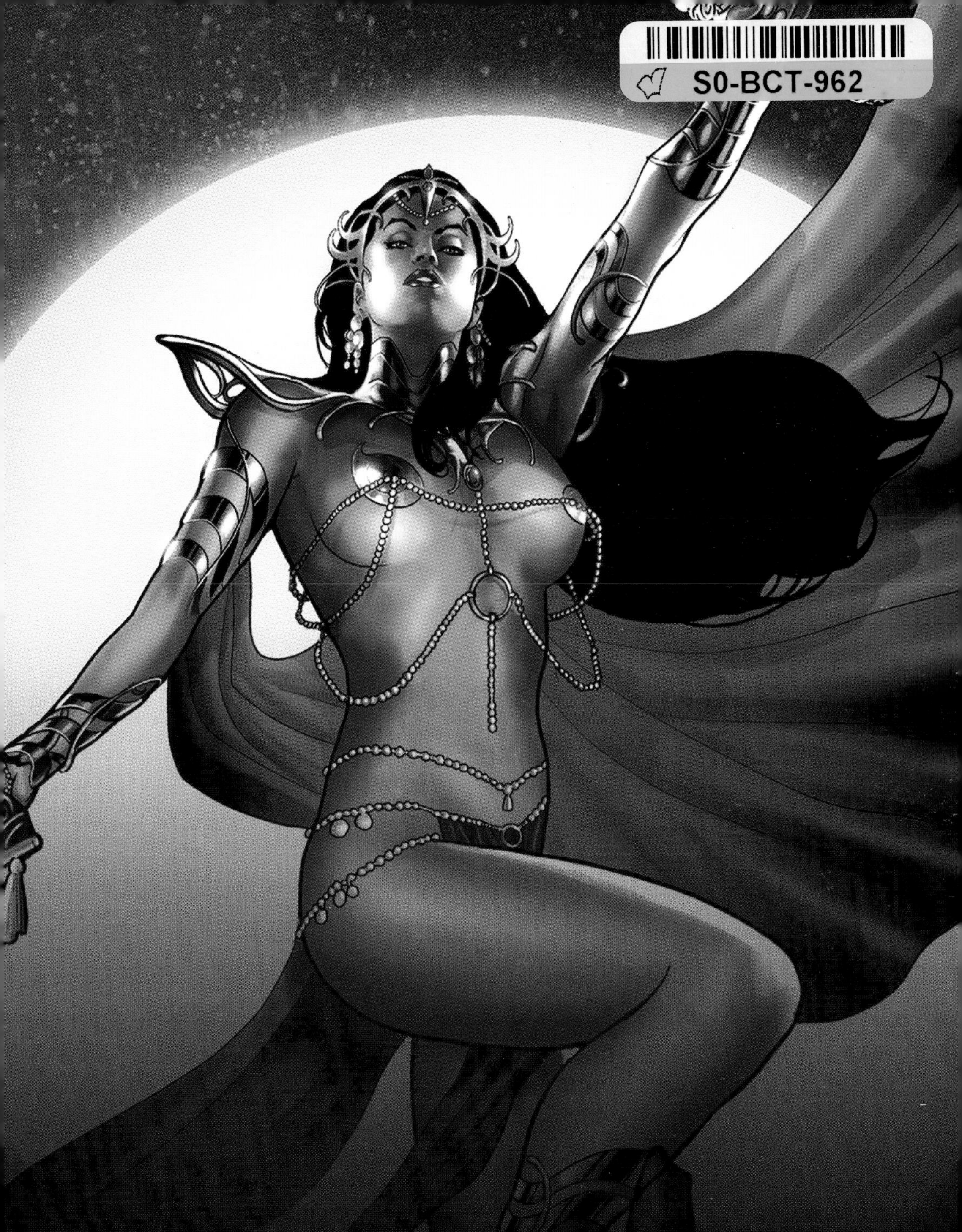

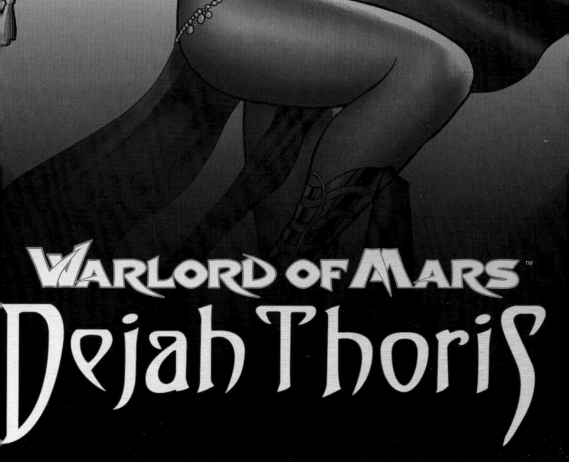

# WARLORD OF MARS™
# Dejah Thoris

# WARLORD
# Dejah Thoris

## volume two:
## PIRATE QUEEN OF MARS

written by
## ARVID NELSON

illustrated by
## CARLOS RAFAEL

colored by
## CARLOS LOPEZ

lettered by
## MARSHALL DILLON

collection cover by
## PAUL RENAUD

based on the stories of
## EDGAR RICE BURROUGHS

collection design by JASON ULLMEYER

This volume collects issues 6-10 of Warlord of Mars: Dejah Thoris
by Dynamite Entertainment

WWW.DYNAMITE.NET

NICK BARRUCCI — PRESIDENT
JUAN COLLADO — CHIEF OPERATING OFFICER
JOSEPH RYBANDT — EDITOR
RICH YOUNG — DIRECTOR BUSINESS DEVELOPMENT
JOSH JOHNSON — CREATIVE DIRECTOR
JASON ULLMEYER — SENIOR DESIGNER
JOSH GREEN — TRAFFIC COORDINATOR
CHRIS CANIANO — PRODUCTION ASSISTANT

WARLORD OF MARS™: DEJAH THORIS VOLUME 2: PIRATE QUEEN OF MARS. Contains materials or
published in Warlord of Mars: Dejah Thoris #6-10. Published by Dynamite Entertainment. 155 Ninth Ave. S
Runnemede, NJ 08078. Warlord of Mars is ™ and © 2012 Savage Tales Entertainment, llc. All rights reserved.
MITE, DYNAMITE ENTERTAINMENT and the Dynamite Entertainment colophon are ® and © 2012 DFI. All name
acters, events, and locales in this publication are entirely fictional. Any resemblance to actual persons (living or
events or places, without satiric intent, is coincidental. No portion of this book may be reproduced by any mean
ital or print) without the written permission of Dynamite Entertainment except for review purposes. The sca
uploading and distribution of this book via the Internet or via any other means without the permission of the pu
is illegal and punishable by law. Please purchase only authorized electronic editions, and do not participat
encourage electronic piracy of copyrighted materials. **Printed in Canada**

For information regarding press, media rights, foreign rights, licensing, promotions, and advertising e-mail:
marketing@dynamite.net

First Edition    ISBN-10: 1-60690-267-9    ISBN-13: 978-1-60690-267-7    10 9 8 7 6 5 4 3 2 1

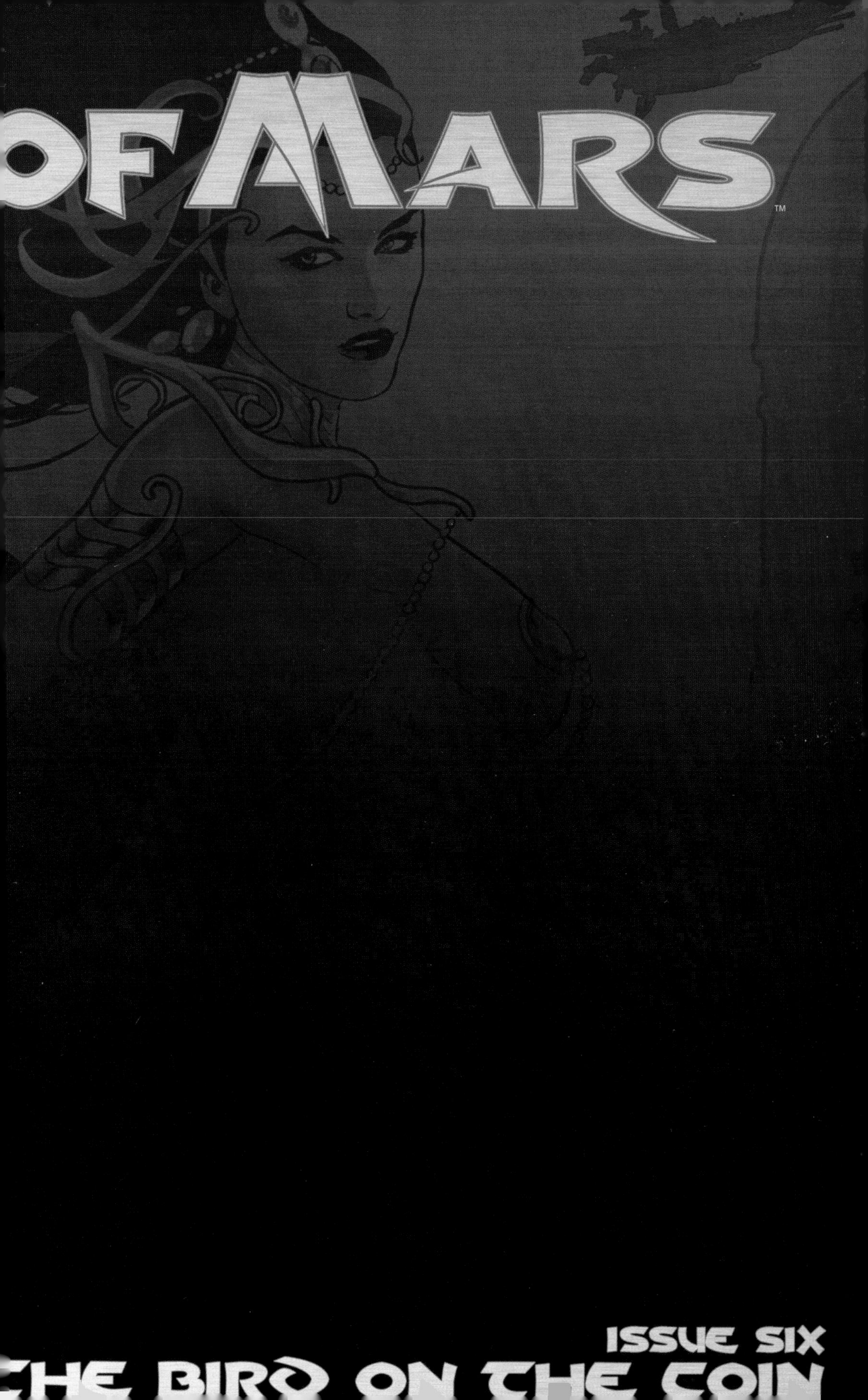
OF MARS™
ISSUE SIX
HE BIRD ON THE COIN

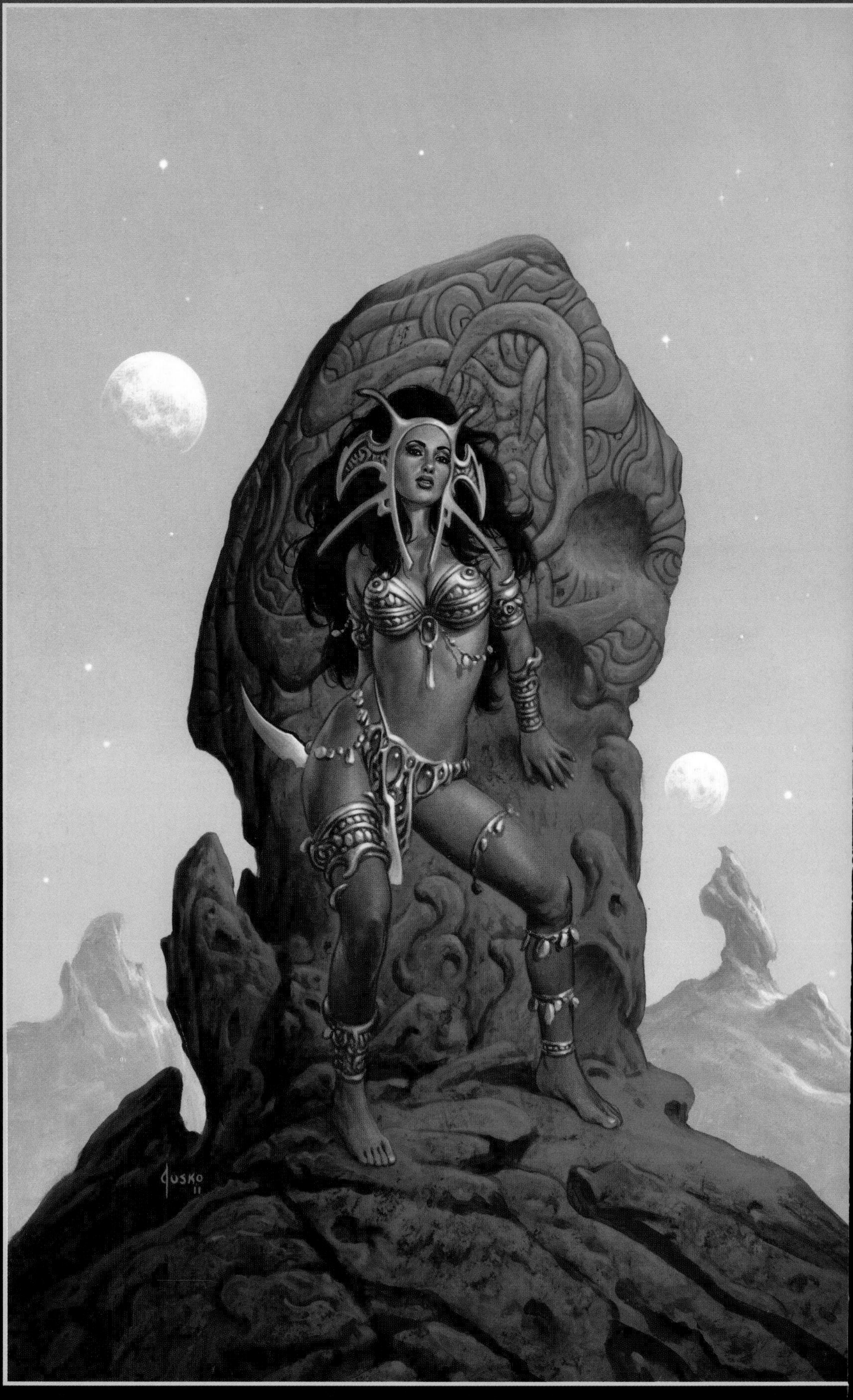

issue # 6 cover by **JOE JUSKO**

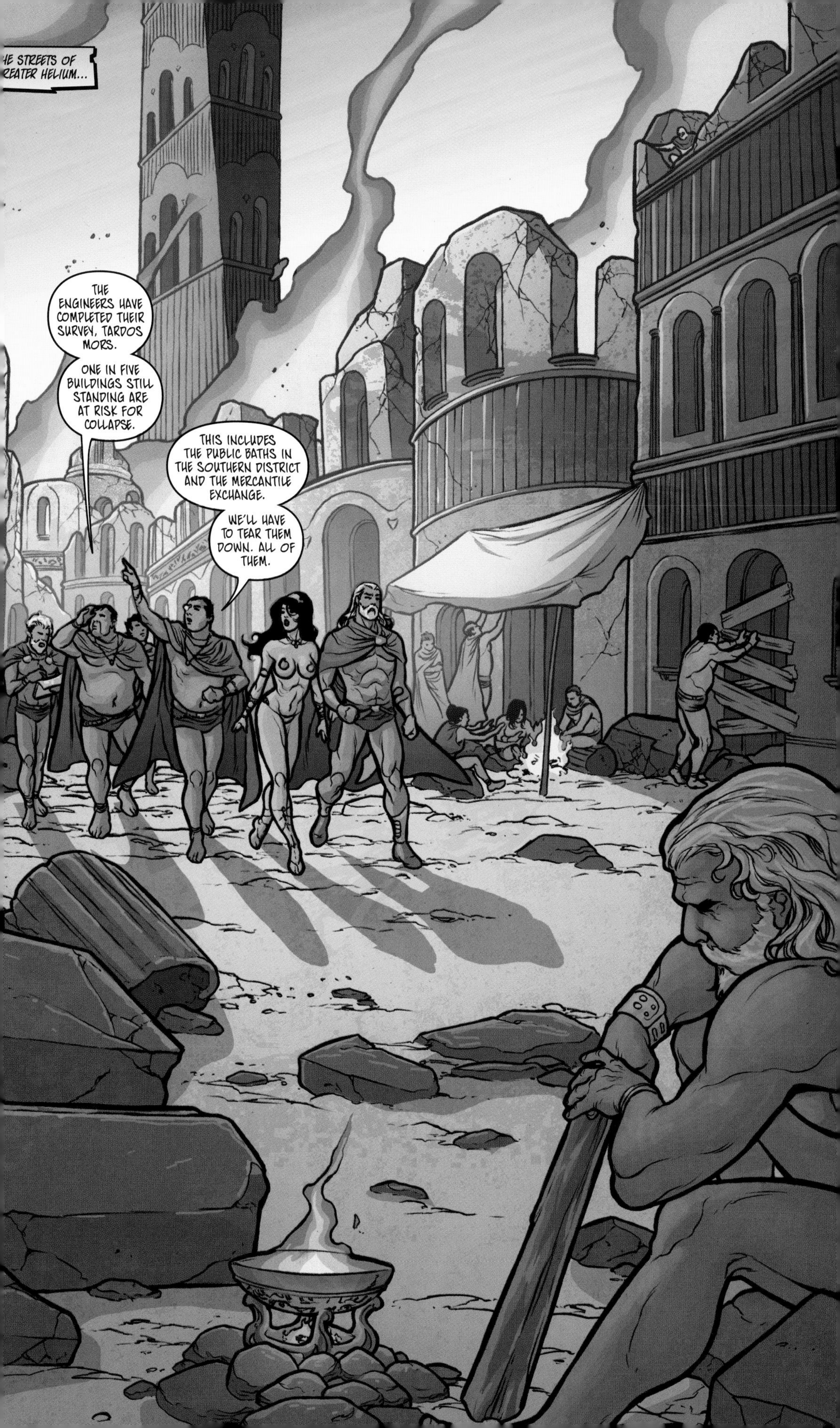
HE STREETS OF
REATER HELIUM...
THE ENGINEERS HAVE COMPLETED THEIR SURVEY, TARDOS MORS.
ONE IN FIVE BUILDINGS STILL STANDING ARE AT RISK FOR COLLAPSE.
THIS INCLUDES THE PUBLIC BATHS IN THE SOUTHERN DISTRICT AND THE MERCANTILE EXCHANGE.
WE'LL HAVE TO TEAR THEM DOWN. ALL OF THEM.

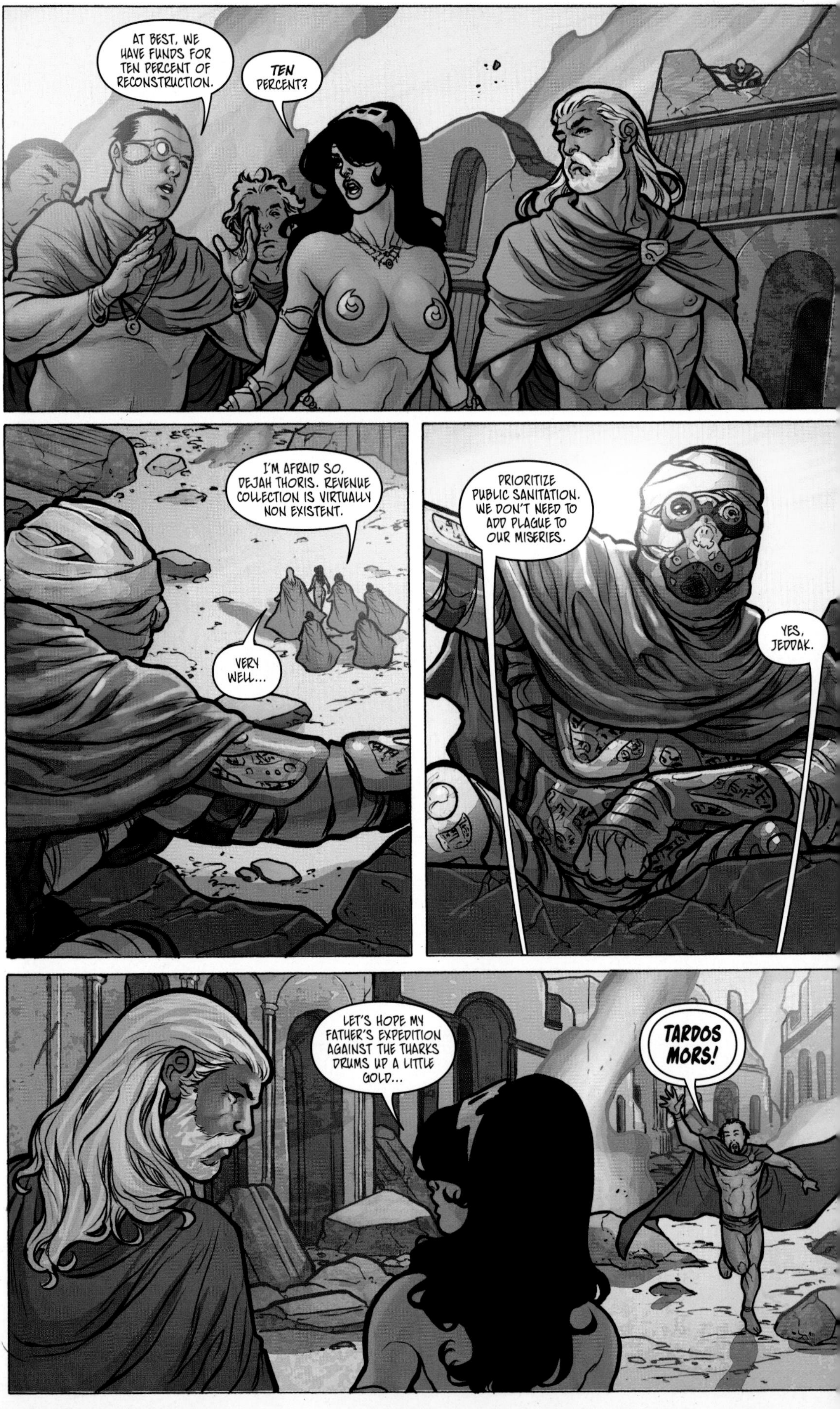
AT BEST, WE HAVE FUNDS FOR TEN PERCENT OF RECONSTRUCTION.
TEN PERCENT?
I'M AFRAID SO, DEJAH THORIS. REVENUE COLLECTION IS VIRTUALLY NON EXISTENT.
VERY WELL...
PRIORITIZE PUBLIC SANITATION. WE DON'T NEED TO ADD PLAGUE TO OUR MISERIES.
YES, JEDDAK.
LET'S HOPE MY FATHER'S EXPEDITION AGAINST THE THARKS DRUMS UP A LITTLE GOLD...
TARDOS MORS!

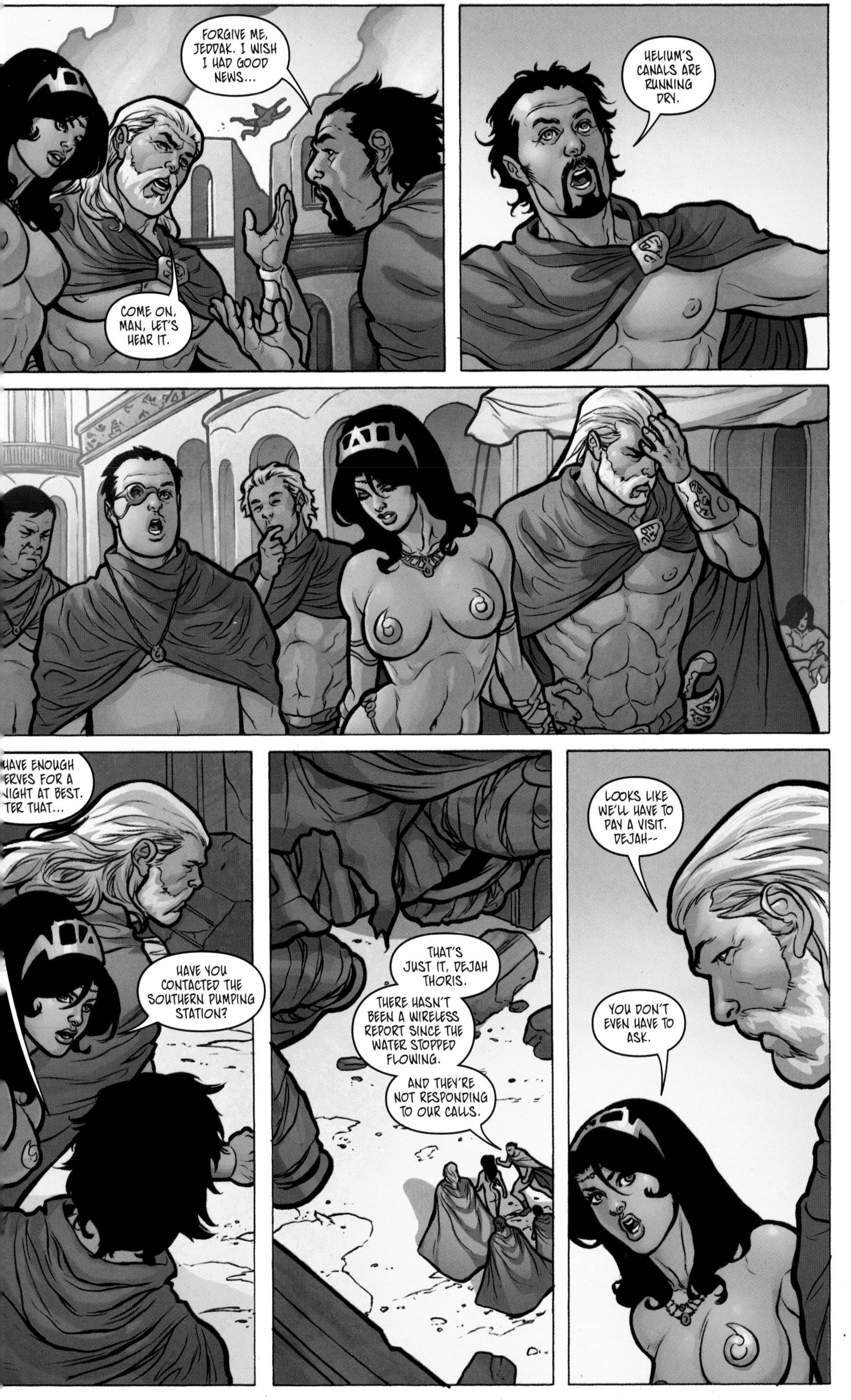
FORGIVE ME, JEDDAK. I WISH I HAD GOOD NEWS...
COME ON, MAN, LET'S HEAR IT.
HELIUM'S CANALS ARE RUNNING DRY.
HAVE ENOUGH ERVES FOR A NIGHT AT BEST. TER THAT...
HAVE YOU CONTACTED THE SOUTHERN PUMPING STATION?
THAT'S JUST IT, DEJAH THORIS.
THERE HASN'T BEEN A WIRELESS REPORT SINCE THE WATER STOPPED FLOWING.
AND THEY'RE NOT RESPONDING TO OUR CALLS.
LOOKS LIKE WE'LL HAVE TO PAY A VISIT. DEJAH--
YOU DON'T EVEN HAVE TO ASK.

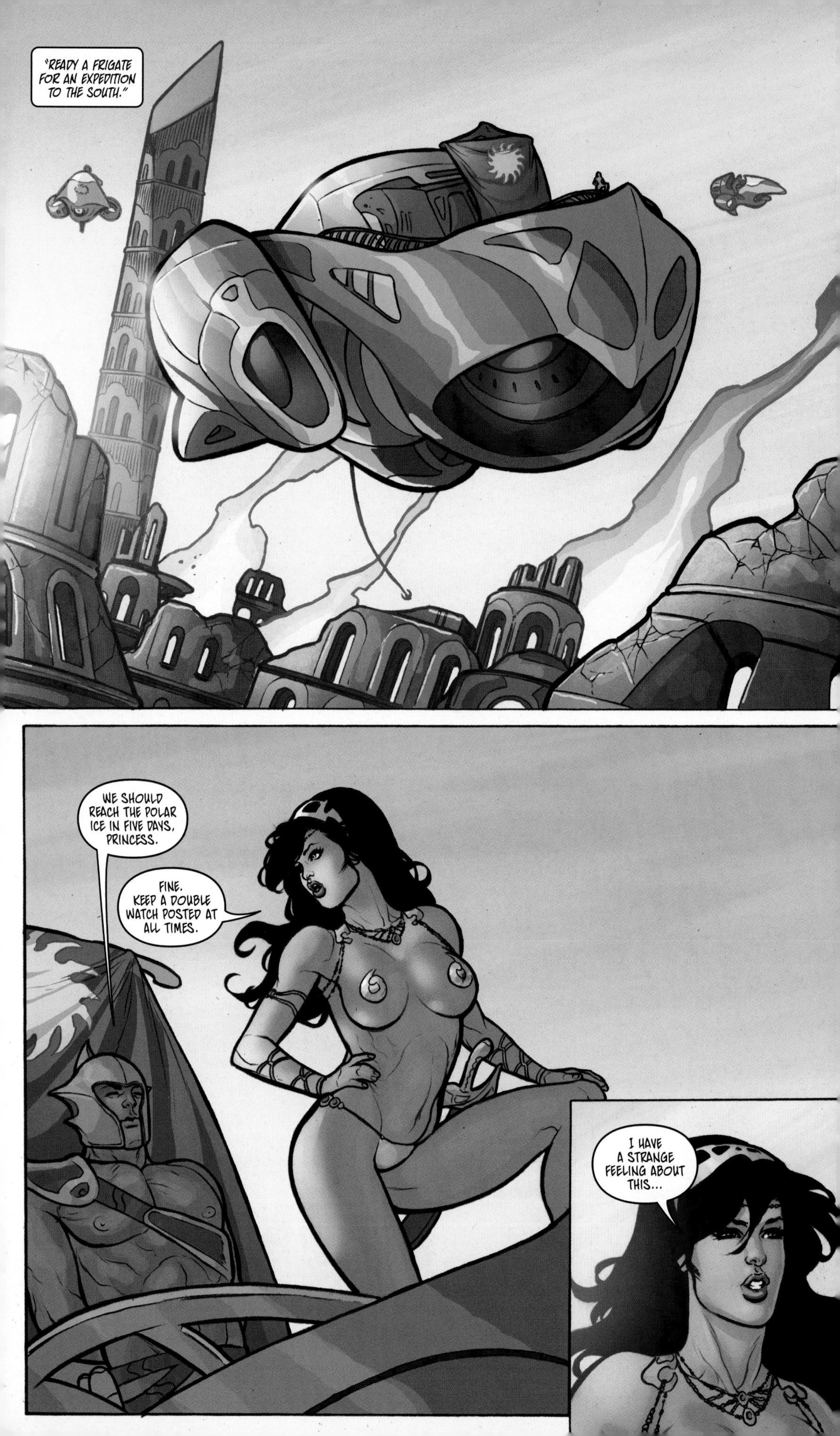
"READY A FRIGATE FOR AN EXPEDITION TO THE SOUTH."
WE SHOULD REACH THE POLAR ICE IN FIVE DAYS, PRINCESS.
FINE. KEEP A DOUBLE WATCH POSTED AT ALL TIMES.
I HAVE A STRANGE FEELING ABOUT THIS...

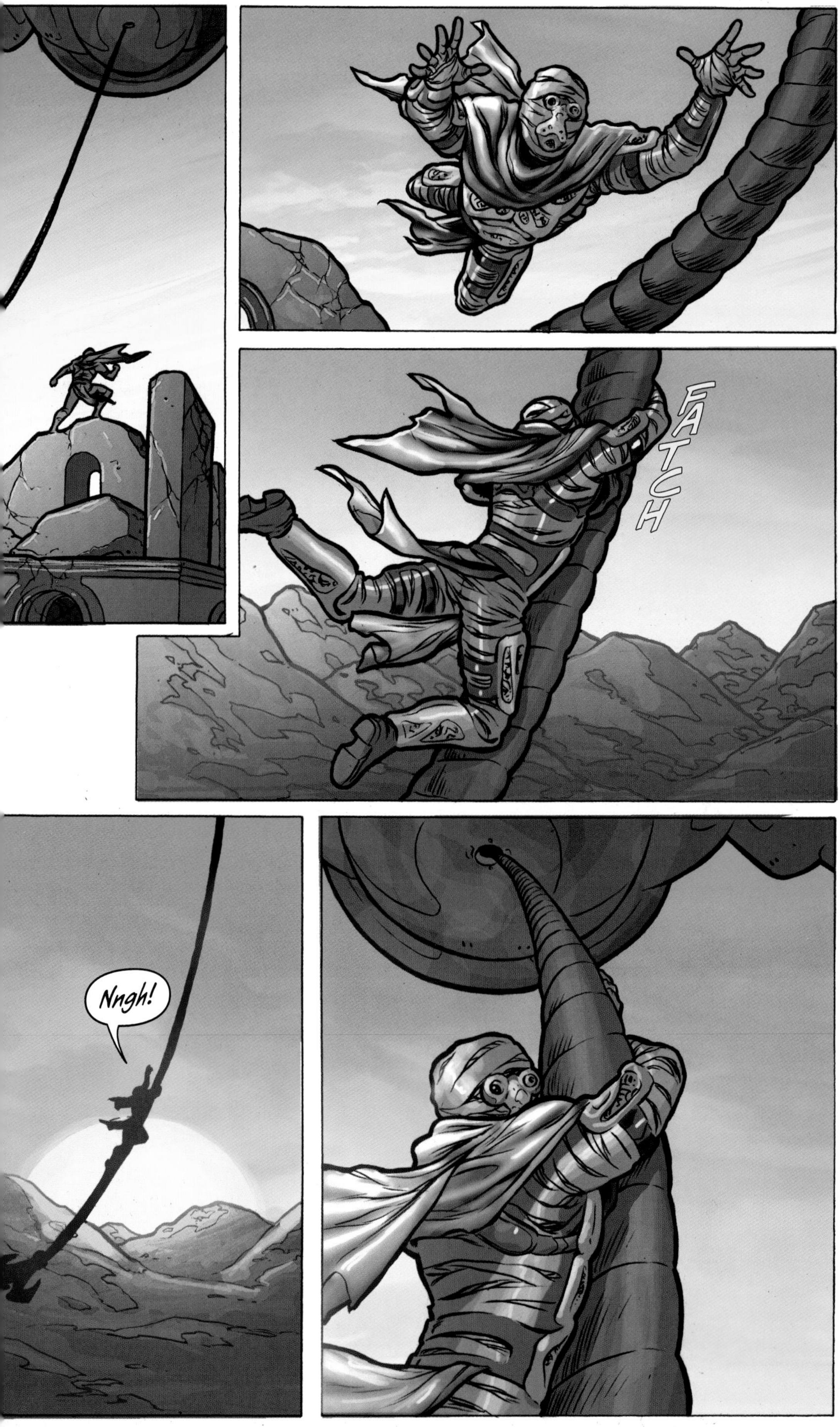
FATCH
Nngh!

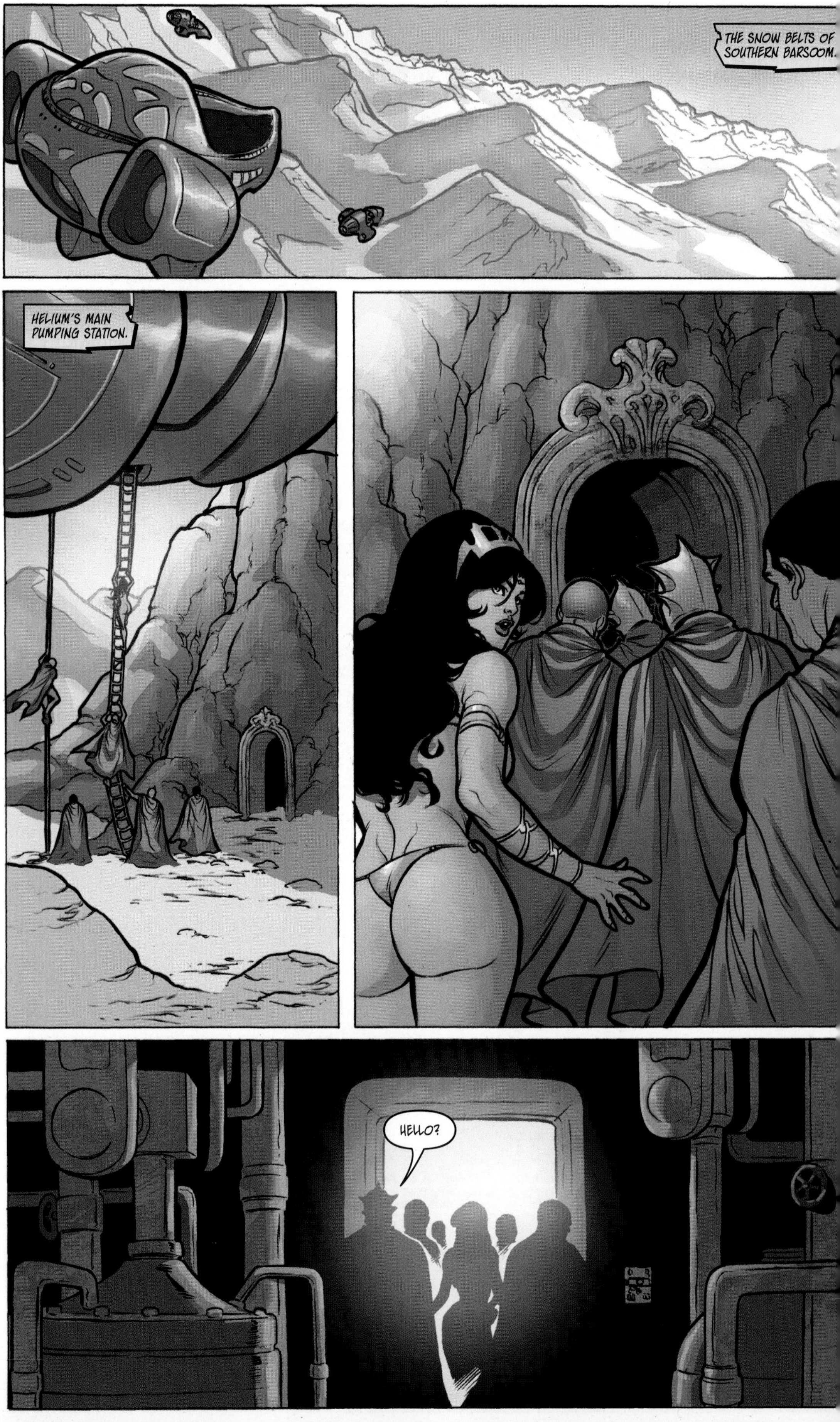
THE SNOW BELTS OF SOUTHERN BARSOOM.
HELIUM'S MAIN PUMPING STATION.
HELLO?

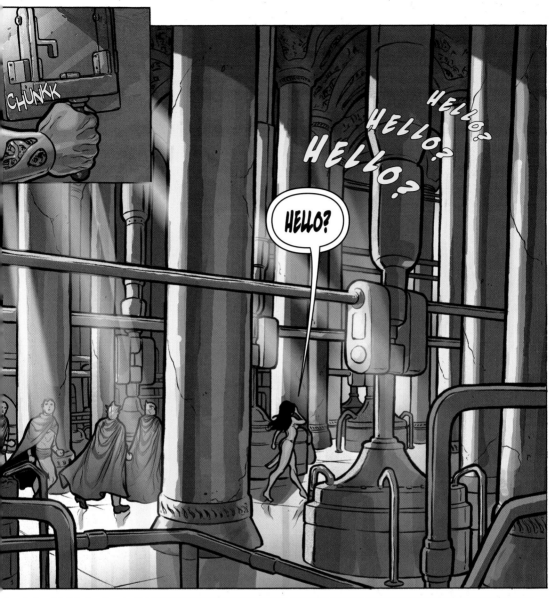

CHUNKK

HELLO?
HELLO?
HELLO?
HELLO?

WHERE COULD EVERYONE BE?

SPREAD OUT.

THE CISTERNS ARE FULL, AT LEAST. ANY DAMAGE TO THE PUMPING APPARATUS?

NO, PRINCESS.

MIGHT AS WELL START IT UP.

AT ONCE.

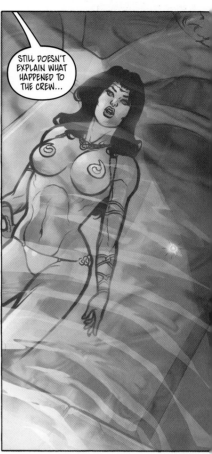

STILL DOESN'T EXPLAIN WHAT HAPPENED TO THE CREW...

WAIT!

THERE'S SOMETHING DOWN THERE, AT THE BOTTOM. SOMETHING SHINY...

THE FILTRATION SYSTEM WILL PICK IT UP, PRINCESS, LET ME--

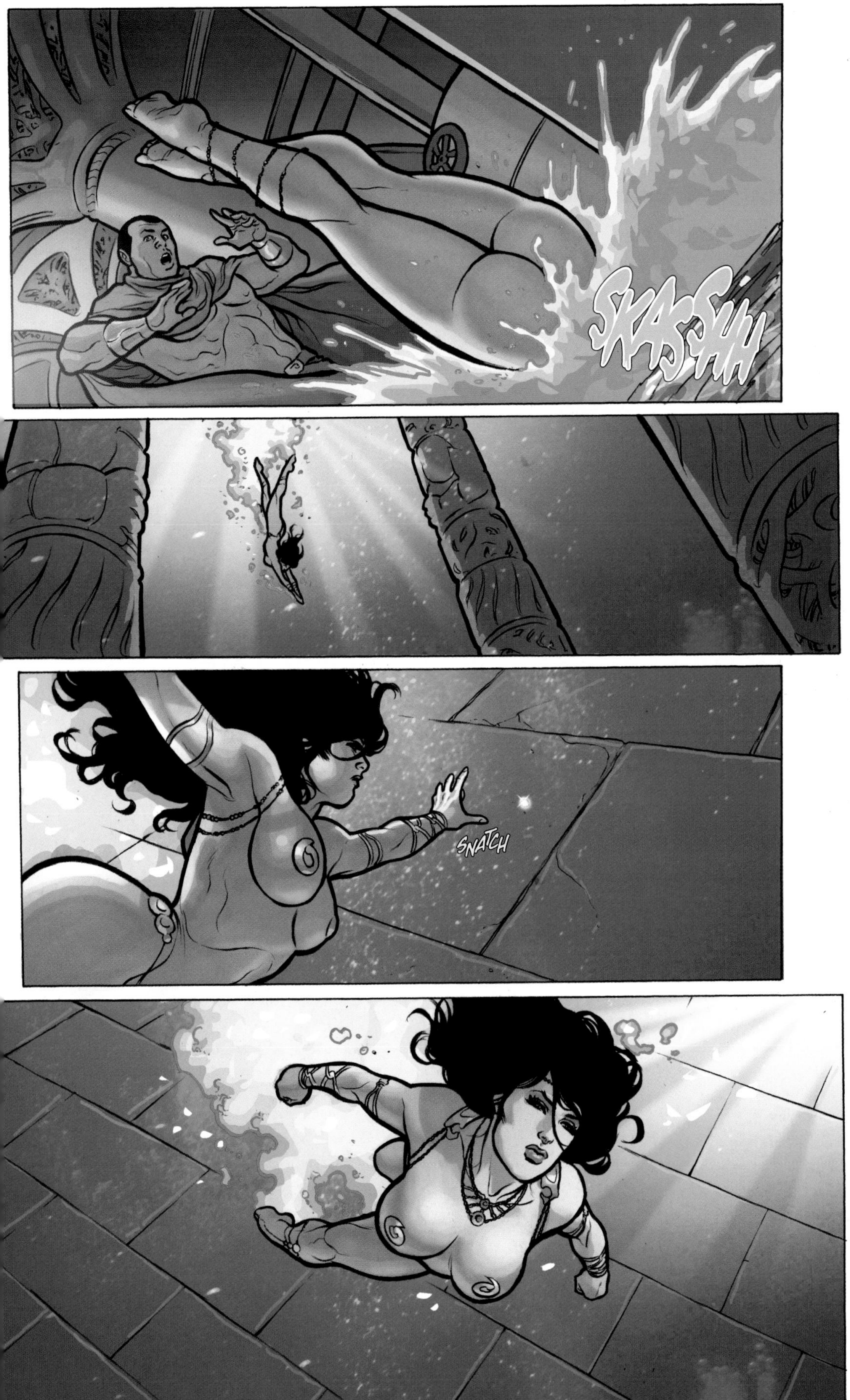
SKASSHH
SNATCH

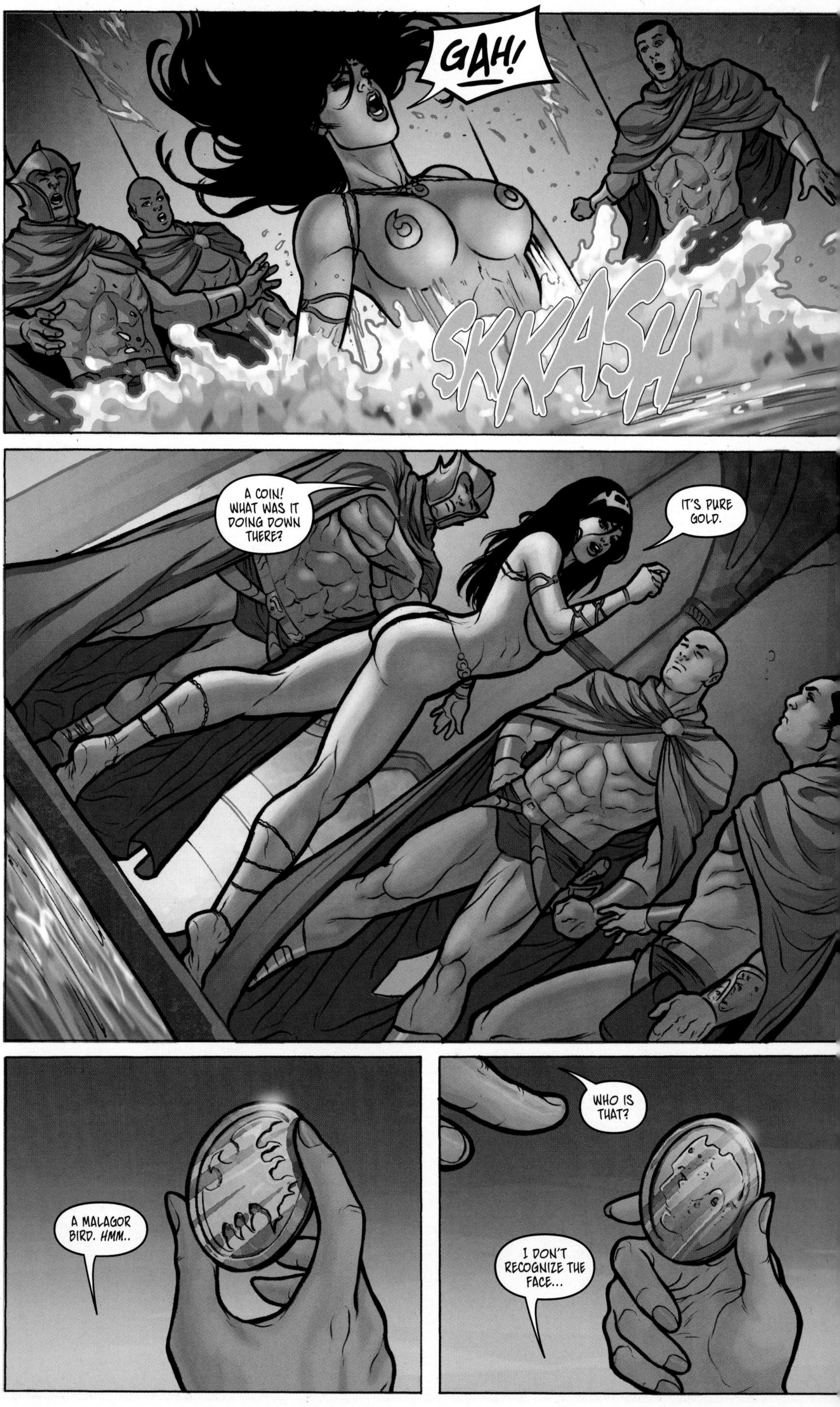
GAH!
SKKASH
A COIN! WHAT WAS IT DOING DOWN THERE?
IT'S PURE GOLD.
A MALAGOR BIRD. HMM..
WHO IS THAT?
I DON'T RECOGNIZE THE FACE...

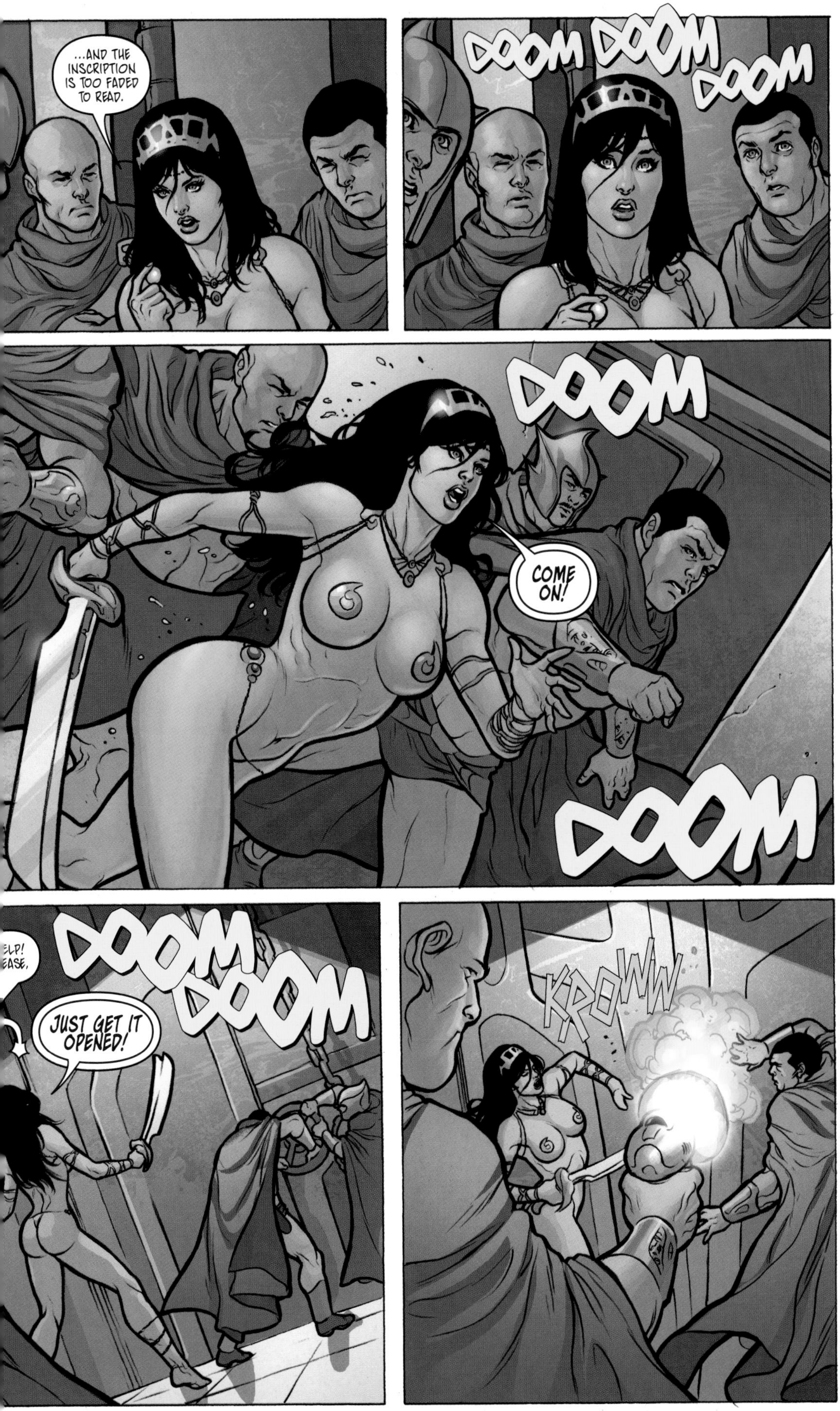
...AND THE INSCRIPTION IS TOO FADED TO READ.
DOOM DOOM DOOM
DOOM
COME ON!
DOOM
DOOM DOOM
JUST GET IT OPENED!
KROWW

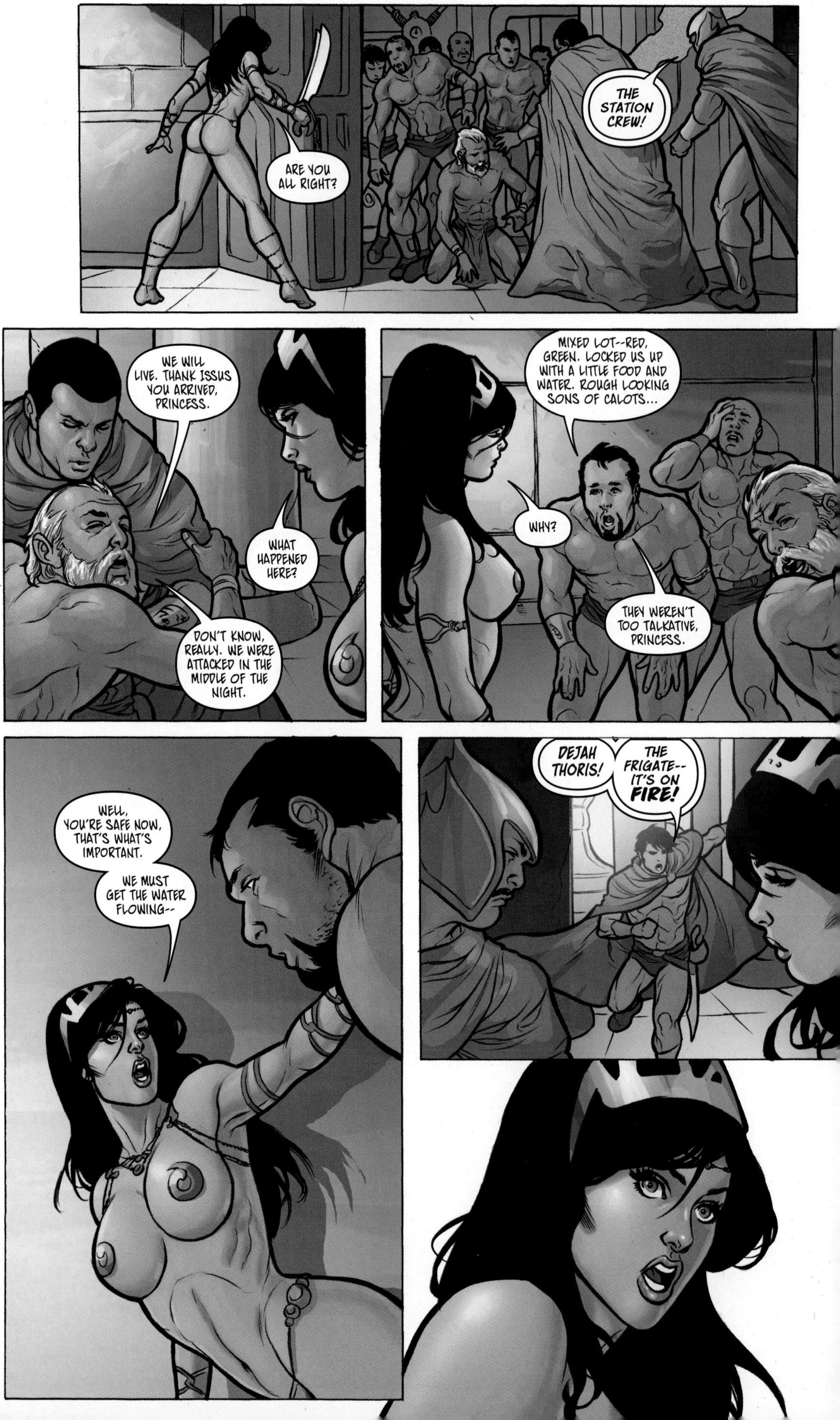
ARE YOU ALL RIGHT?
THE STATION CREW!
WE WILL LIVE. THANK ISSUS YOU ARRIVED, PRINCESS.
WHAT HAPPENED HERE?
DON'T KNOW, REALLY. WE WERE ATTACKED IN THE MIDDLE OF THE NIGHT.
MIXED LOT--RED, GREEN. LOCKED US UP WITH A LITTLE FOOD AND WATER. ROUGH LOOKING SONS OF CALOTS...
WHY?
THEY WEREN'T TOO TALKATIVE, PRINCESS.
WELL, YOU'RE SAFE NOW, THAT'S WHAT'S IMPORTANT.
WE MUST GET THE WATER FLOWING--
DEJAH THORIS!
THE FRIGATE-- IT'S ON FIRE!

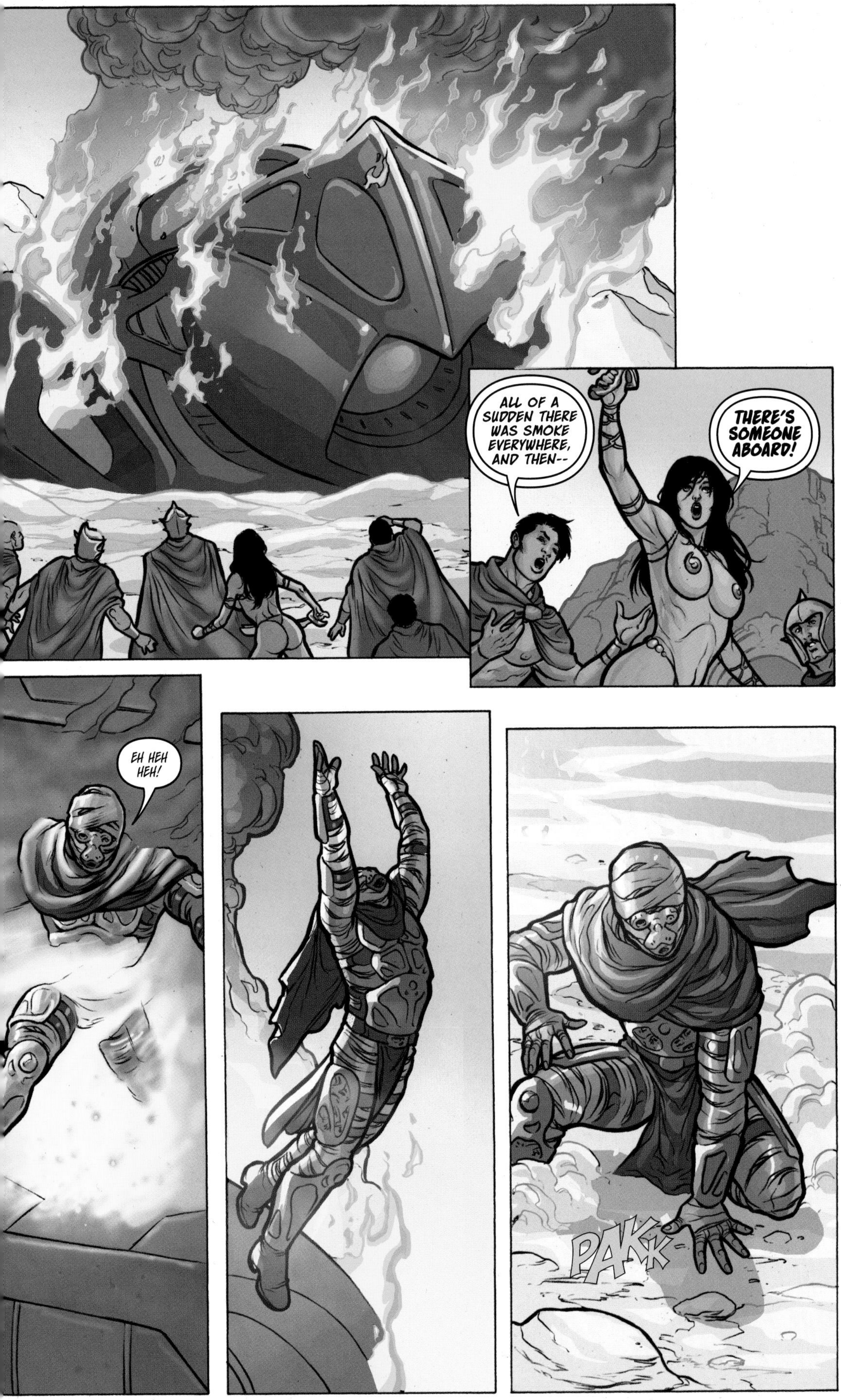
ALL OF A SUDDEN THERE WAS SMOKE EVERYWHERE, AND THEN--
THERE'S SOMEONE ABOARD!
EH HEH HEH!
PAKK

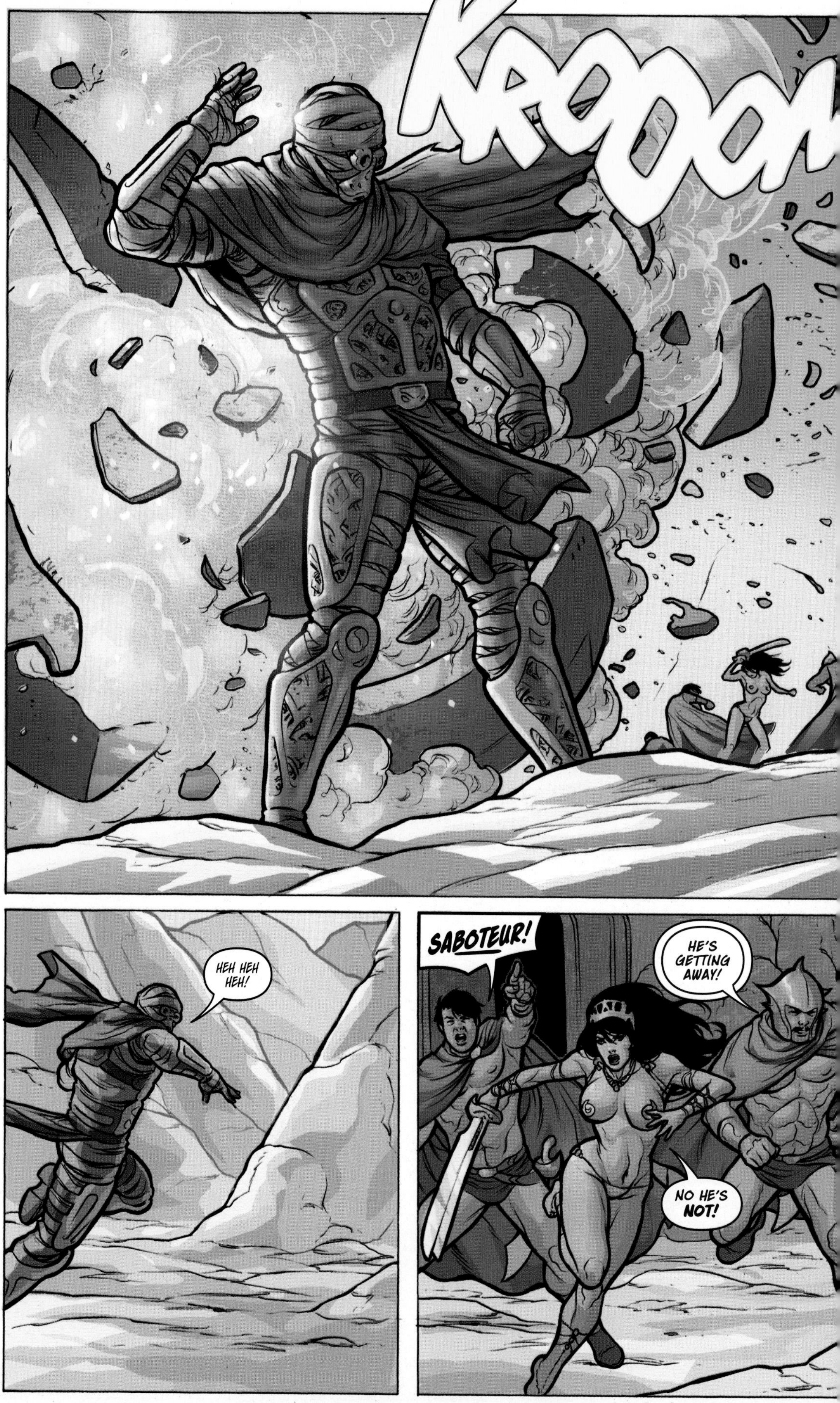
KROOOM
HEH HEH HEH!
SABOTEUR!
HE'S GETTING AWAY!
NO HE'S NOT!

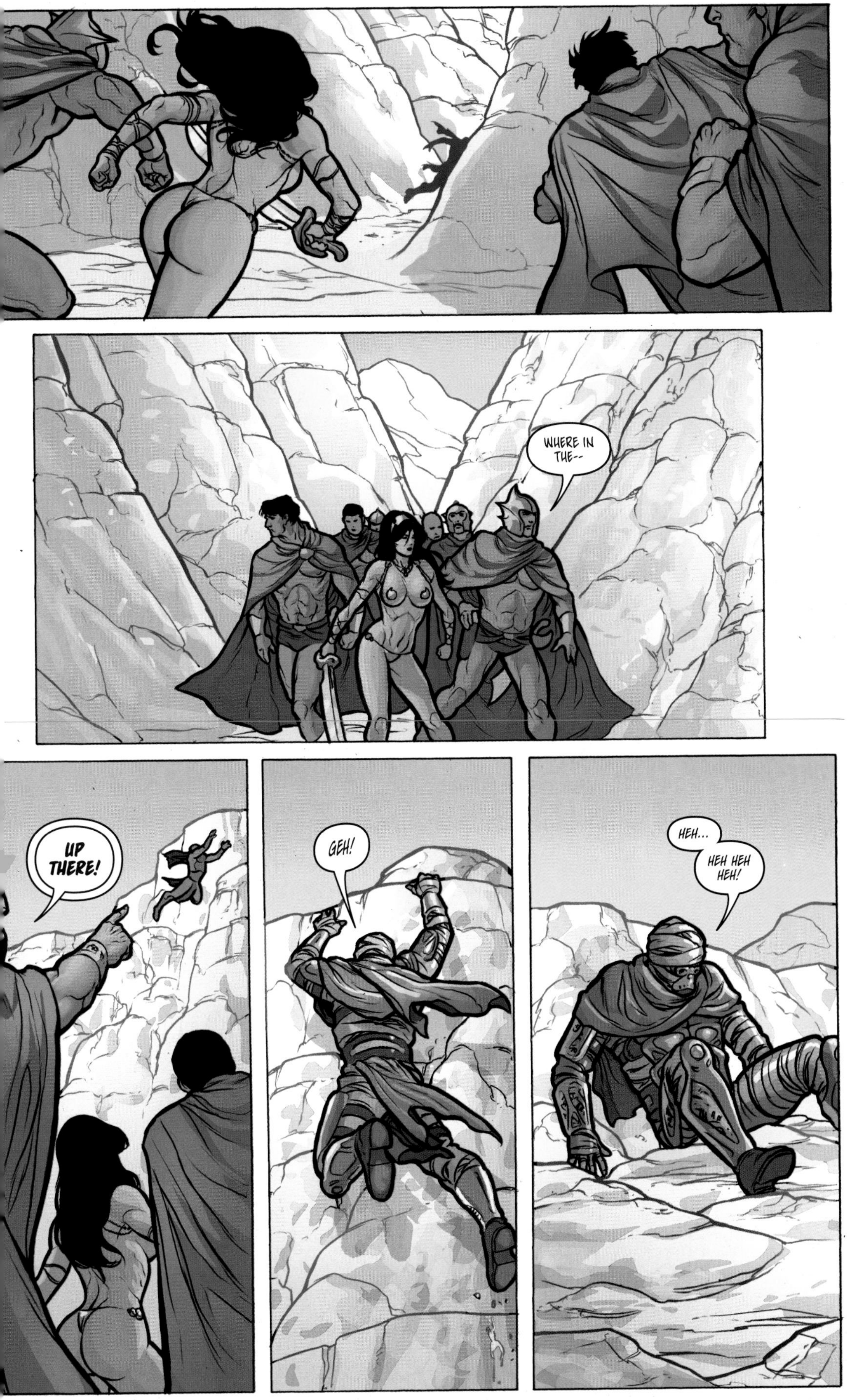
WHERE IN THE--
UP THERE!
GEH!
HEH...
HEH HEH HEH!

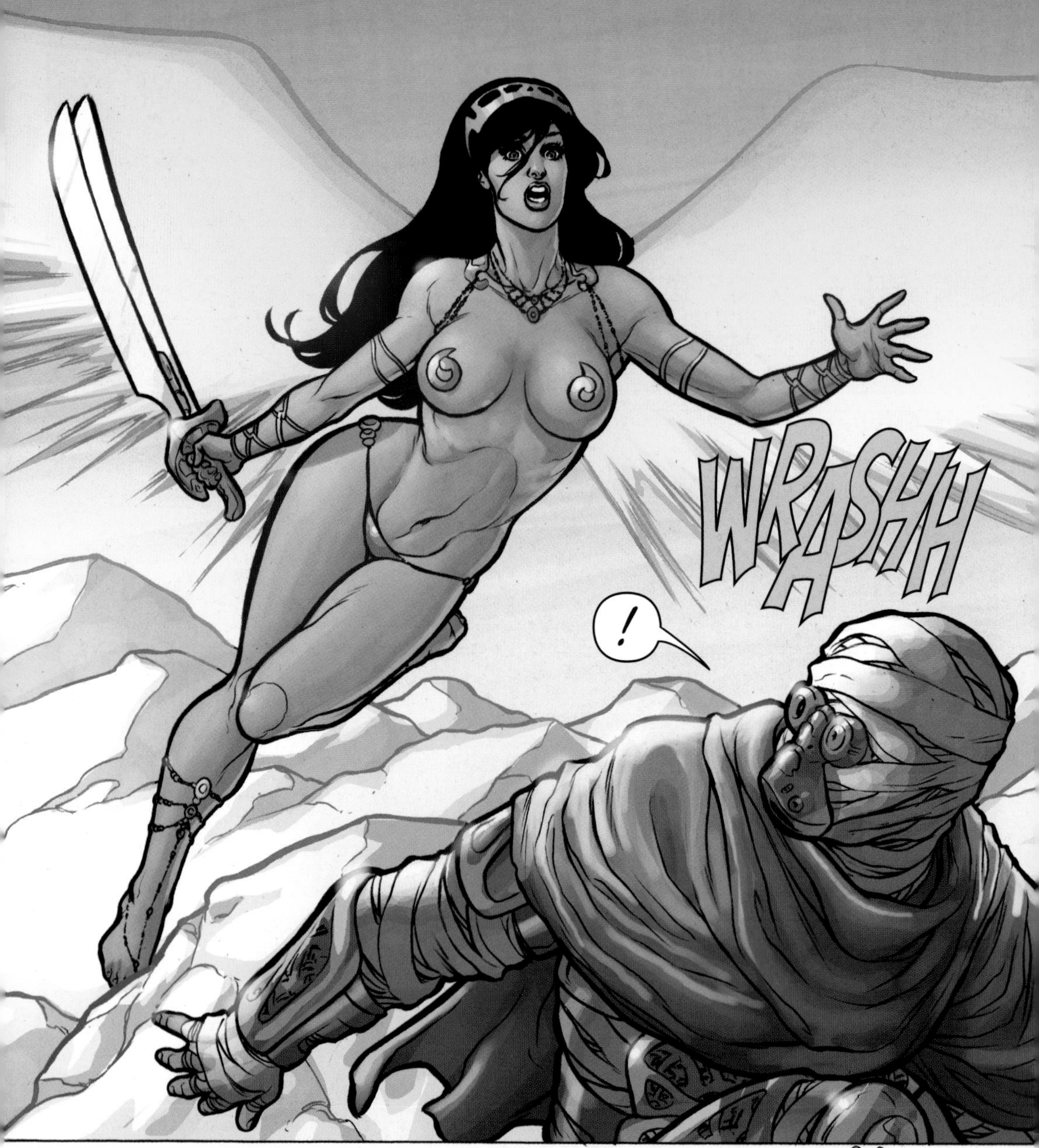
WRASHH
!

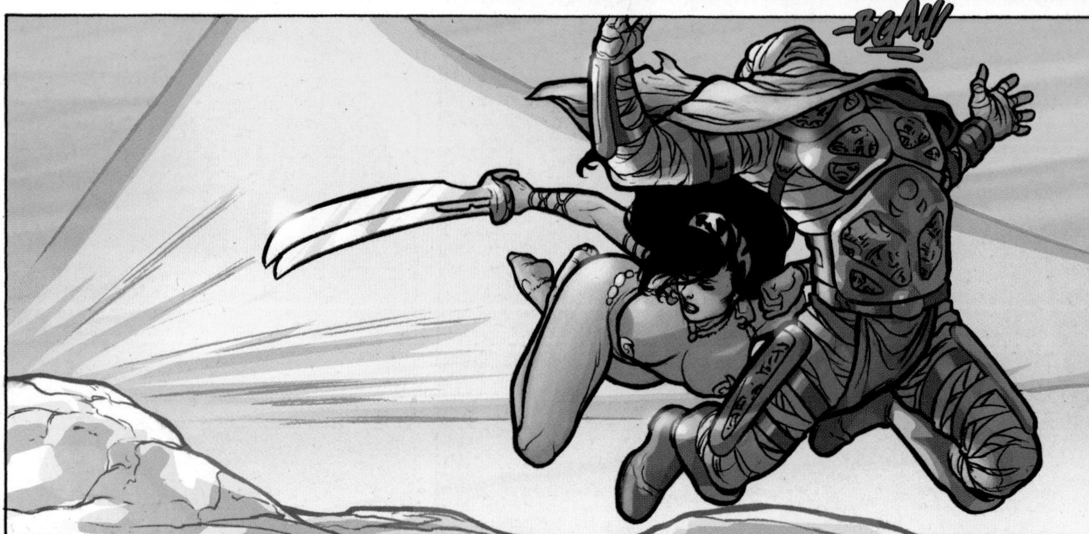
-BGAH!

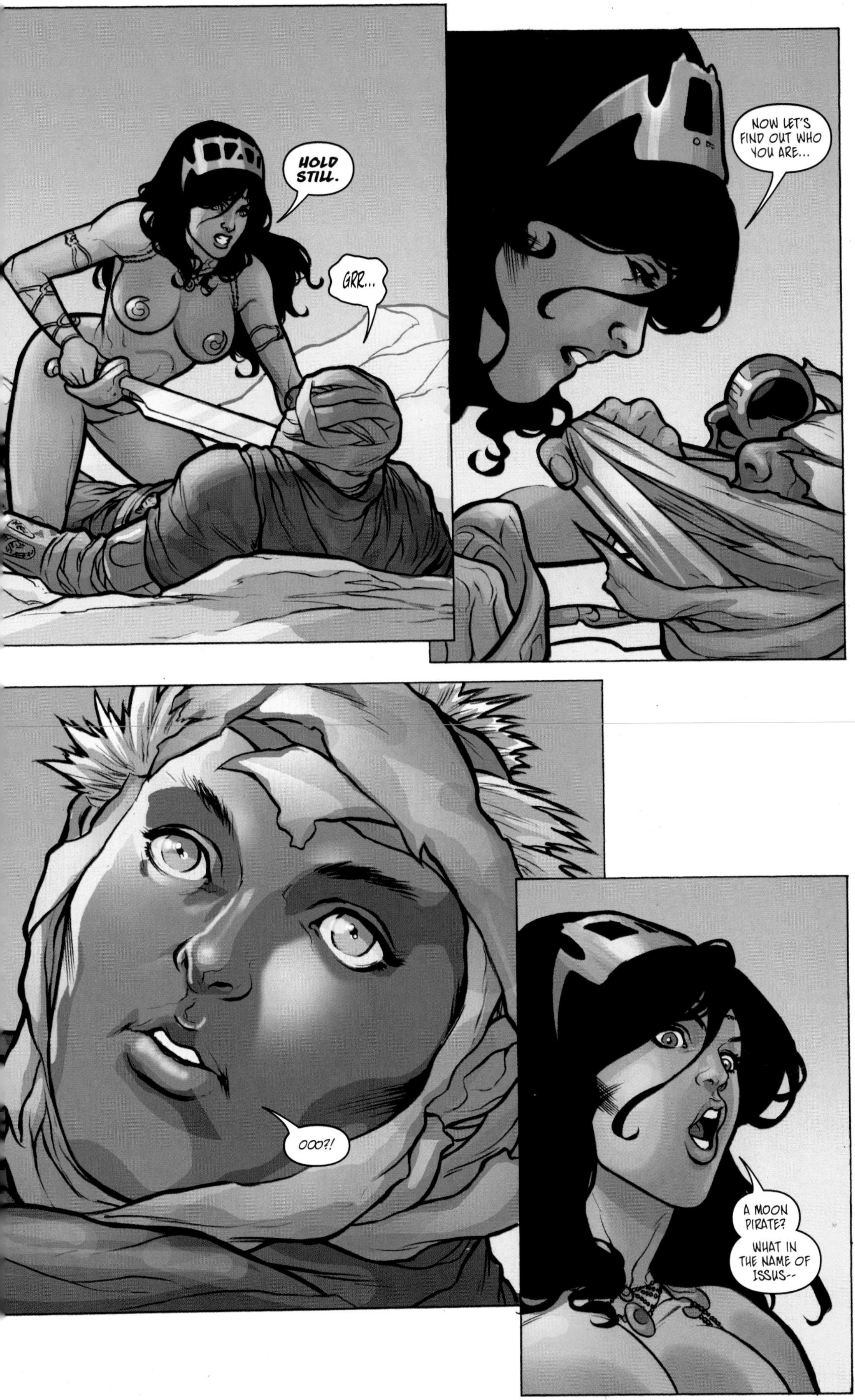
HOLD STILL.
GRR...
NOW LET'S FIND OUT WHO YOU ARE...
OOO?!
A MOON PIRATE?
WHAT IN THE NAME OF ISSUS--

AH!

CHOMP

WHAP

GAA HAH HAH!

LITTLE ULSIO! GET OFF OF ME!

GET--

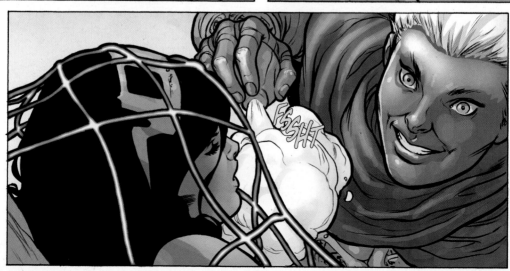

FSSHT

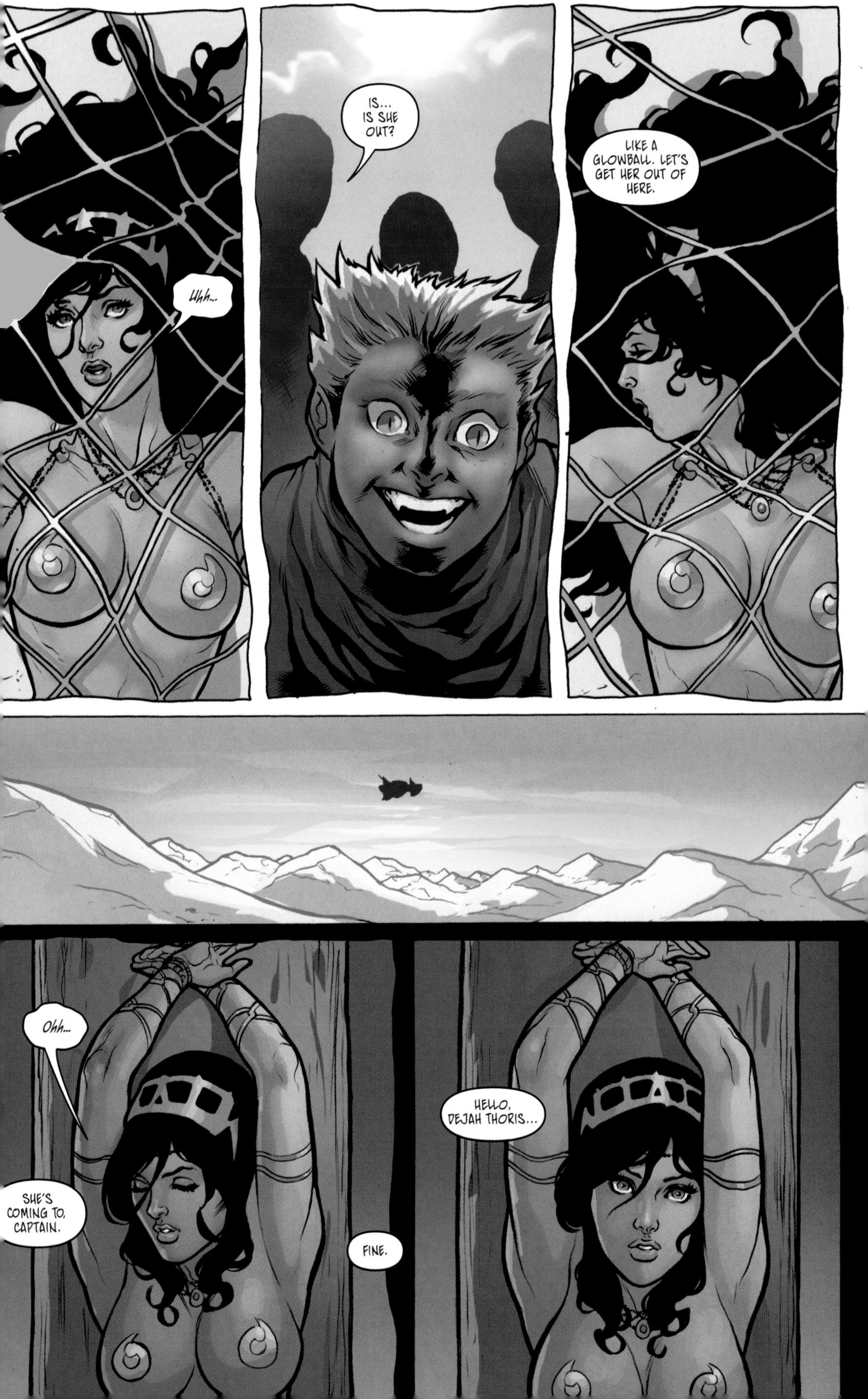
Uhh...
IS... IS SHE OUT?
LIKE A GLOWBALL. LET'S GET HER OUT OF HERE.
Ohh...
SHE'S COMING TO, CAPTAIN.
FINE.
HELLO, DEJAH THORIS...

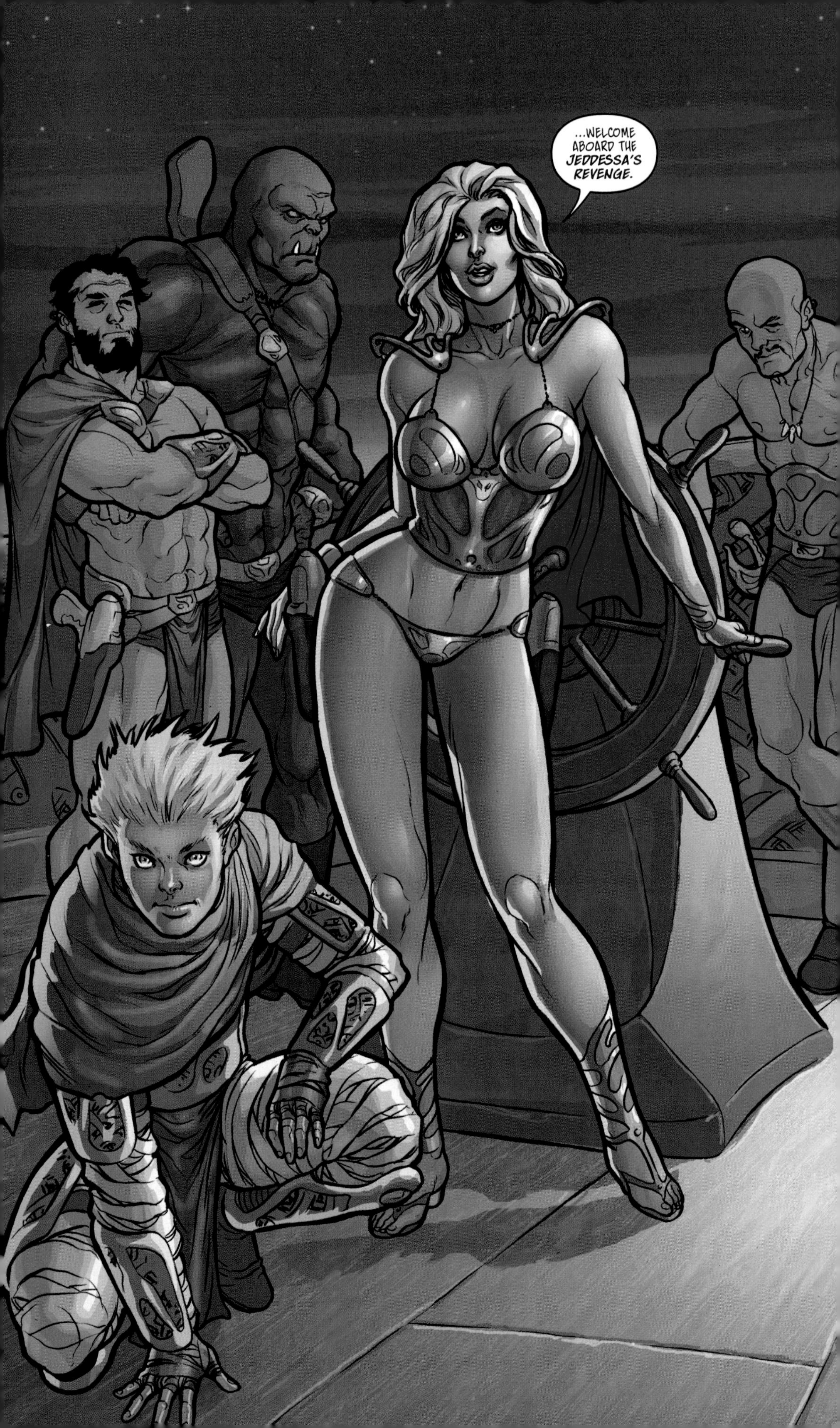
...WELCOME ABOARD THE JEDDESSA'S REVENGE.

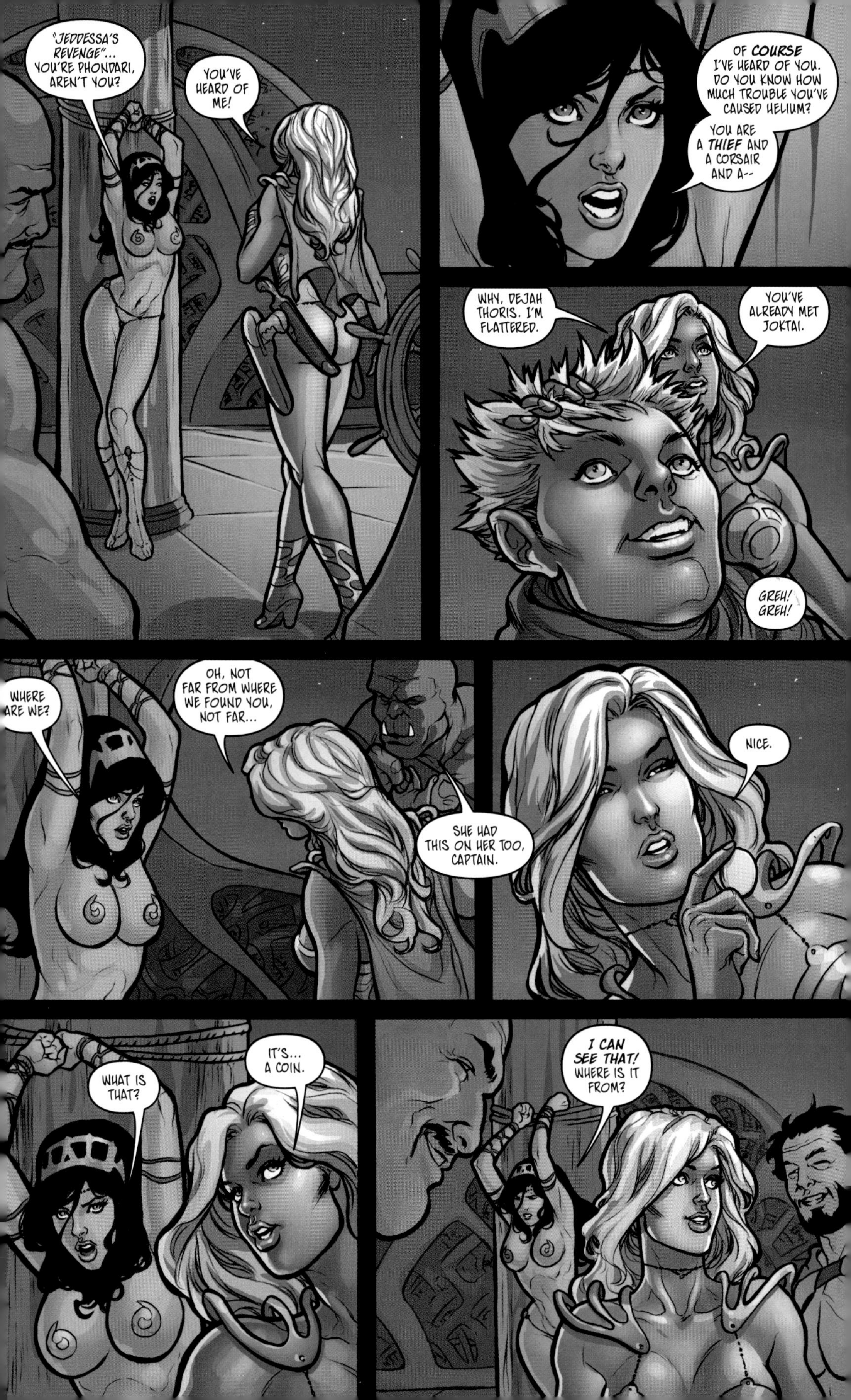

"JEDDESSA'S REVENGE"... YOU'RE PHONDARI, AREN'T YOU?
YOU'VE HEARD OF ME!
OF **COURSE** I'VE HEARD OF YOU. DO YOU KNOW HOW MUCH TROUBLE YOU'VE CAUSED HELIUM?
YOU ARE A ***THIEF*** AND A CORSAIR AND A--
WHY, DEJAH THORIS. I'M FLATTERED.
YOU'VE ALREADY MET JOKTAI.
GREH! GREH!
WHERE ARE WE?
OH, NOT FAR FROM WHERE WE FOUND YOU, NOT FAR...
SHE HAD THIS ON HER TOO, CAPTAIN.
NICE.
WHAT IS THAT?
IT'S... A COIN.
***I CAN SEE THAT!*** WHERE IS IT FROM?

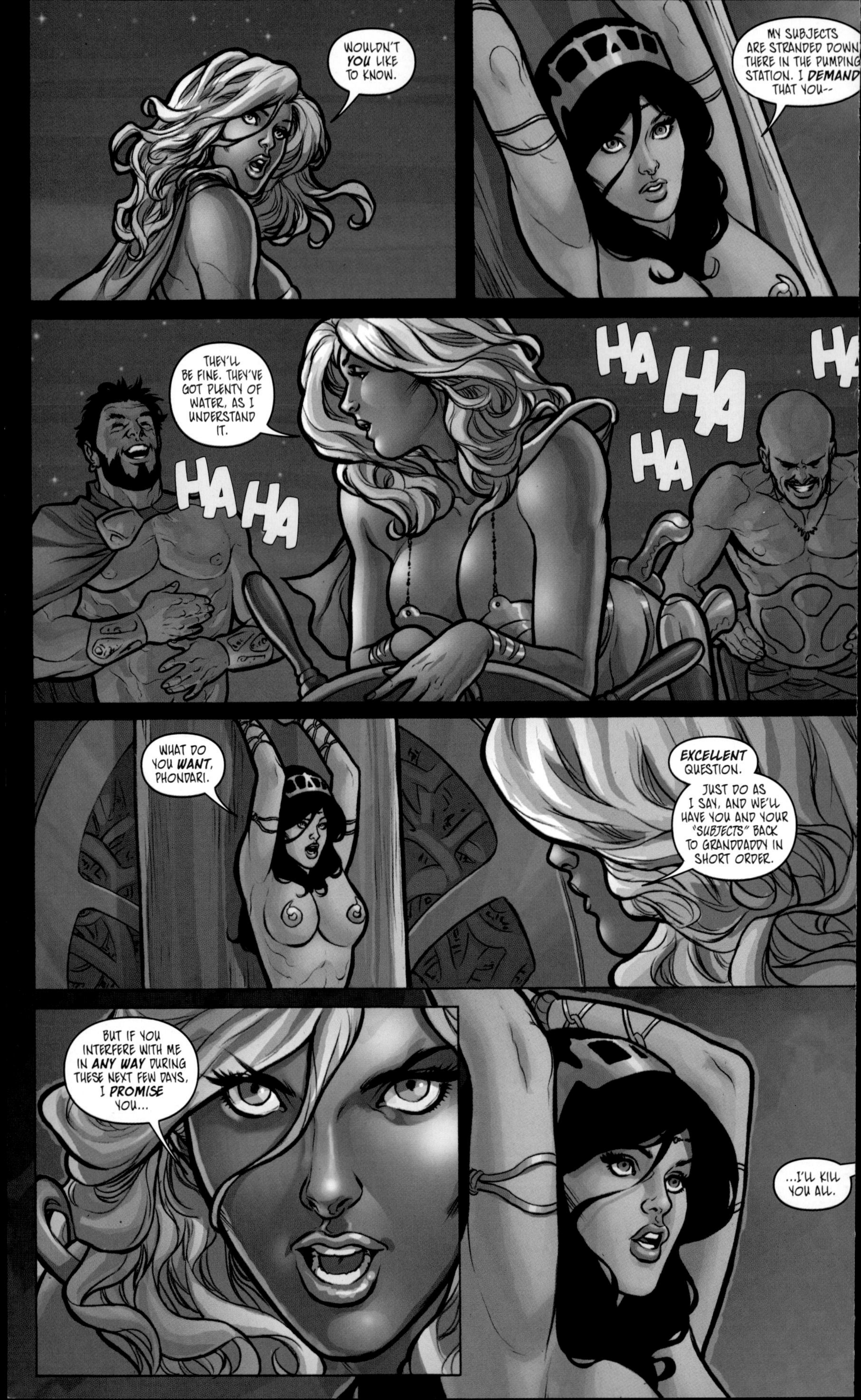
WOULDN'T YOU LIKE TO KNOW.
MY SUBJECTS ARE STRANDED DOWN THERE IN THE PUMPING STATION. I DEMAND THAT YOU--
THEY'LL BE FINE. THEY'VE GOT PLENTY OF WATER, AS I UNDERSTAND IT.
HA HA
HA HA HA
HA
WHAT DO YOU WANT, PHONDARI.
EXCELLENT QUESTION.
JUST DO AS I SAY, AND WE'LL HAVE YOU AND YOUR "SUBJECTS" BACK TO GRANDDADDY IN SHORT ORDER.
BUT IF YOU INTERFERE WITH ME IN ANY WAY DURING THESE NEXT FEW DAYS, I PROMISE YOU...
...I'LL KILL YOU ALL.

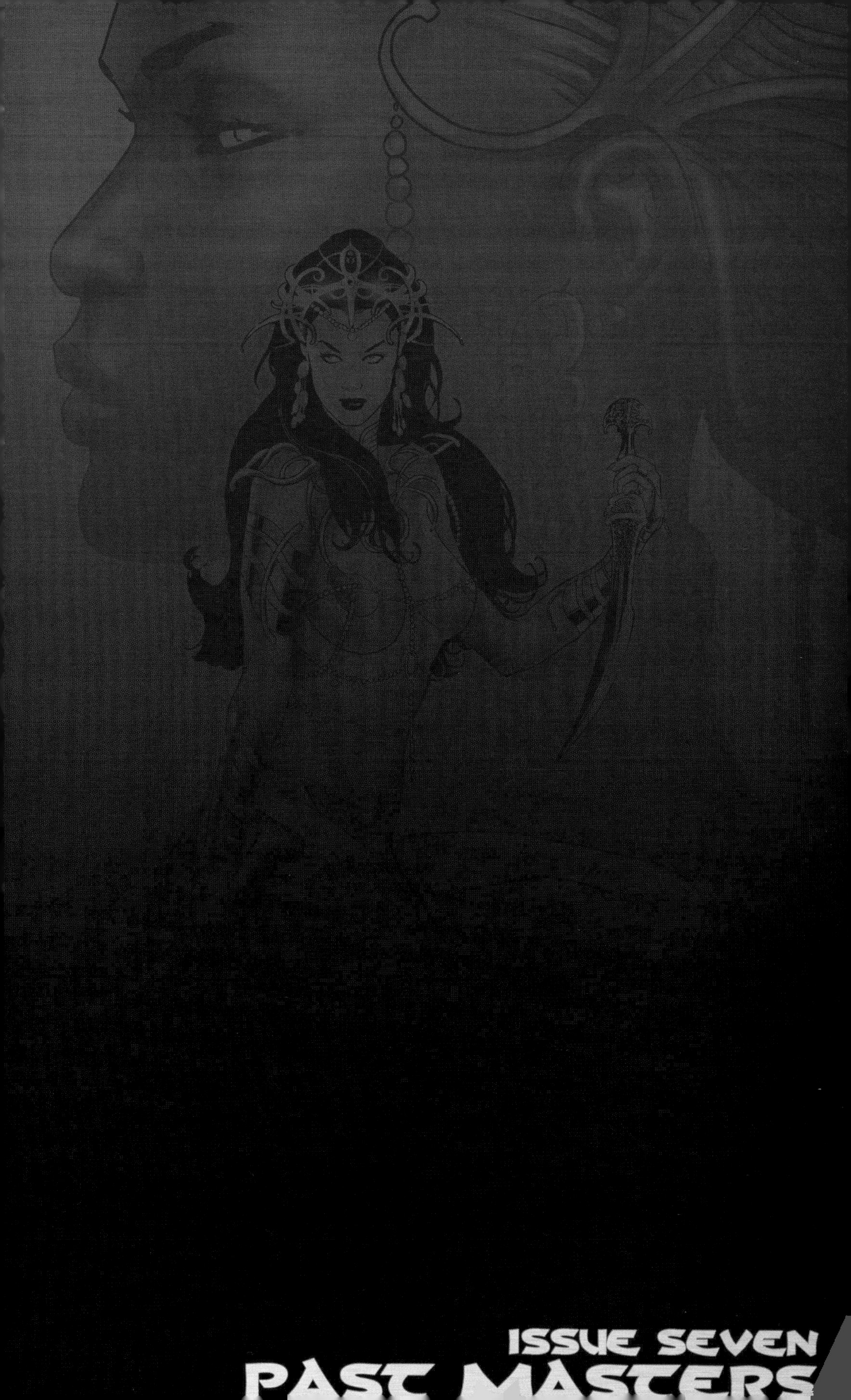
ISSUE SEVEN
PAST MASTERS

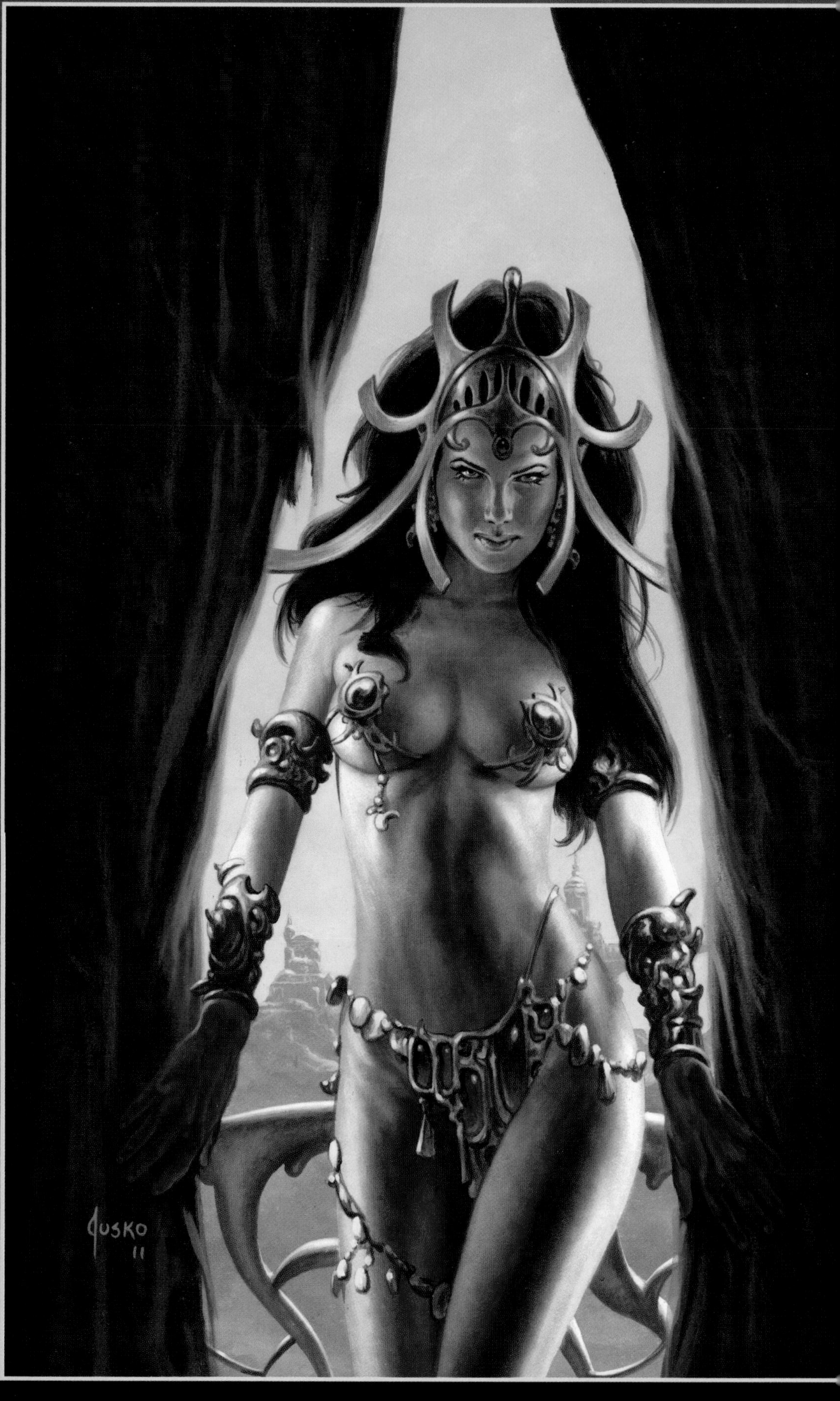
JUSKO
11

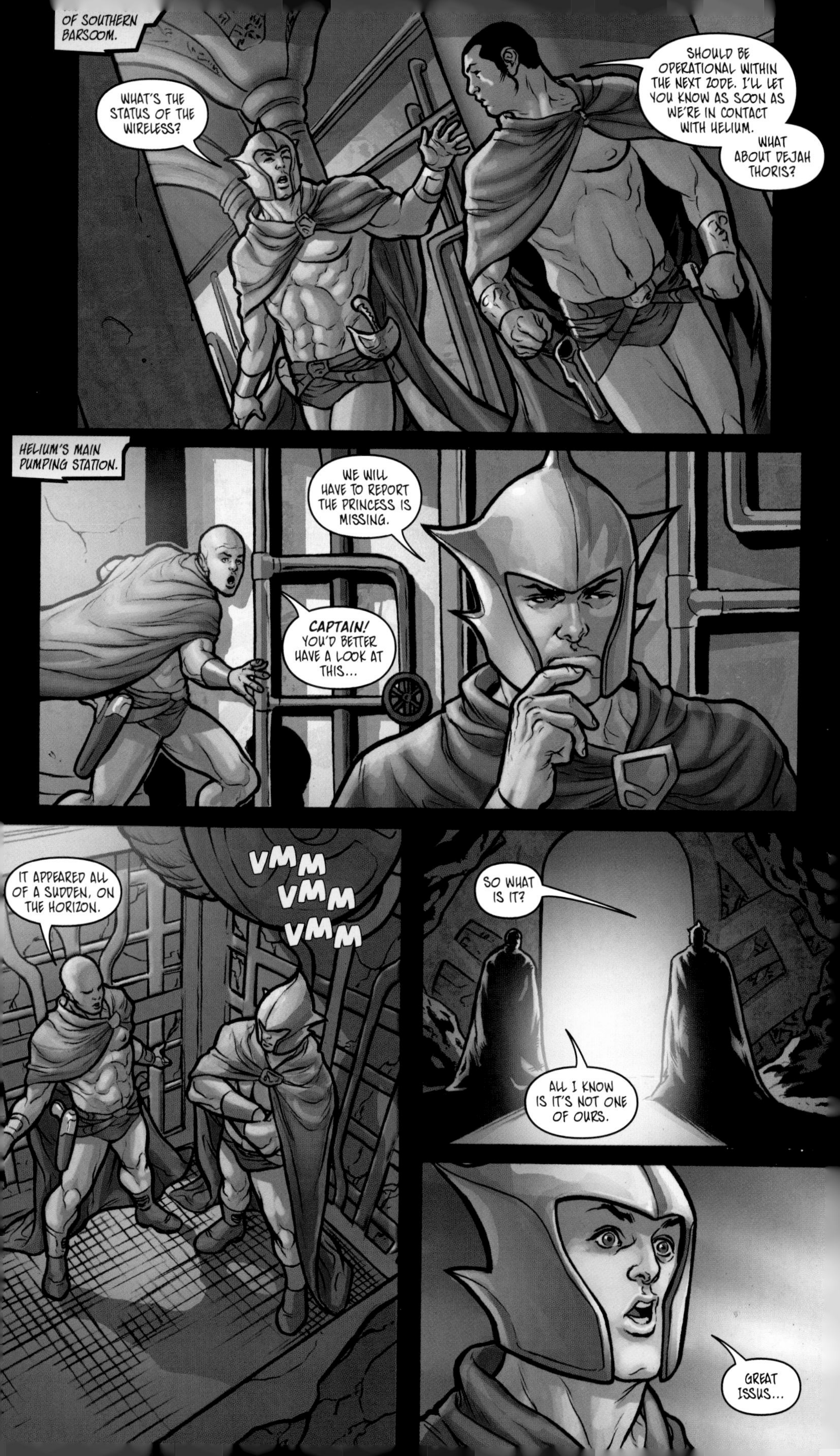
OF SOUTHERN BARSOOM.
WHAT'S THE STATUS OF THE WIRELESS?
SHOULD BE OPERATIONAL WITHIN THE NEXT ZODE. I'LL LET YOU KNOW AS SOON AS WE'RE IN CONTACT WITH HELIUM.
WHAT ABOUT DEJAH THORIS?
HELIUM'S MAIN PUMPING STATION.
WE WILL HAVE TO REPORT THE PRINCESS IS MISSING.
CAPTAIN! YOU'D BETTER HAVE A LOOK AT THIS...
IT APPEARED ALL OF A SUDDEN, ON THE HORIZON.
VMM VMM VMM
SO WHAT IS IT?
ALL I KNOW IS IT'S NOT ONE OF OURS.
GREAT ISSUS...

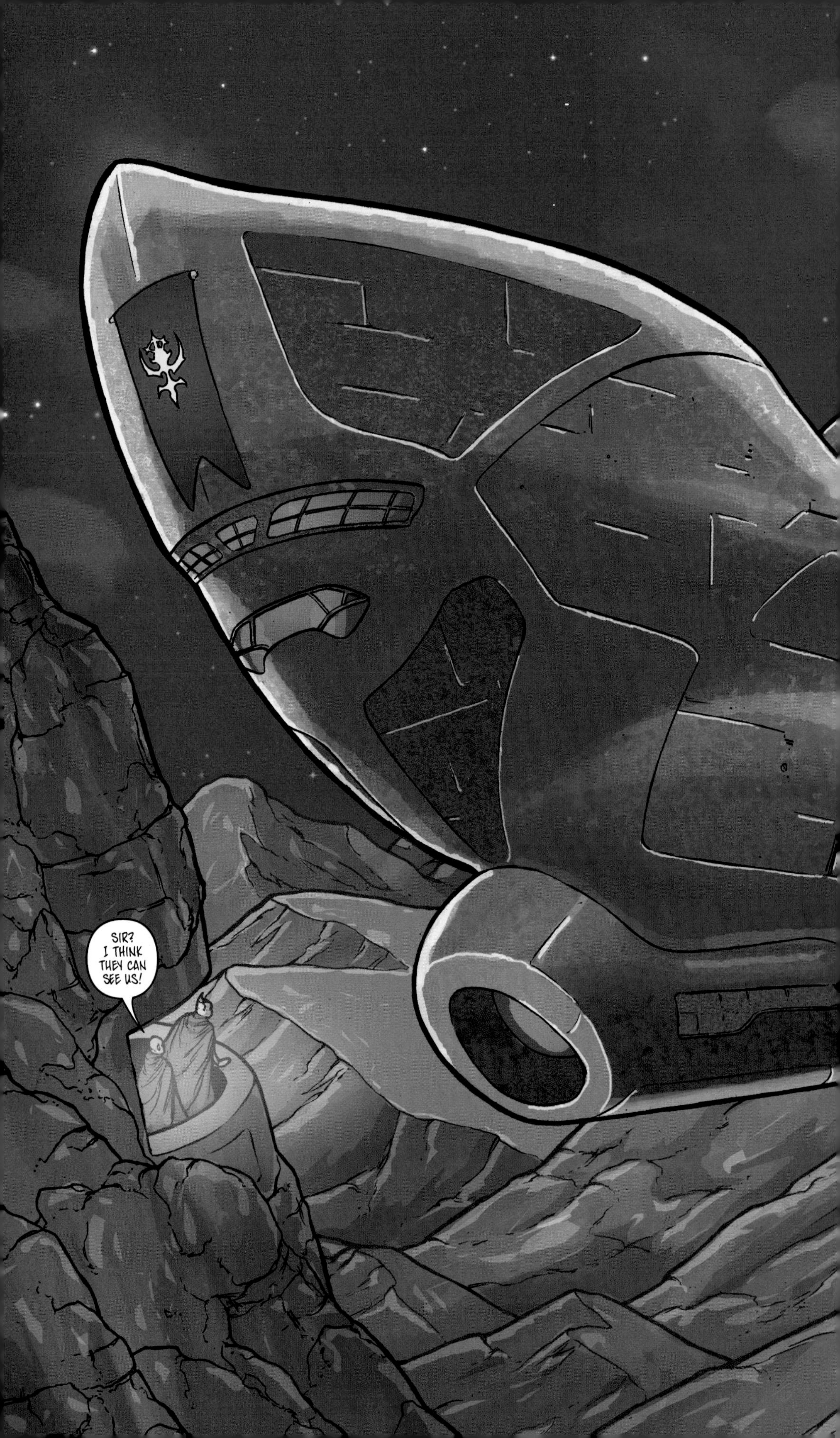
SIR? I THINK THEY CAN SEE US!

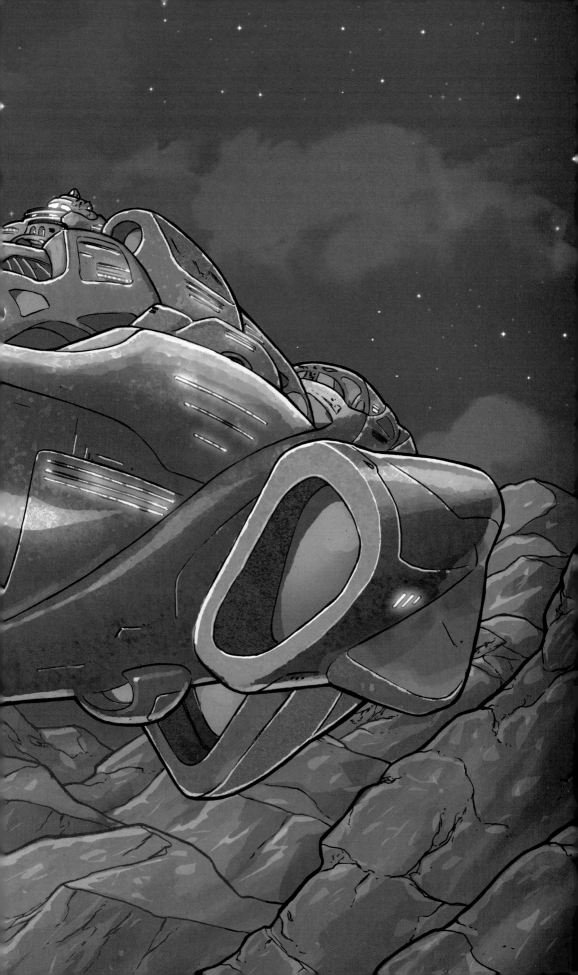

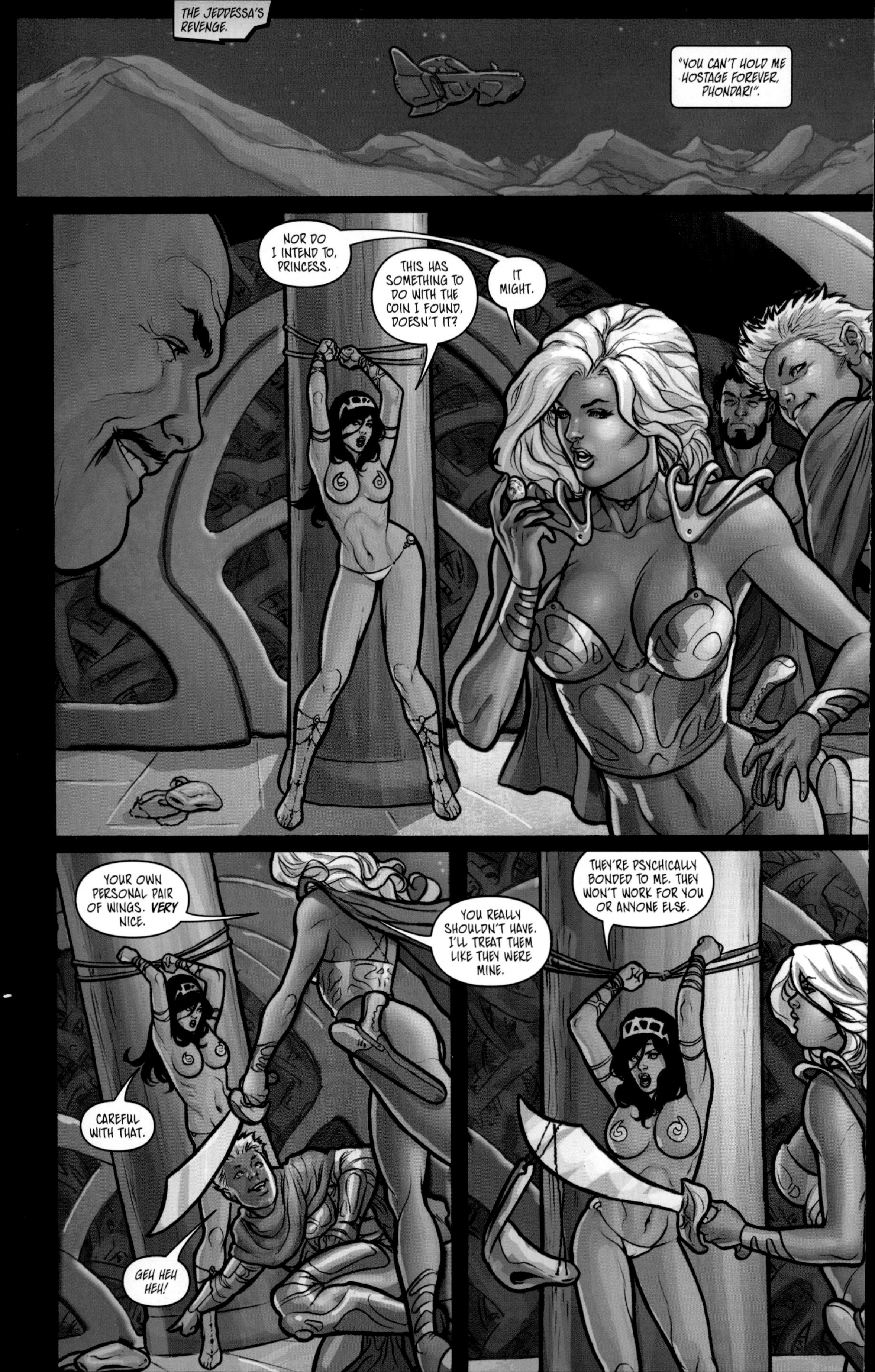
THE JEDDESSA'S REVENGE.
"YOU CAN'T HOLD ME HOSTAGE FOREVER, PHONDARI".
NOR DO I INTEND TO, PRINCESS.
THIS HAS SOMETHING TO DO WITH THE COIN I FOUND, DOESN'T IT?
IT MIGHT.
YOUR OWN PERSONAL PAIR OF WINGS. VERY NICE.
YOU REALLY SHOULDN'T HAVE. I'LL TREAT THEM LIKE THEY WERE MINE.
CAREFUL WITH THAT.
GEH HEH HEH!
THEY'RE PSYCHICALLY BONDED TO ME. THEY WON'T WORK FOR YOU OR ANYONE ELSE.

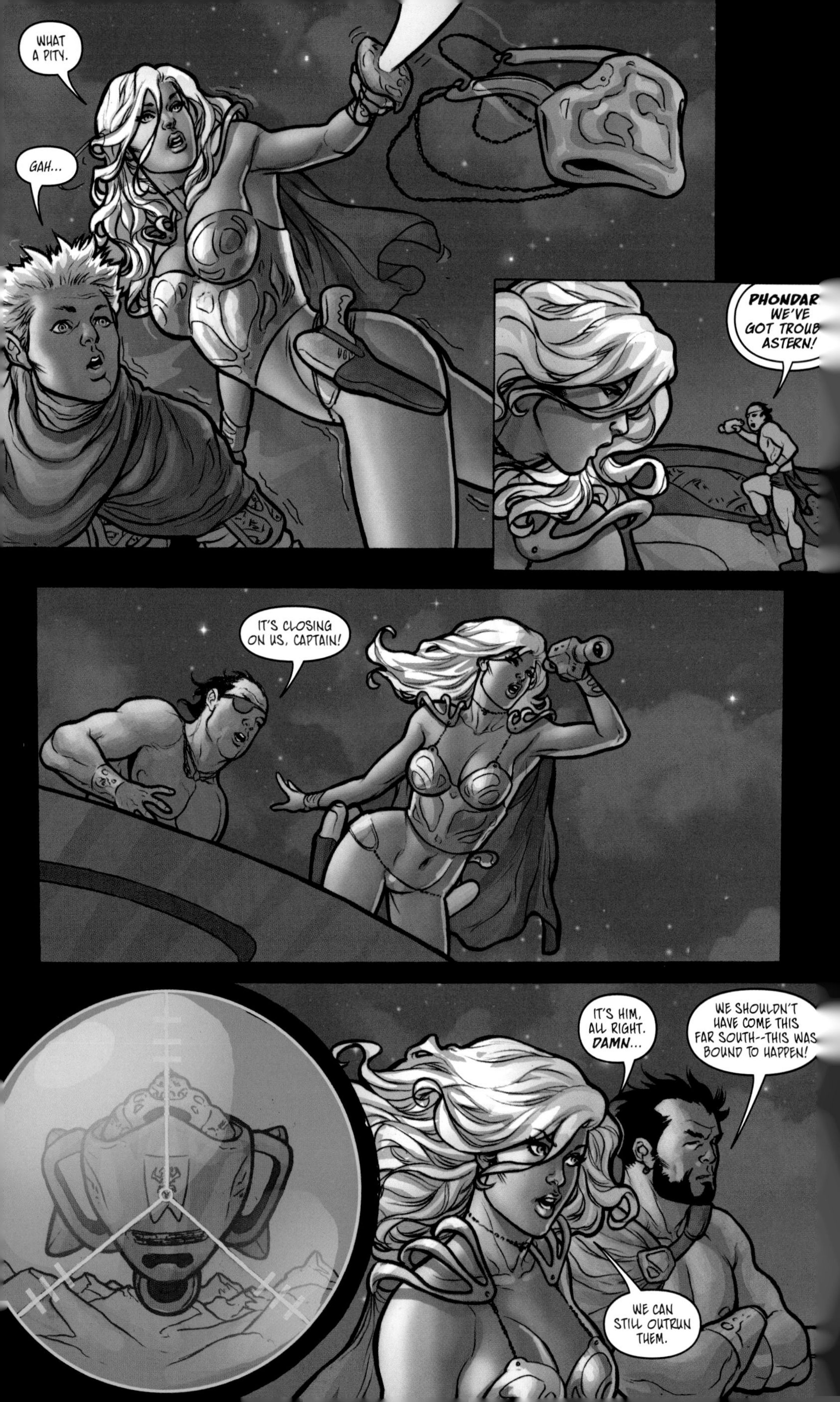
WHAT A PITY.
GAH...
PHONDAR! WE'VE GOT TROUB ASTERN!
IT'S CLOSING ON US, CAPTAIN!
IT'S HIM, ALL RIGHT. DAMN...
WE SHOULDN'T HAVE COME THIS FAR SOUTH--THIS WAS BOUND TO HAPPEN!
WE CAN STILL OUTRUN THEM.

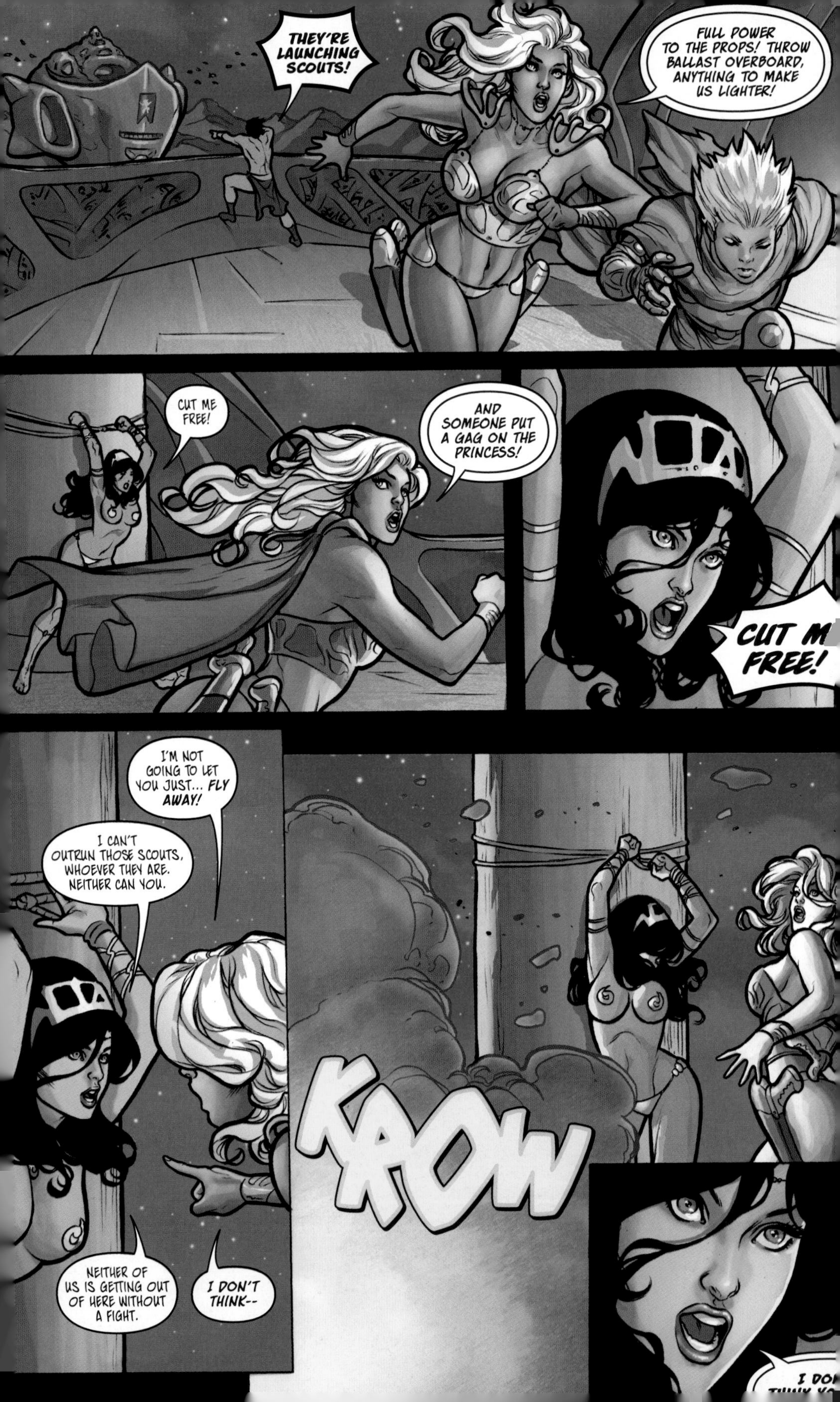

THEY'RE LAUNCHING SCOUTS!
FULL POWER TO THE PROPS! THROW BALLAST OVERBOARD, ANYTHING TO MAKE US LIGHTER!
CUT ME FREE!
AND SOMEONE PUT A GAG ON THE PRINCESS!
CUT M FREE!
I'M NOT GOING TO LET YOU JUST... FLY AWAY!
I CAN'T OUTRUN THOSE SCOUTS, WHOEVER THEY ARE. NEITHER CAN YOU.
NEITHER OF US IS GETTING OUT OF HERE WITHOUT A FIGHT.
I DON'T THINK--
KROW

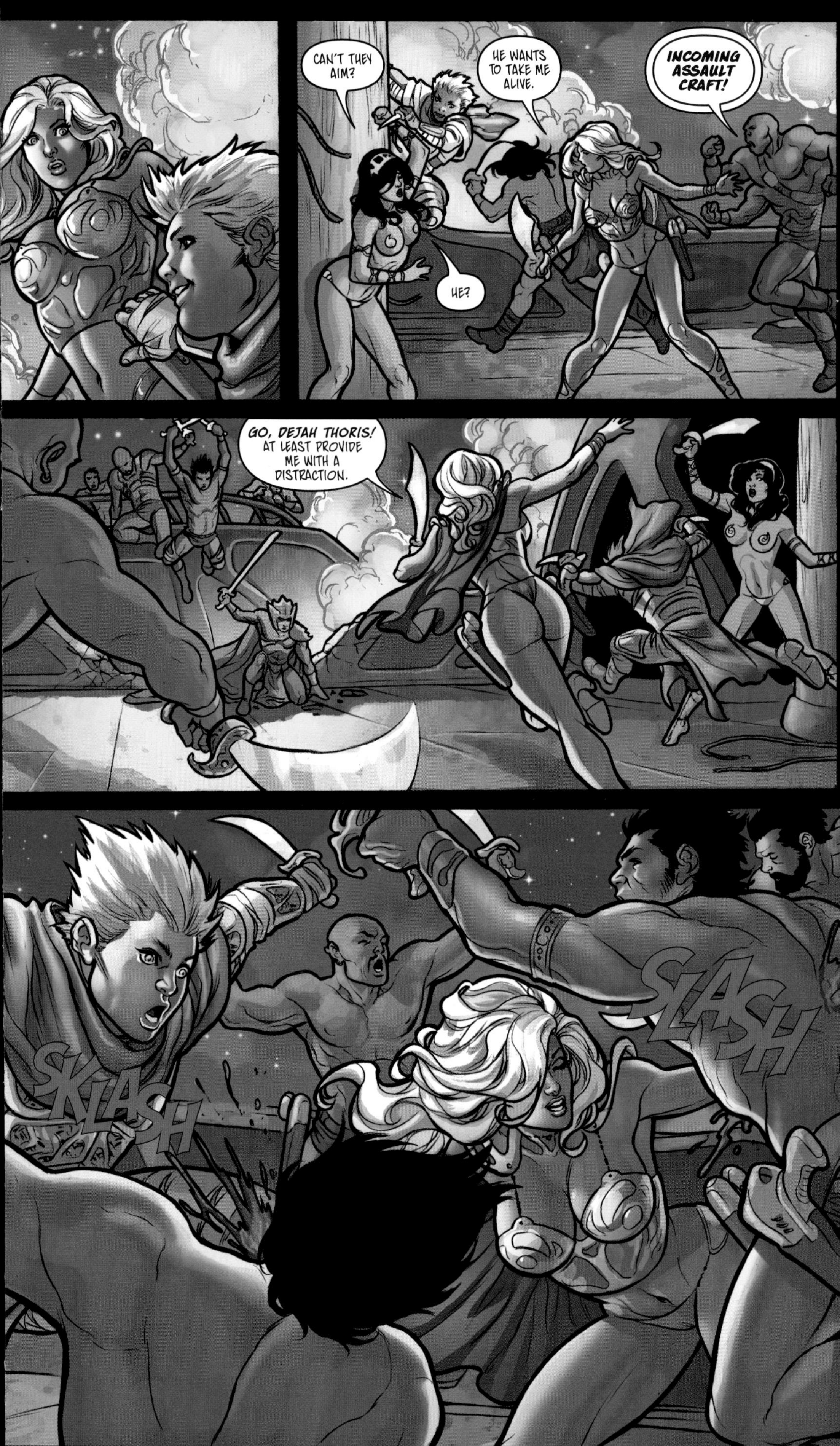
CAN'T THEY AIM?
HE WANTS TO TAKE ME ALIVE.
HE?
INCOMING ASSAULT CRAFT!
GO, DEJAH THORIS! AT LEAST PROVIDE ME WITH A DISTRACTION.
SKLASH
SLASH

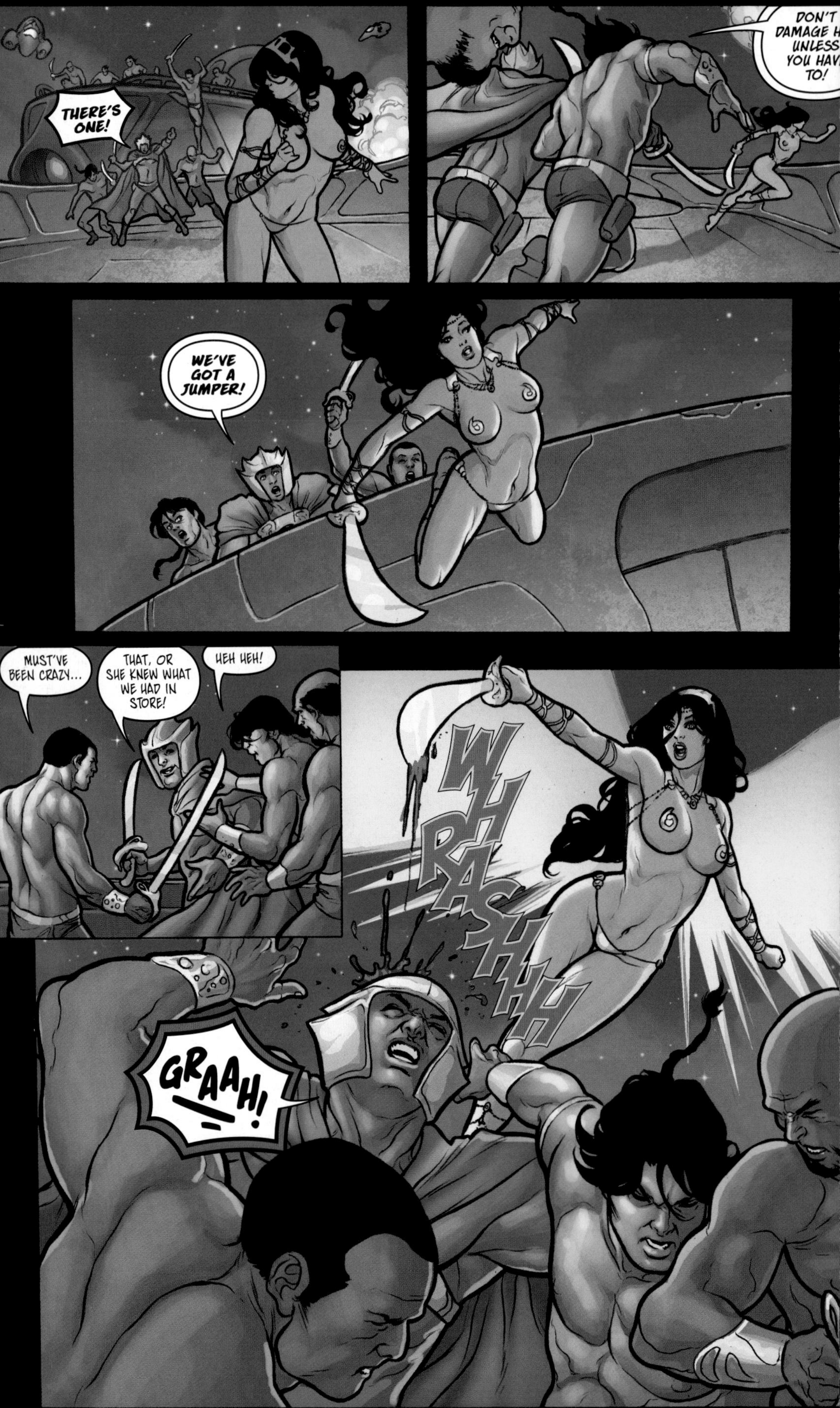
THERE'S ONE!
DON'T DAMAGE H UNLESS YOU HAV TO!
WE'VE GOT A JUMPER!
MUST'VE BEEN CRAZY...
THAT, OR SHE KNEW WHAT WE HAD IN STORE!
HEH HEH!
WHRASHHH
GRAAH!

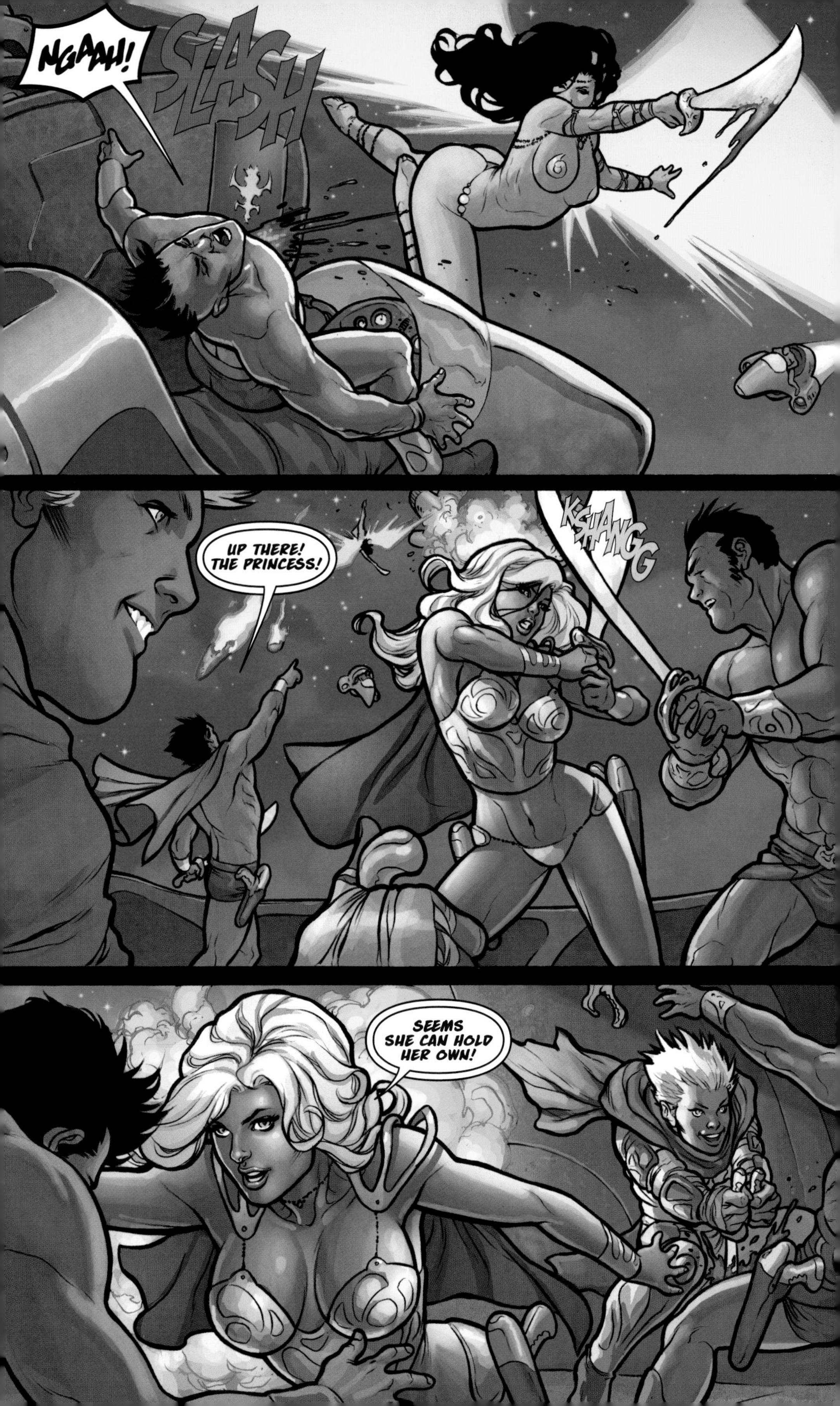
NGAAH!
SLASH
UP THERE! THE PRINCESS!
K-SHANGG
SEEMS SHE CAN HOLD HER OWN!

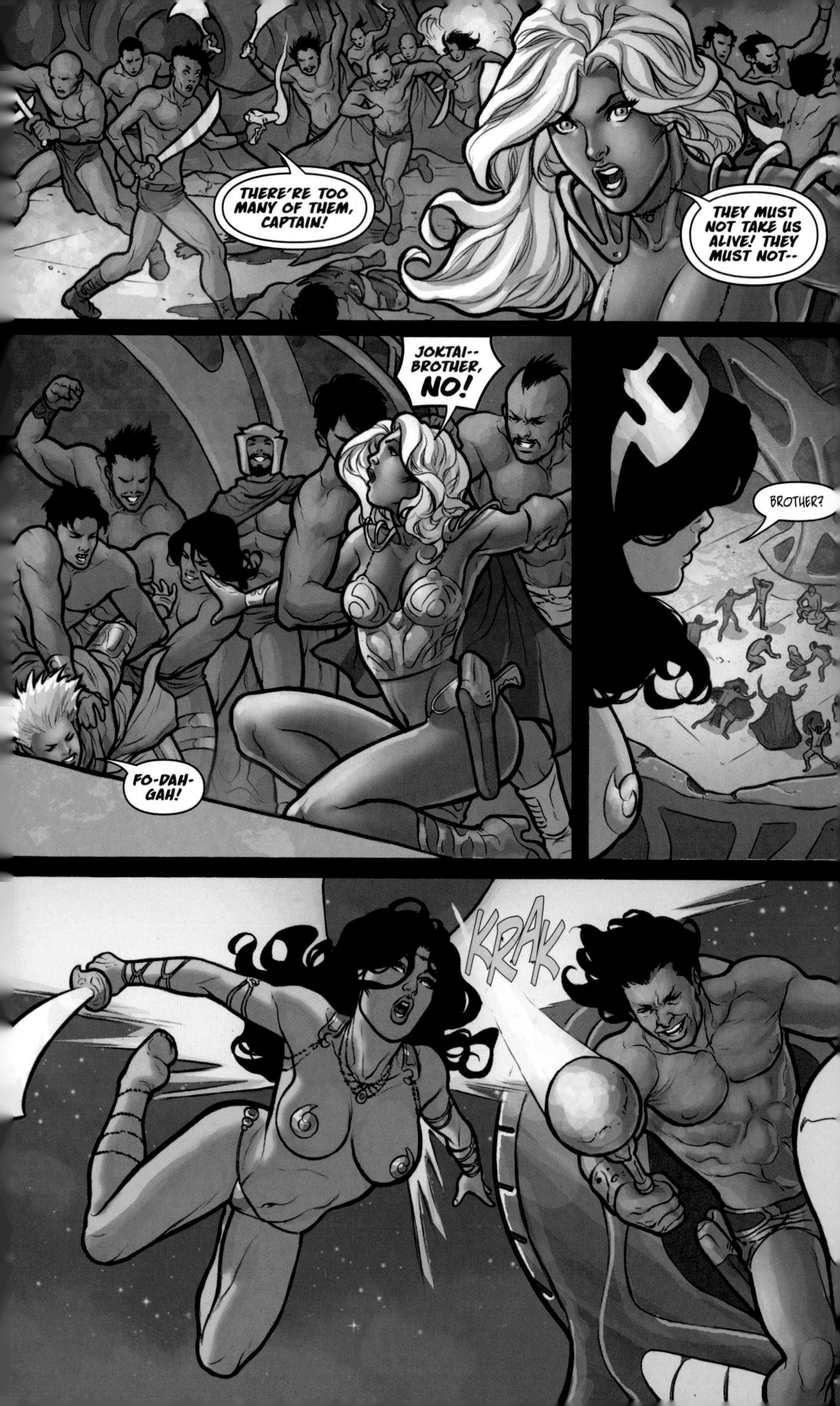
THERE'RE TOO MANY OF THEM, CAPTAIN!
THEY MUST NOT TAKE US ALIVE! THEY MUST NOT--
JOKTAI-- BROTHER, NO!
FO-DAH-GAH!
BROTHER?
KRAK

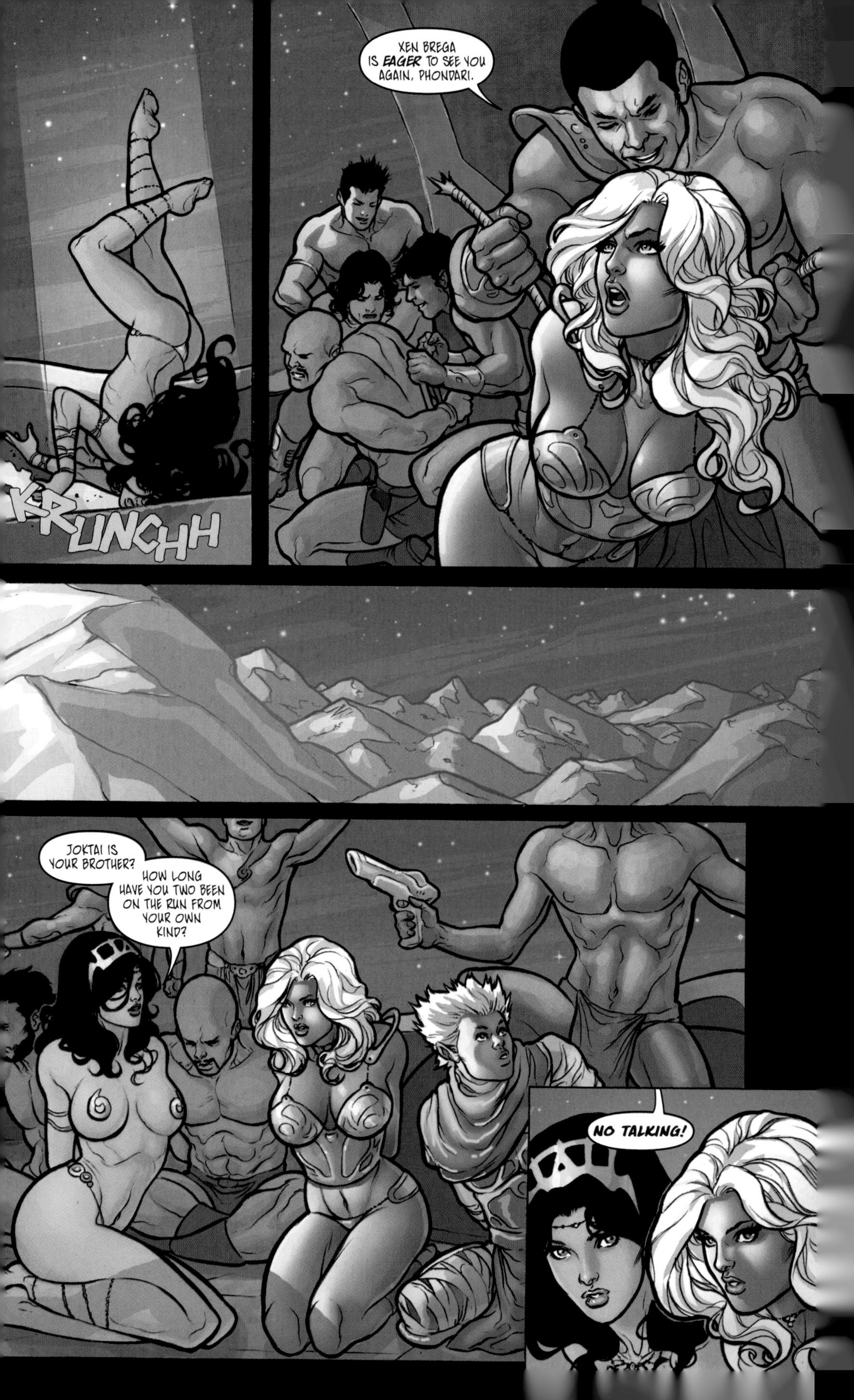
KRUNCHH
XEN BREGA IS **EAGER** TO SEE YOU AGAIN, PHONDARI.
JOKTAI IS YOUR BROTHER?
HOW LONG HAVE YOU TWO BEEN ON THE RUN FROM YOUR OWN KIND?
NO TALKING!

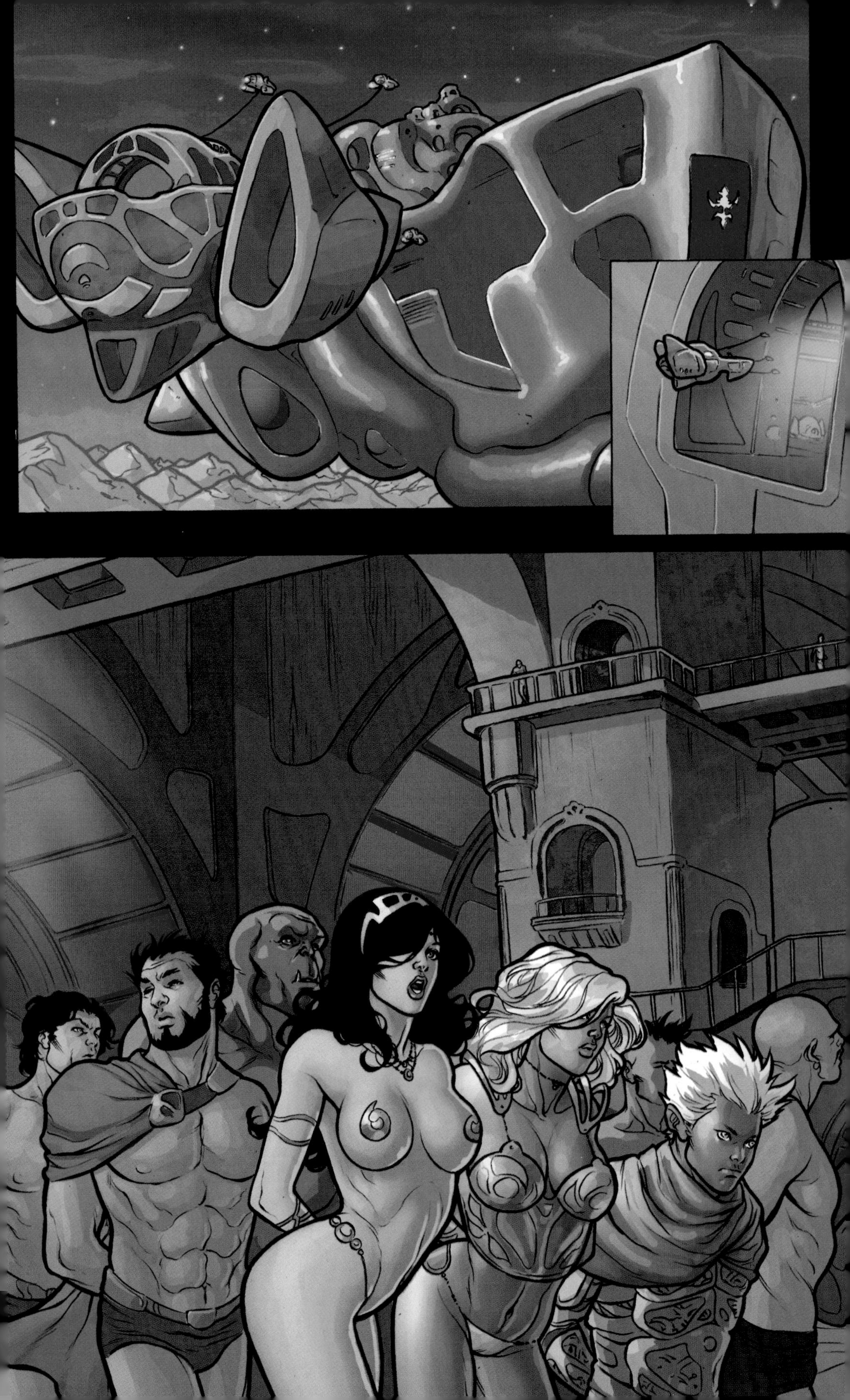

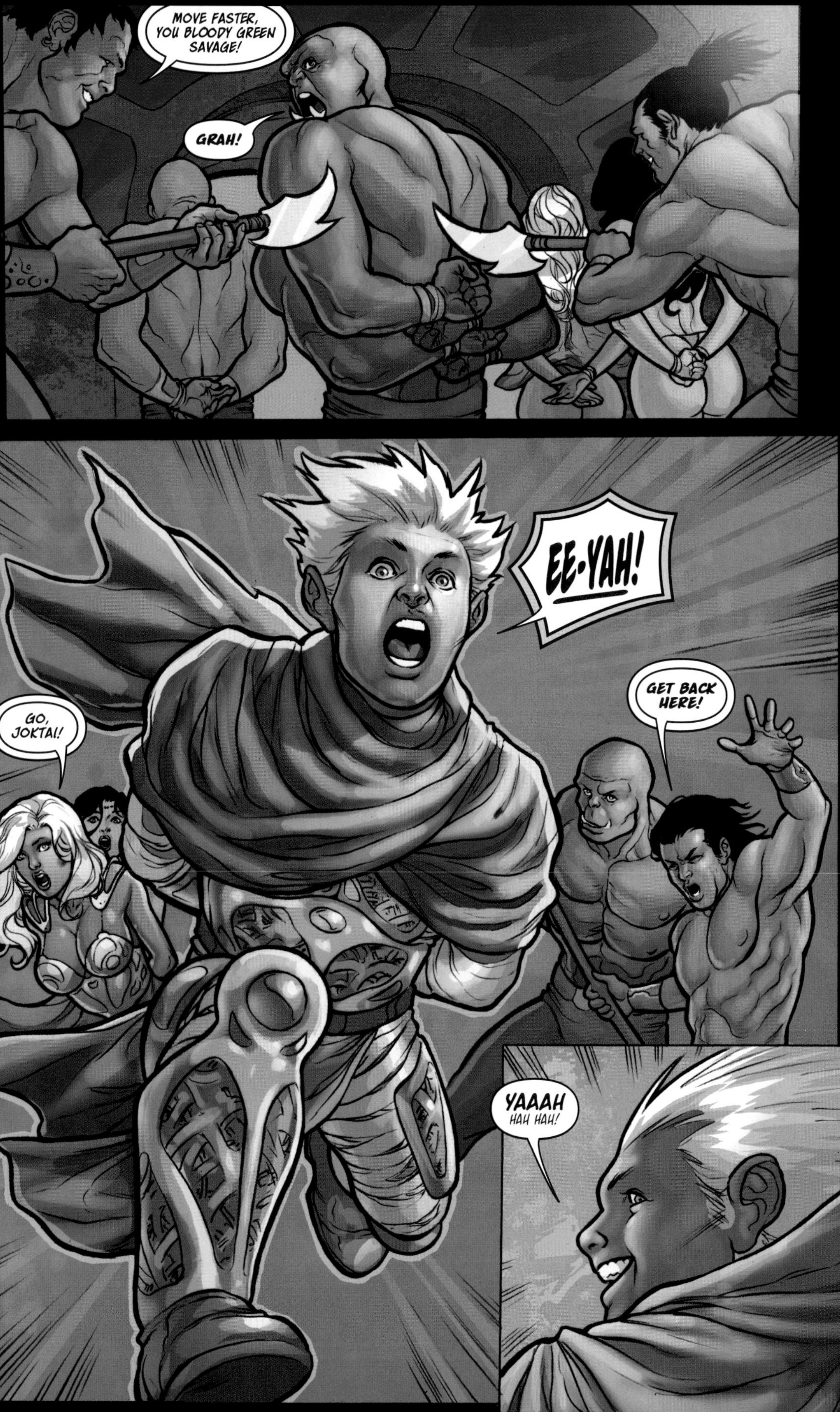
MOVE FASTER, YOU BLOODY GREEN SAVAGE!
GRAH!
EE-YAH!
GET BACK HERE!
GO, JOKTAI!
YAAAH HAH HAH!

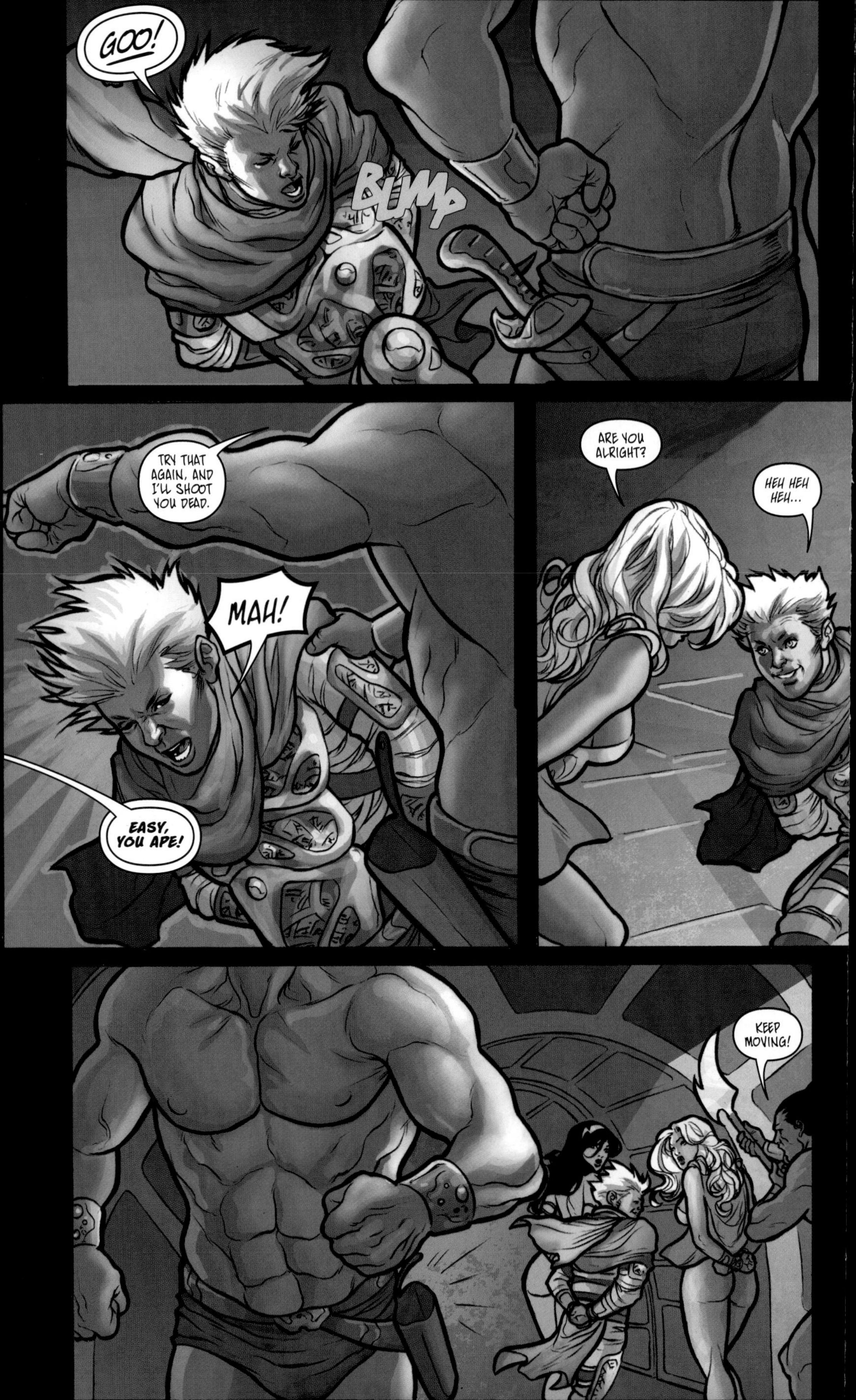
GOO!
BUMP
TRY THAT AGAIN, AND I'LL SHOOT YOU DEAD.
MAH!
EASY, YOU APE!
ARE YOU ALRIGHT?
HEH HEH HEH...
KEEP MOVING!

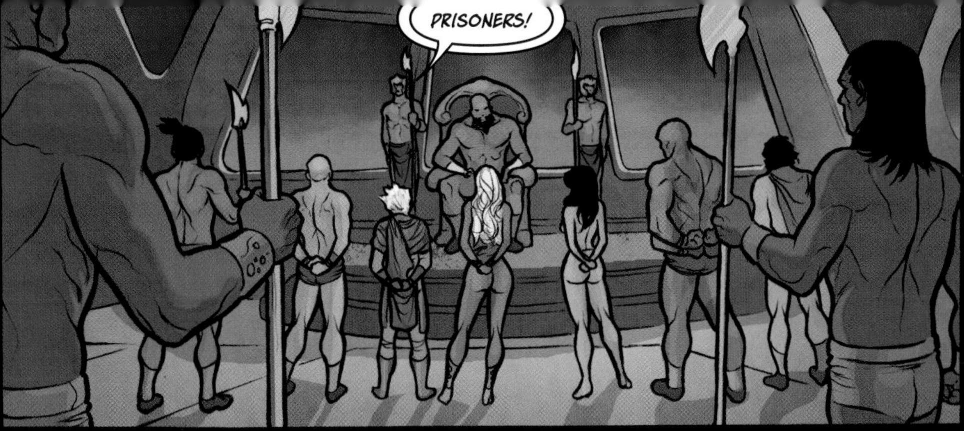
PRISONERS!

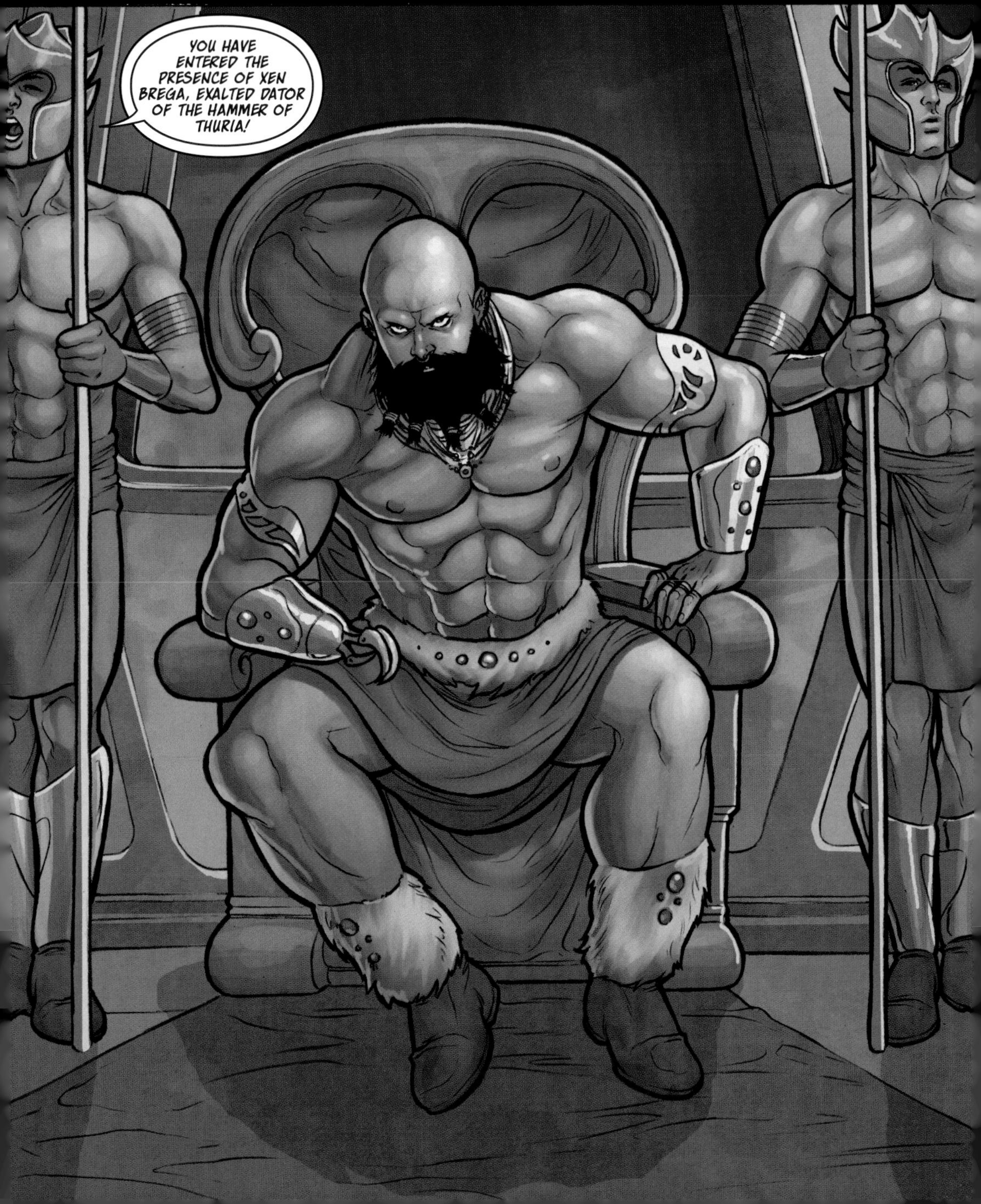
YOU HAVE ENTERED THE PRESENCE OF XEN BREGA, EXALTED DATOR OF THE HAMMER OF THURIA!

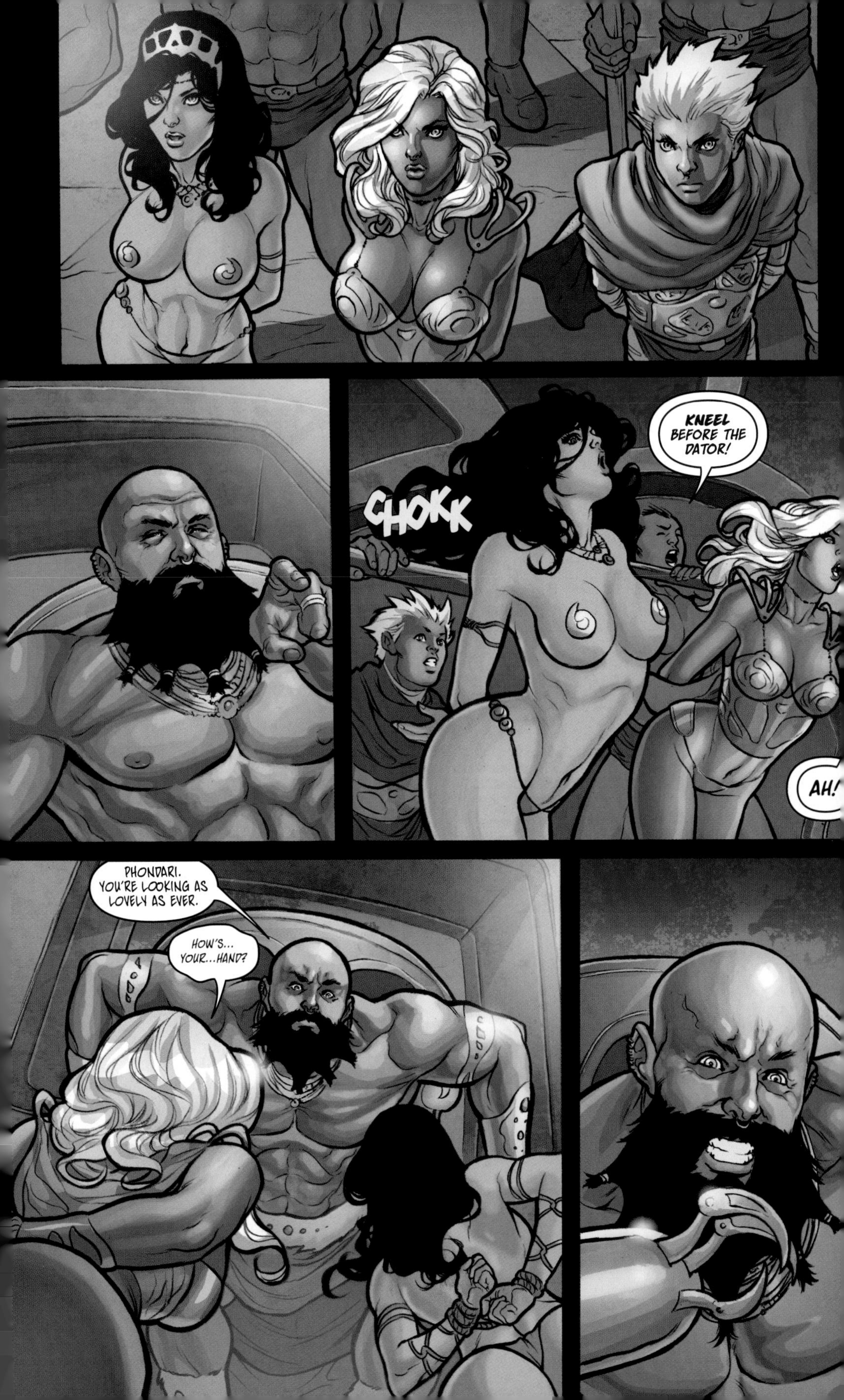
CHOKK
KNEEL BEFORE THE DATOR!
AH!
PHONDARI. YOU'RE LOOKING AS LOVELY AS EVER.
HOW'S... YOUR...HAND?

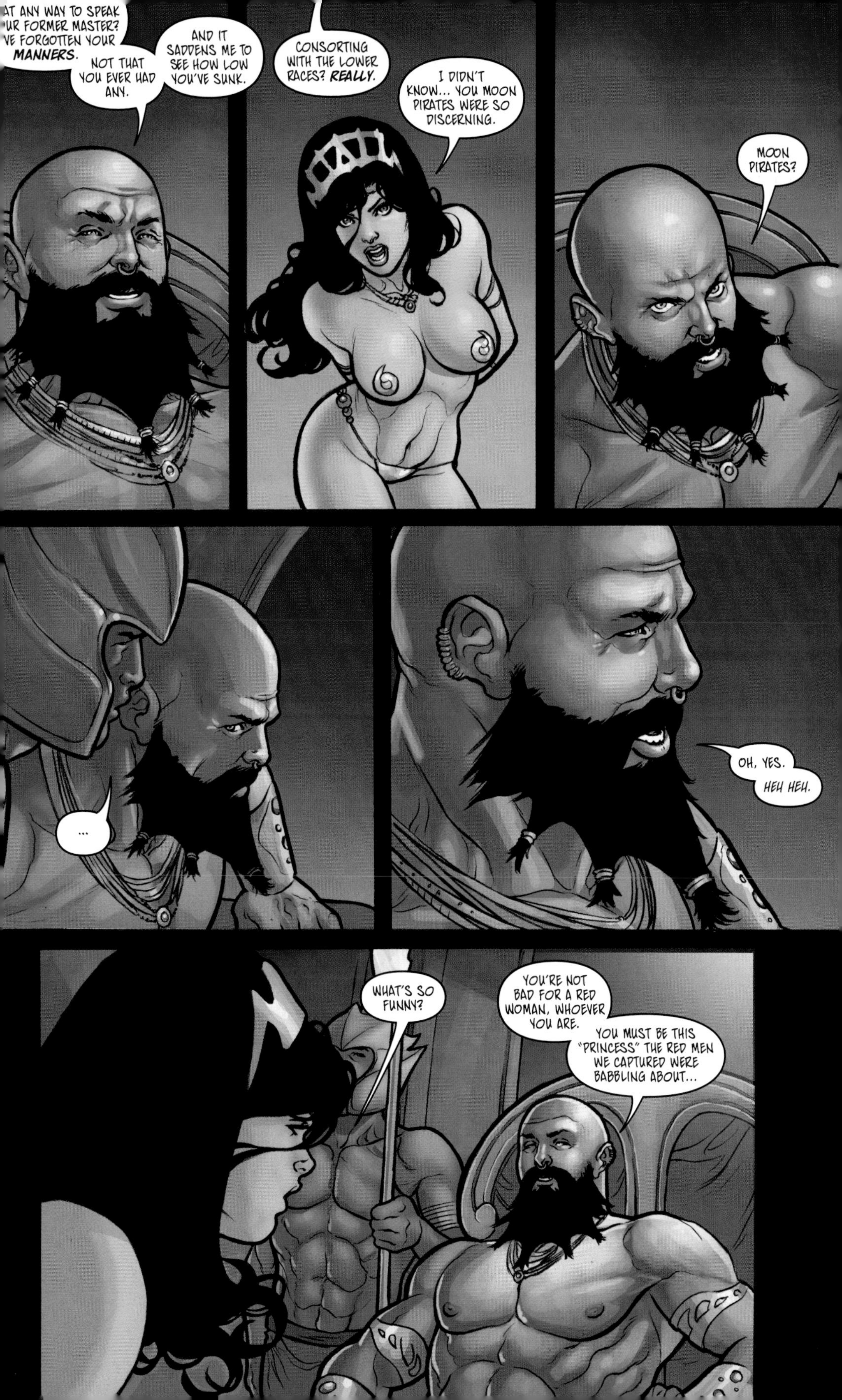
AT ANY WAY TO SPEAK UR FORMER MASTER? VE FORGOTTEN YOUR **MANNERS**.
NOT THAT YOU EVER HAD ANY.
AND IT SADDENS ME TO SEE HOW LOW YOU'VE SUNK.
CONSORTING WITH THE LOWER RACES? **REALLY**.
I DIDN'T KNOW... YOU MOON PIRATES WERE SO DISCERNING.
MOON PIRATES?
...
OH, YES.
HEH HEH.
WHAT'S SO FUNNY?
YOU'RE NOT BAD FOR A RED WOMAN, WHOEVER YOU ARE.
YOU MUST BE THIS "PRINCESS" THE RED MEN WE CAPTURED WERE BABBLING ABOUT...

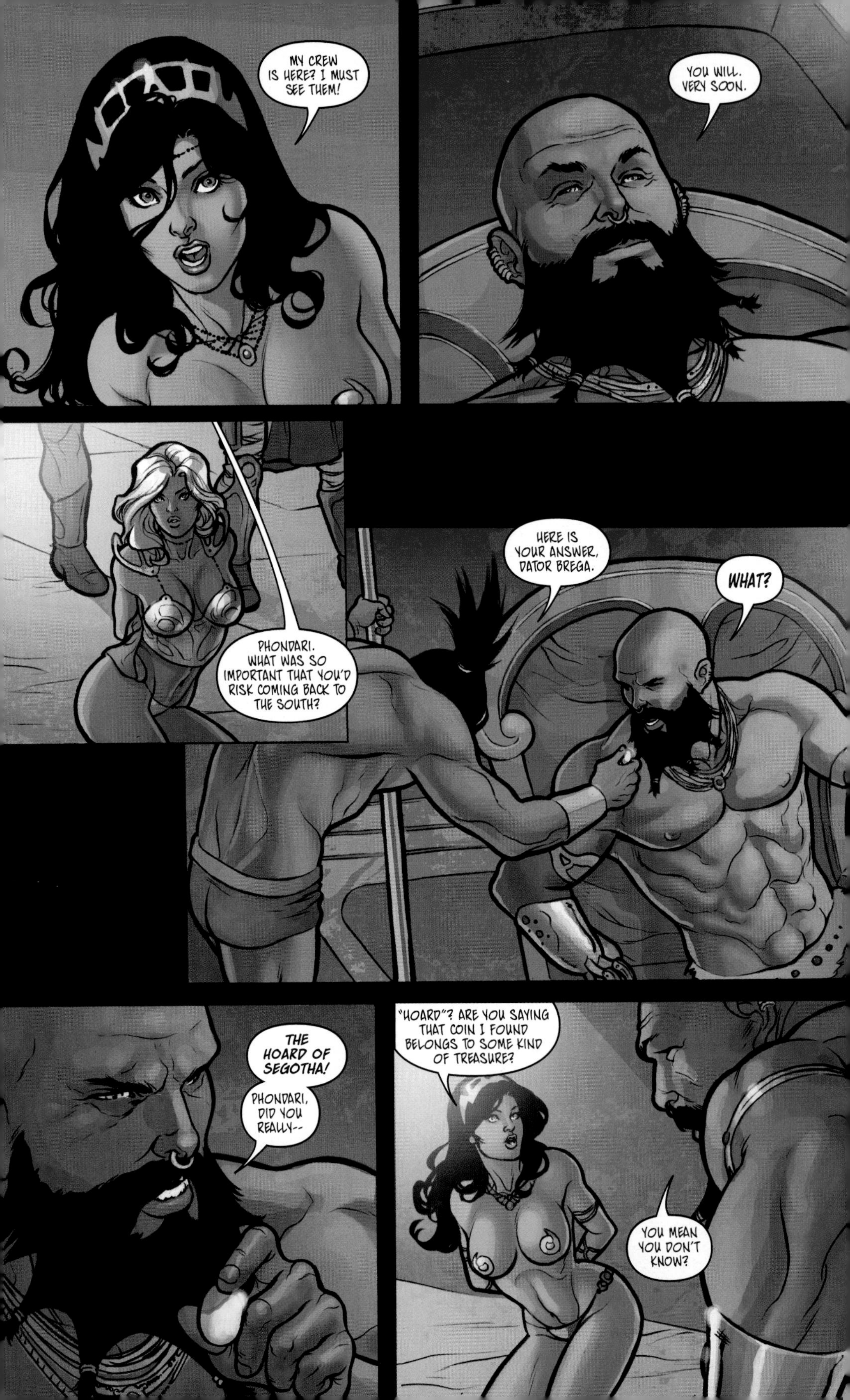
MY CREW IS HERE? I MUST SEE THEM!
YOU WILL. VERY SOON.
PHONDARI. WHAT WAS SO IMPORTANT THAT YOU'D RISK COMING BACK TO THE SOUTH?
HERE IS YOUR ANSWER, DATOR BREGA.
WHAT?
THE HOARD OF SEGOTHA!
PHONDARI, DID YOU REALLY--
"HOARD"? ARE YOU SAYING THAT COIN I FOUND BELONGS TO SOME KIND OF TREASURE?
YOU MEAN YOU DON'T KNOW?

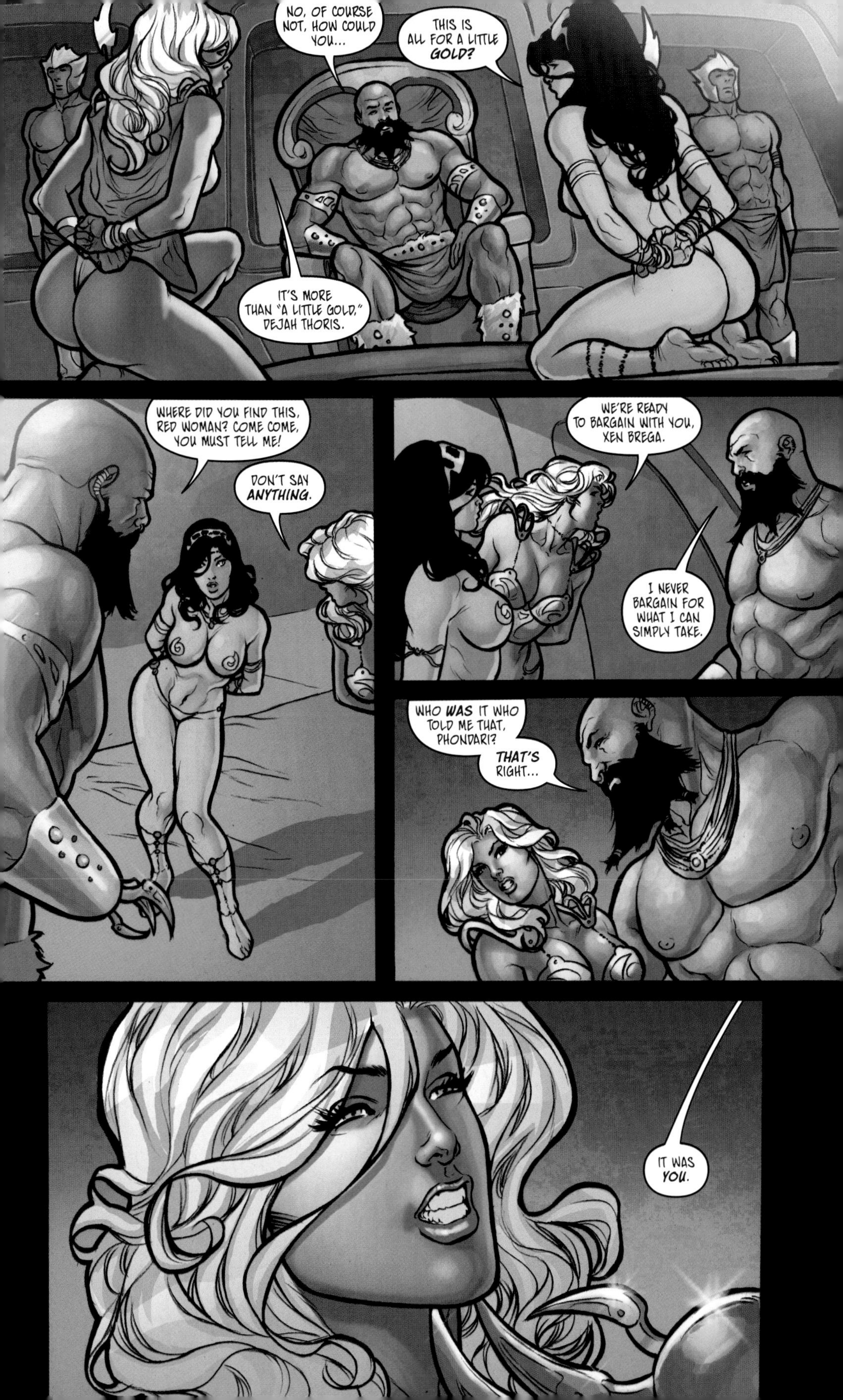
NO, OF COURSE NOT, HOW COULD YOU...
THIS IS ALL FOR A LITTLE GOLD?
IT'S MORE THAN "A LITTLE GOLD," DEJAH THORIS.
WHERE DID YOU FIND THIS, RED WOMAN? COME COME, YOU MUST TELL ME!
DON'T SAY ANYTHING.
WE'RE READY TO BARGAIN WITH YOU, XEN BREGA.
I NEVER BARGAIN FOR WHAT I CAN SIMPLY TAKE.
WHO WAS IT WHO TOLD ME THAT, PHONDARI?
THAT'S RIGHT...
IT WAS YOU.

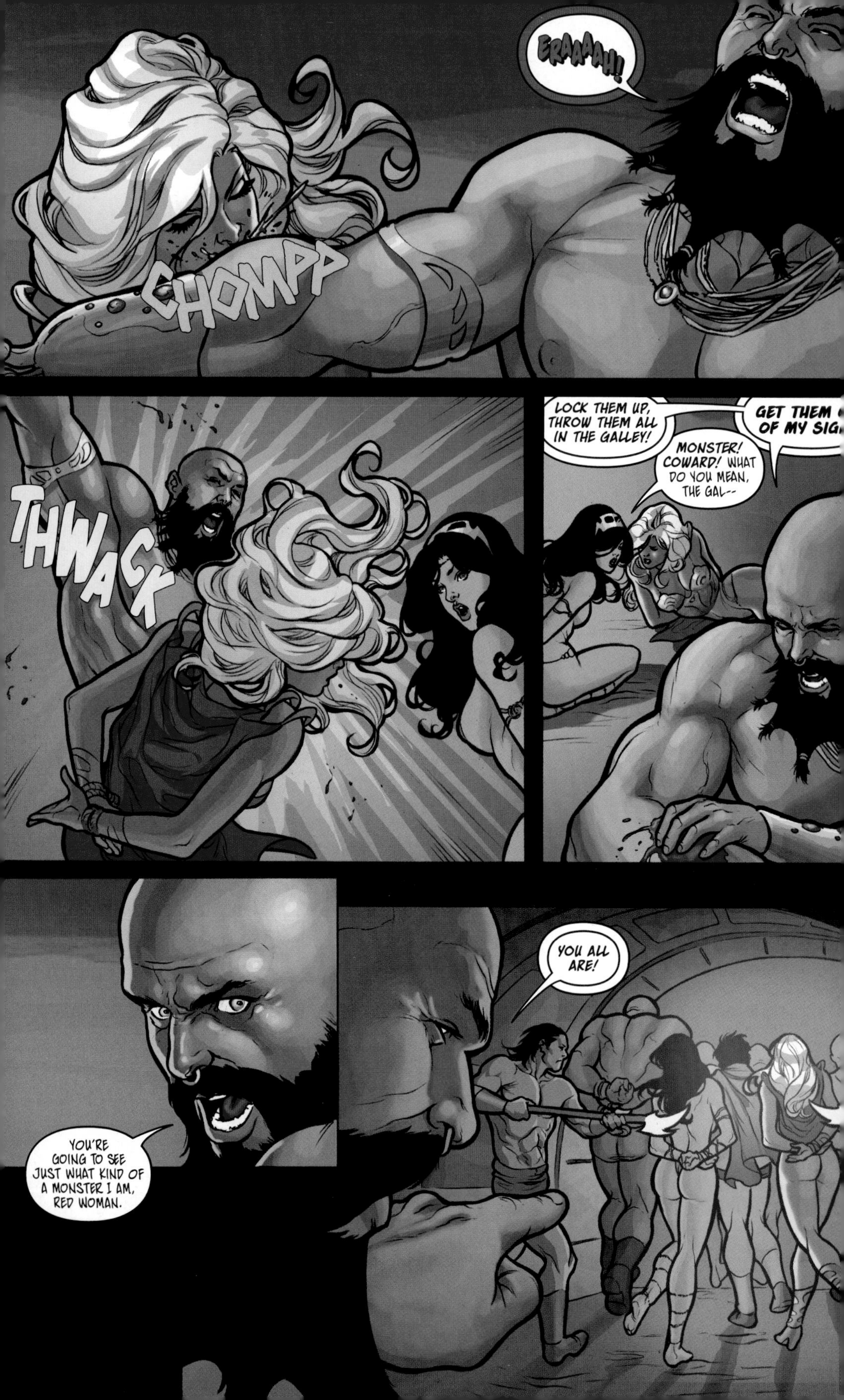
ERAAAAH!
CHOMPP
THWACK
LOCK THEM UP, THROW THEM ALL IN THE GALLEY!
GET THEM OUT OF MY SIGHT
MONSTER! COWARD! WHAT DO YOU MEAN, THE GAL--
YOU'RE GOING TO SEE JUST WHAT KIND OF A MONSTER I AM, RED WOMAN.
YOU ALL ARE!

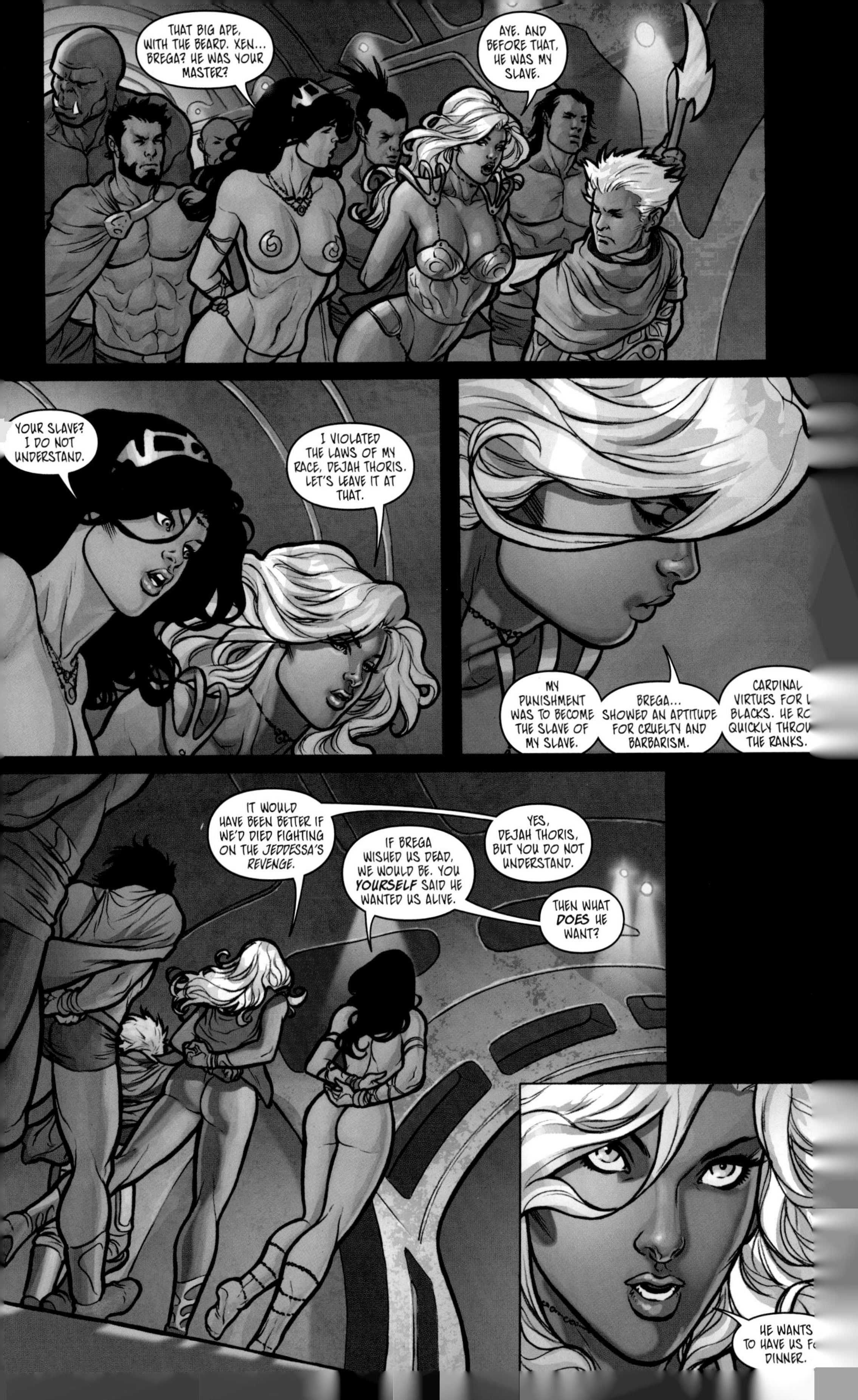
THAT BIG APE, WITH THE BEARD. XEN... BREGA? HE WAS YOUR MASTER?
AYE. AND BEFORE THAT, HE WAS MY SLAVE.
YOUR SLAVE? I DO NOT UNDERSTAND.
I VIOLATED THE LAWS OF MY RACE, DEJAH THORIS. LET'S LEAVE IT AT THAT.
MY PUNISHMENT WAS TO BECOME THE SLAVE OF MY SLAVE.
BREGA... SHOWED AN APTITUDE FOR CRUELTY AND BARBARISM.
CARDINAL VIRTUES FOR L BLACKS. HE RO QUICKLY THROU THE RANKS.
IT WOULD HAVE BEEN BETTER IF WE'D DIED FIGHTING ON THE JEDDESSA'S REVENGE.
YES, DEJAH THORIS, BUT YOU DO NOT UNDERSTAND.
IF BREGA WISHED US DEAD, WE WOULD BE. YOU YOURSELF SAID HE WANTED US ALIVE.
THEN WHAT DOES HE WANT?
HE WANTS TO HAVE US F DINNER.

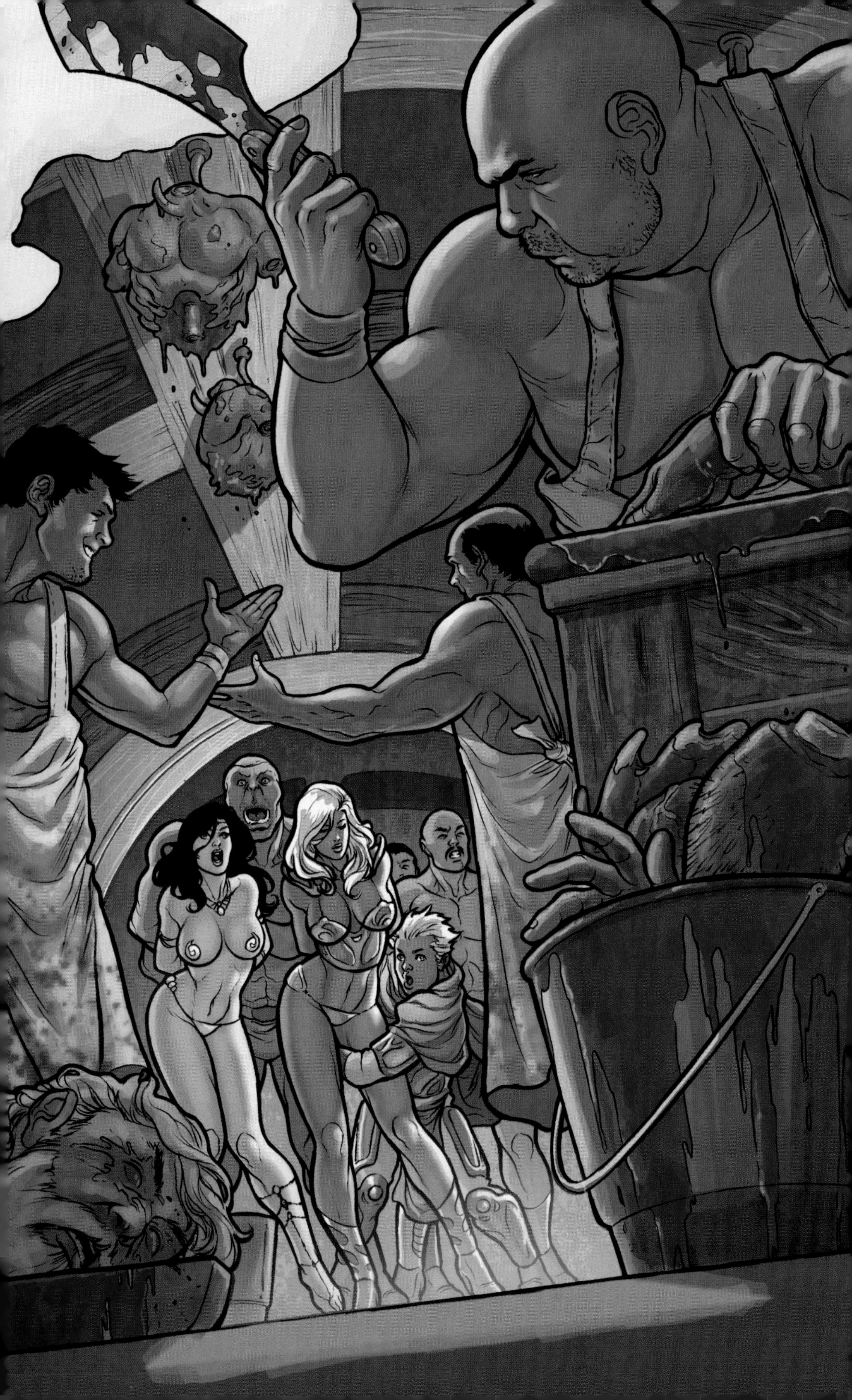

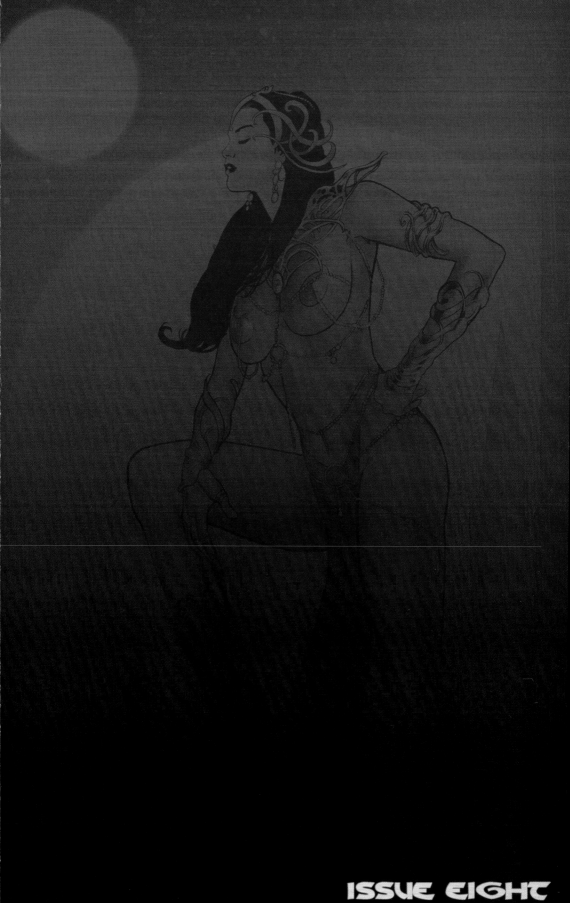

ISSUE EIGHT
THE HOARD OF SAGOTHA

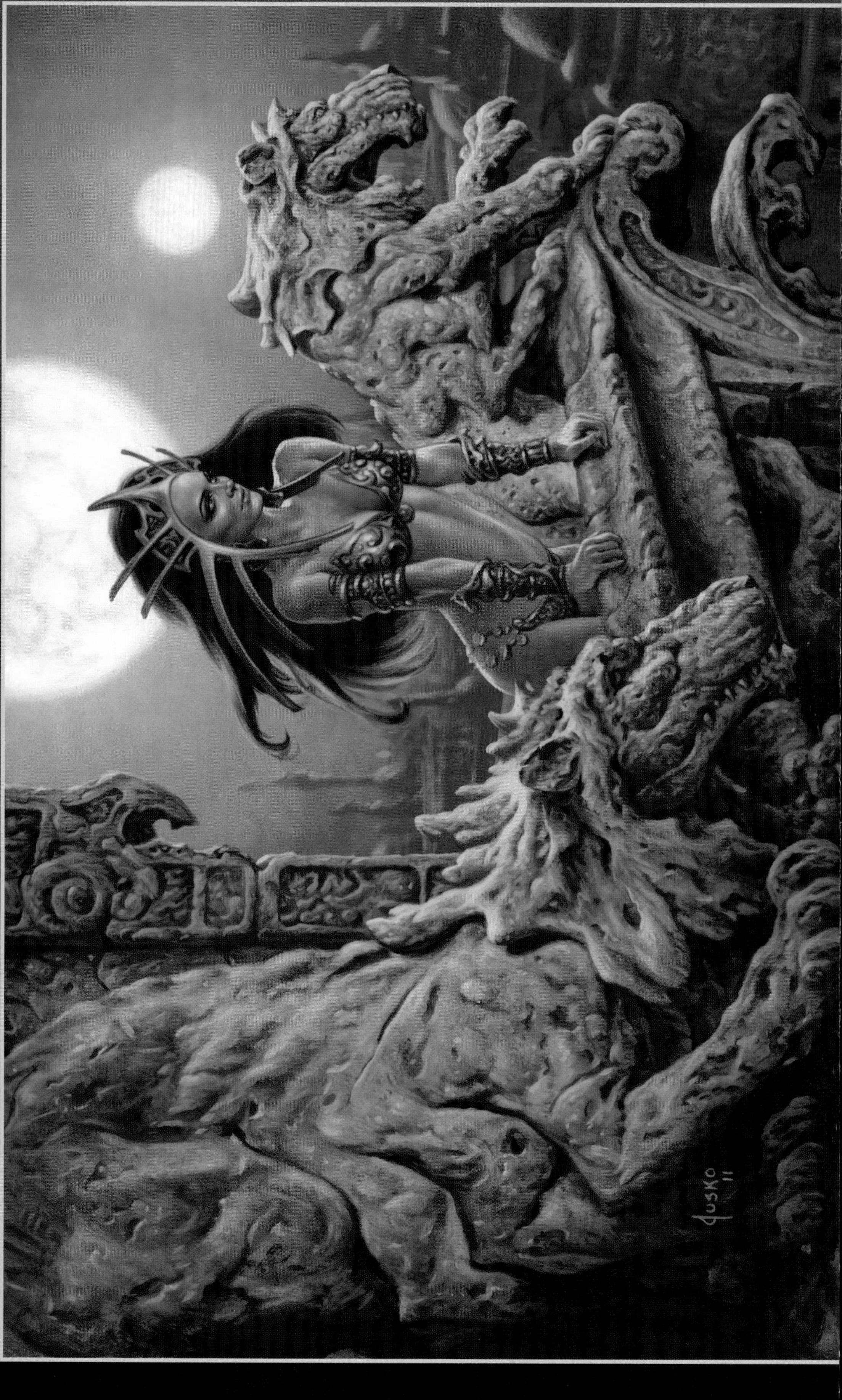

issue #8 cover by **JOE JUSKO**

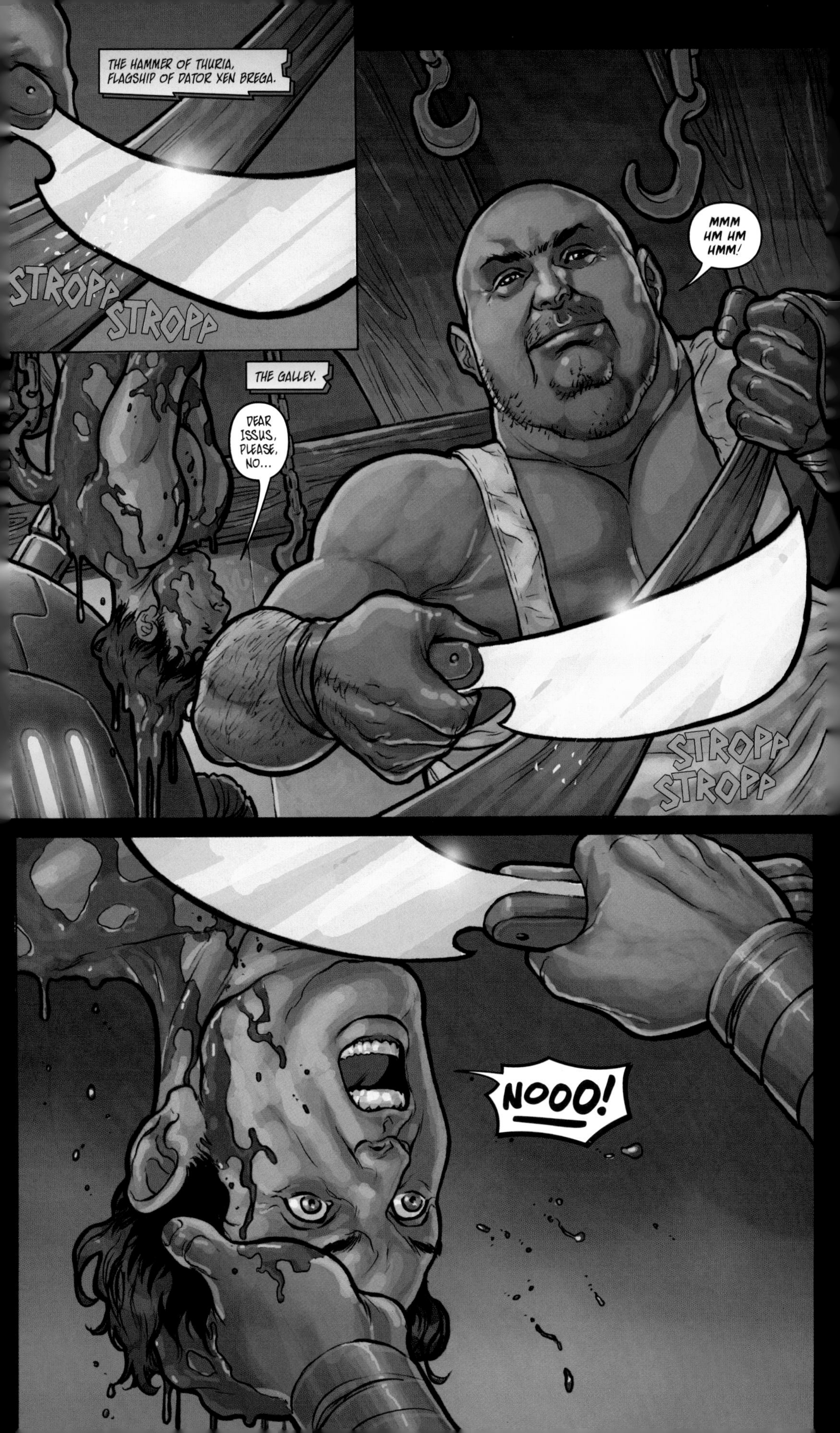
THE HAMMER OF THURIA, FLAGSHIP OF DATOR XEN BREGA.
STROPP STROPP
MMM HM HM HMM!
THE GALLEY.
DEAR ISSUS, PLEASE, NO...
STROPP STROPP
NOOO!

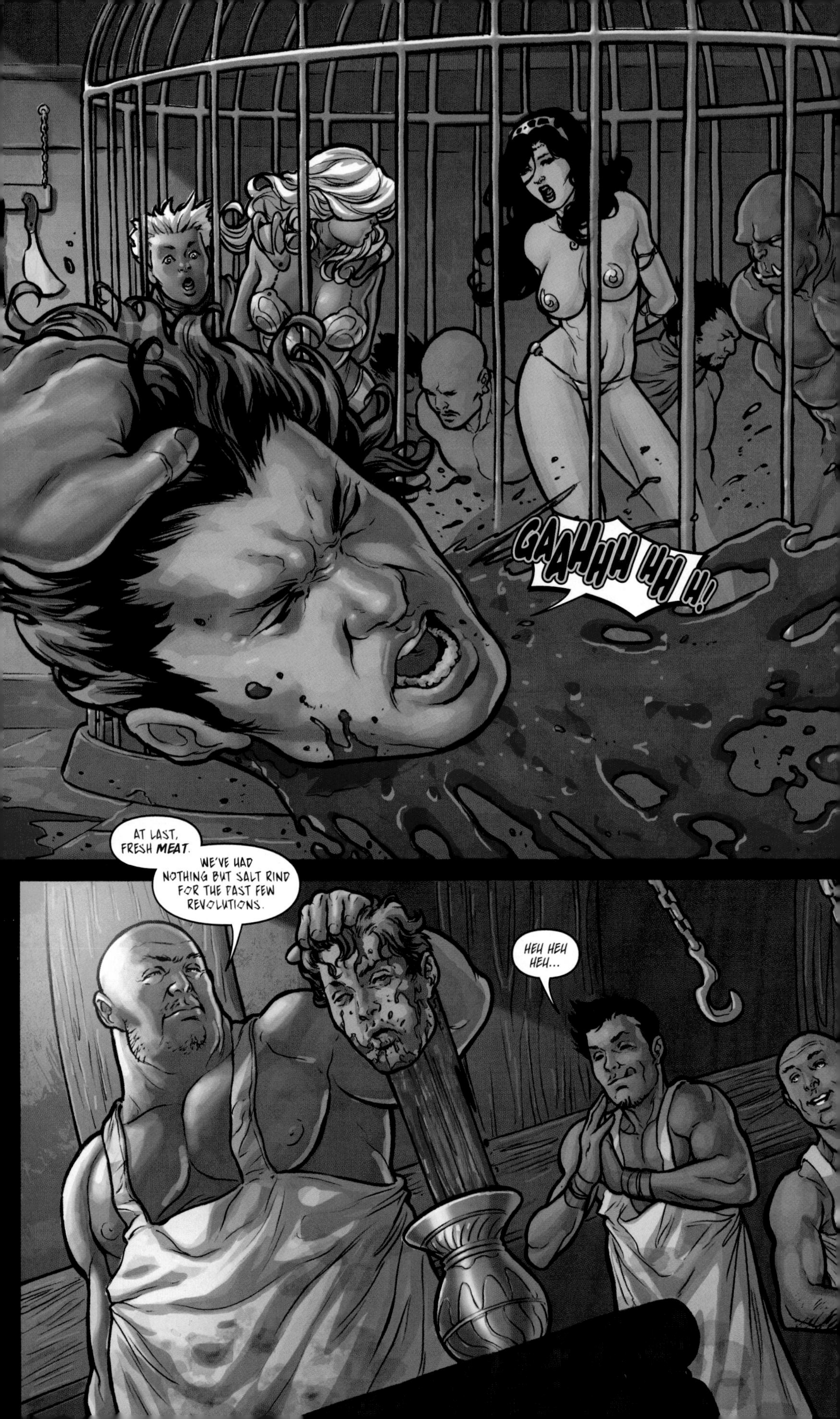
GAAHHH HH H!
AT LAST, FRESH MEAT.
WE'VE HAD NOTHING BUT SALT RIND FOR THE PAST FEW REVOLUTIONS.
HEH HEH HEH...

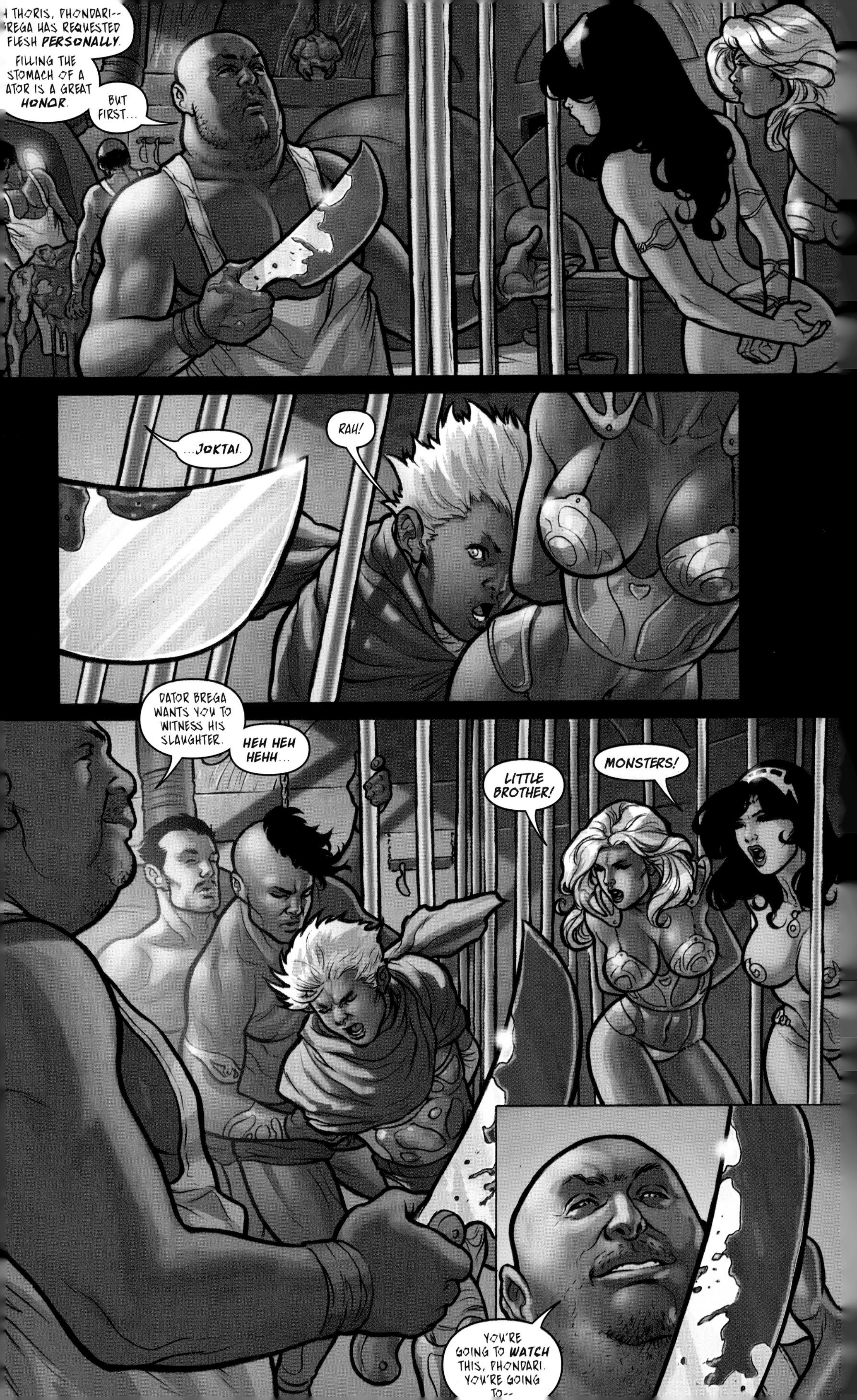

H THORIS, PHONDARI-- BREGA HAS REQUESTED FLESH PERSONALLY.
FILLING THE STOMACH OF A ATOR IS A GREAT HONOR.
BUT FIRST...
...JOKTAI.
RAH!
DATOR BREGA WANTS YOU TO WITNESS HIS SLAUGHTER.
HEH HEH HEHH...
LITTLE BROTHER!
MONSTERS!
YOU'RE GOING TO WATCH THIS, PHONDARI. YOU'RE GOING TO--

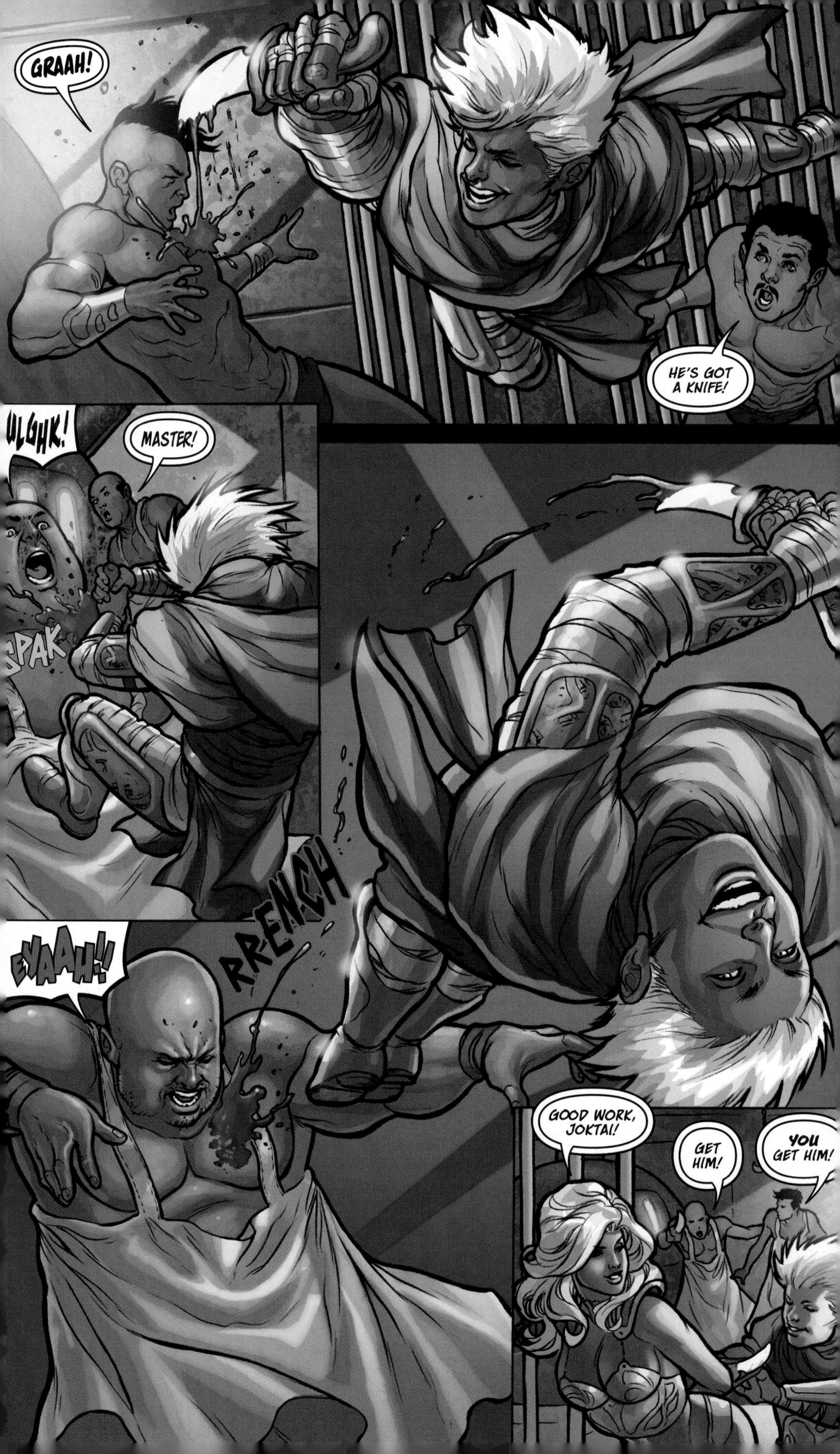
GRAAH!
HE'S GOT A KNIFE!
ULGHK!
MASTER!
SPAK
RRENCH
EYAAH!!
GOOD WORK, JOKTAI!
GET HIM!
YOU GET HIM!

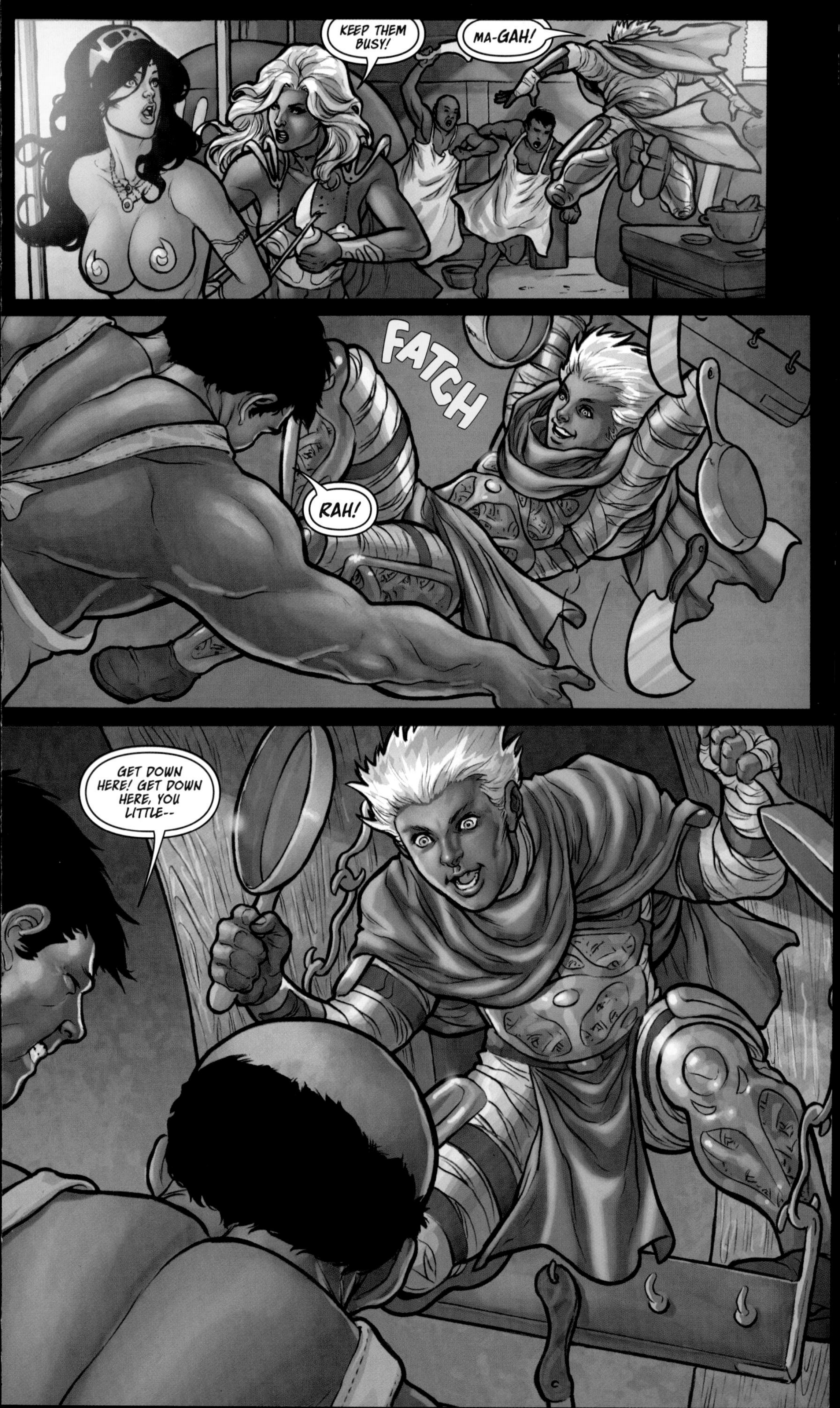
KEEP THEM BUSY!
MA-GAH!
FATCH
RAH!
GET DOWN HERE! GET DOWN HERE, YOU LITTLE--

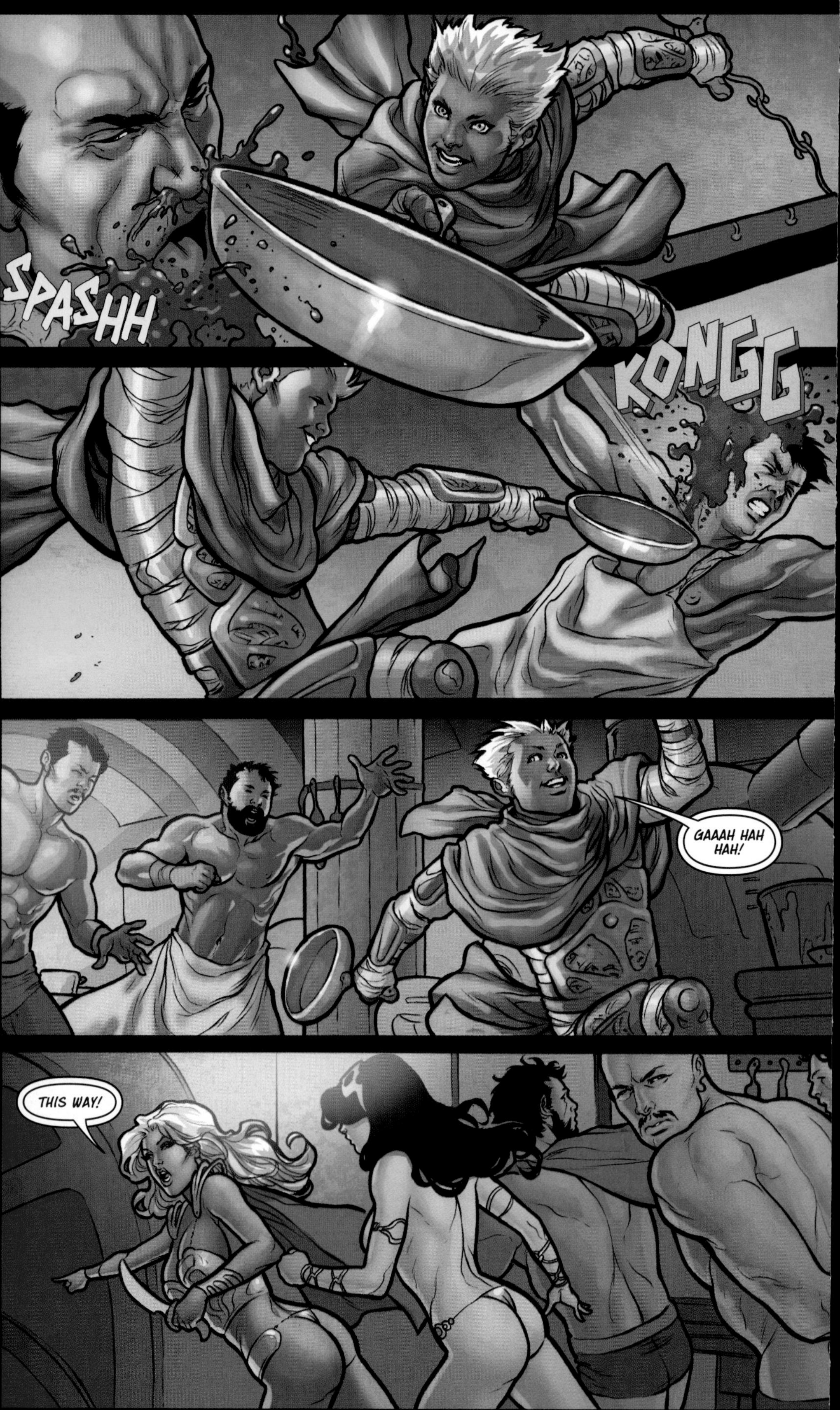
SPASHH
KONGG
GAAAH HAH HAH!
THIS WAY!

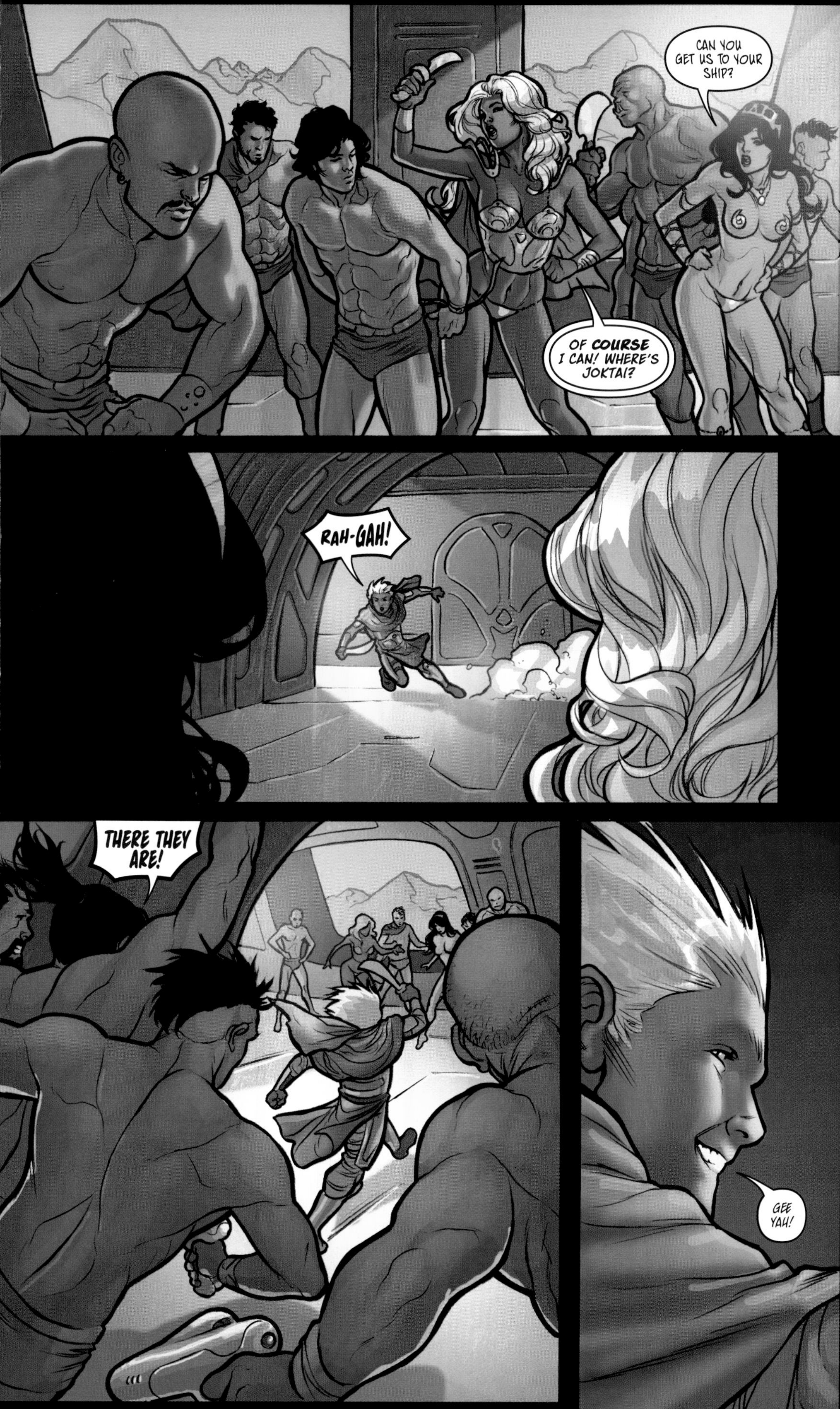
CAN YOU GET US TO YOUR SHIP?
OF COURSE I CAN! WHERE'S JOKTAI?
RAH-GAH!
THERE THEY ARE!
GEE YAH!

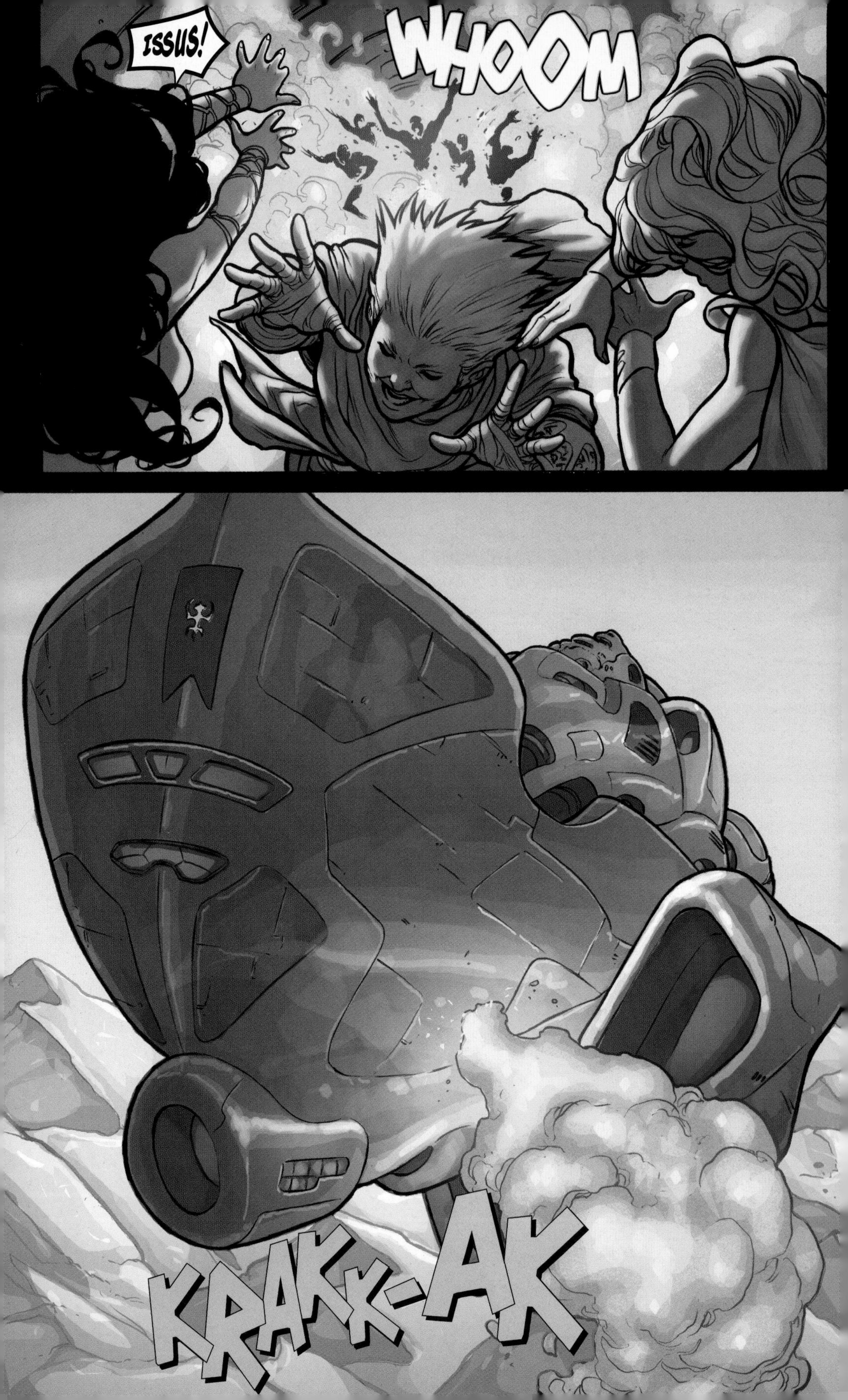
ISSUS!
WHOOM
KRAKK-AK

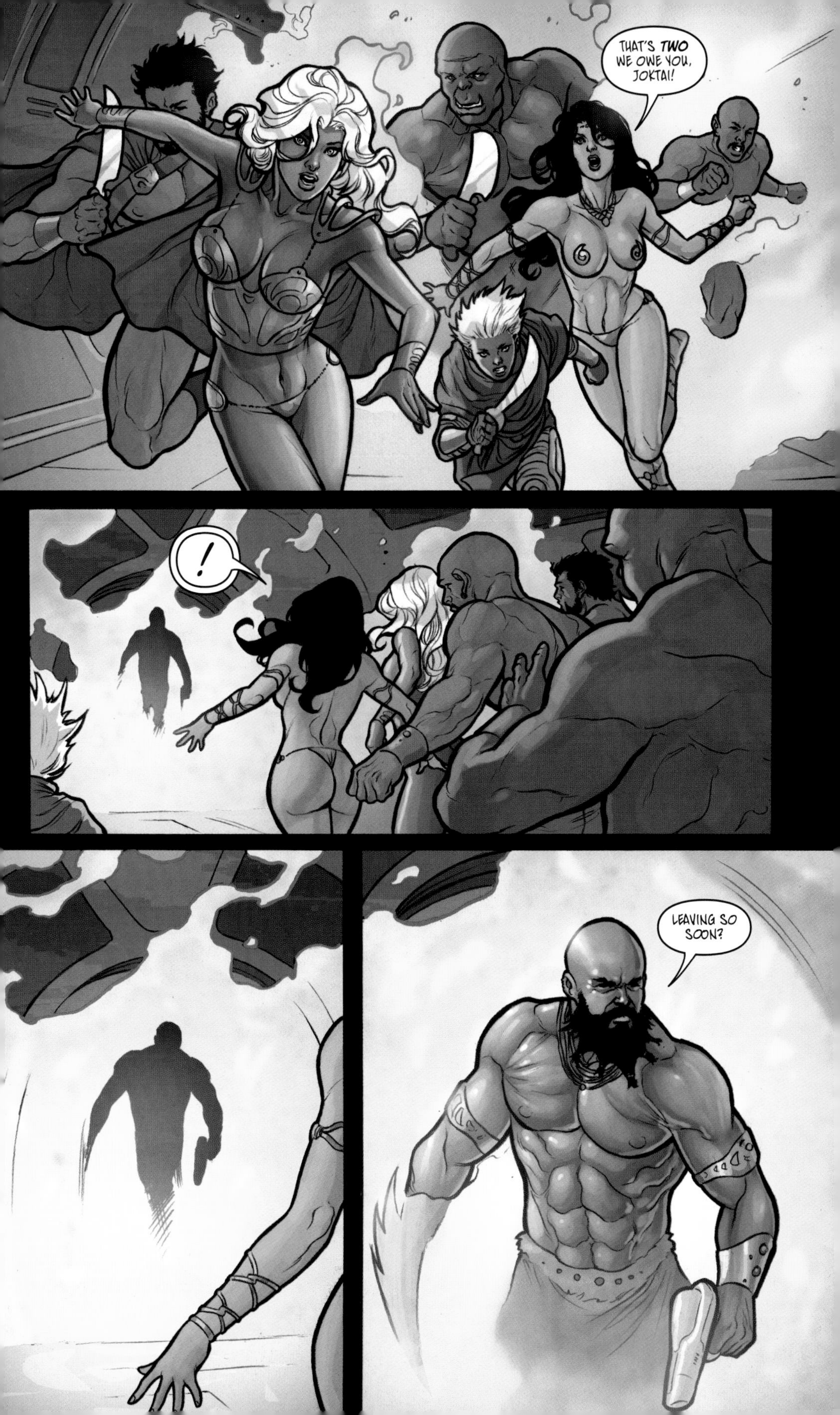
THAT'S TWO WE OWE YOU, JOKTAI!
!
LEAVING SO SOON?

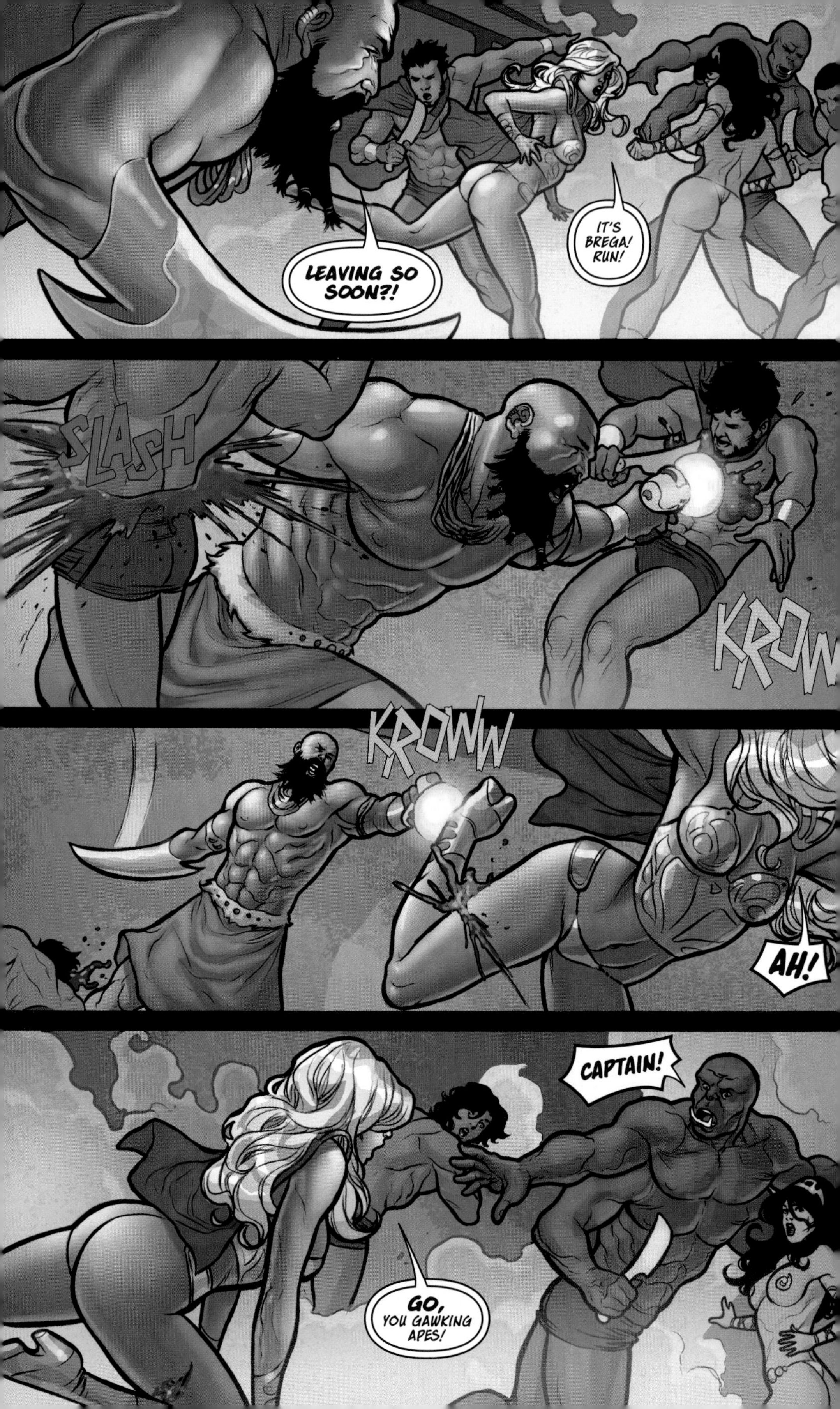
LEAVING SO SOON?!
IT'S BREGA! RUN!
SLASH
KROW
KROWW
AH!
CAPTAIN!
GO, YOU GAWKING APES!

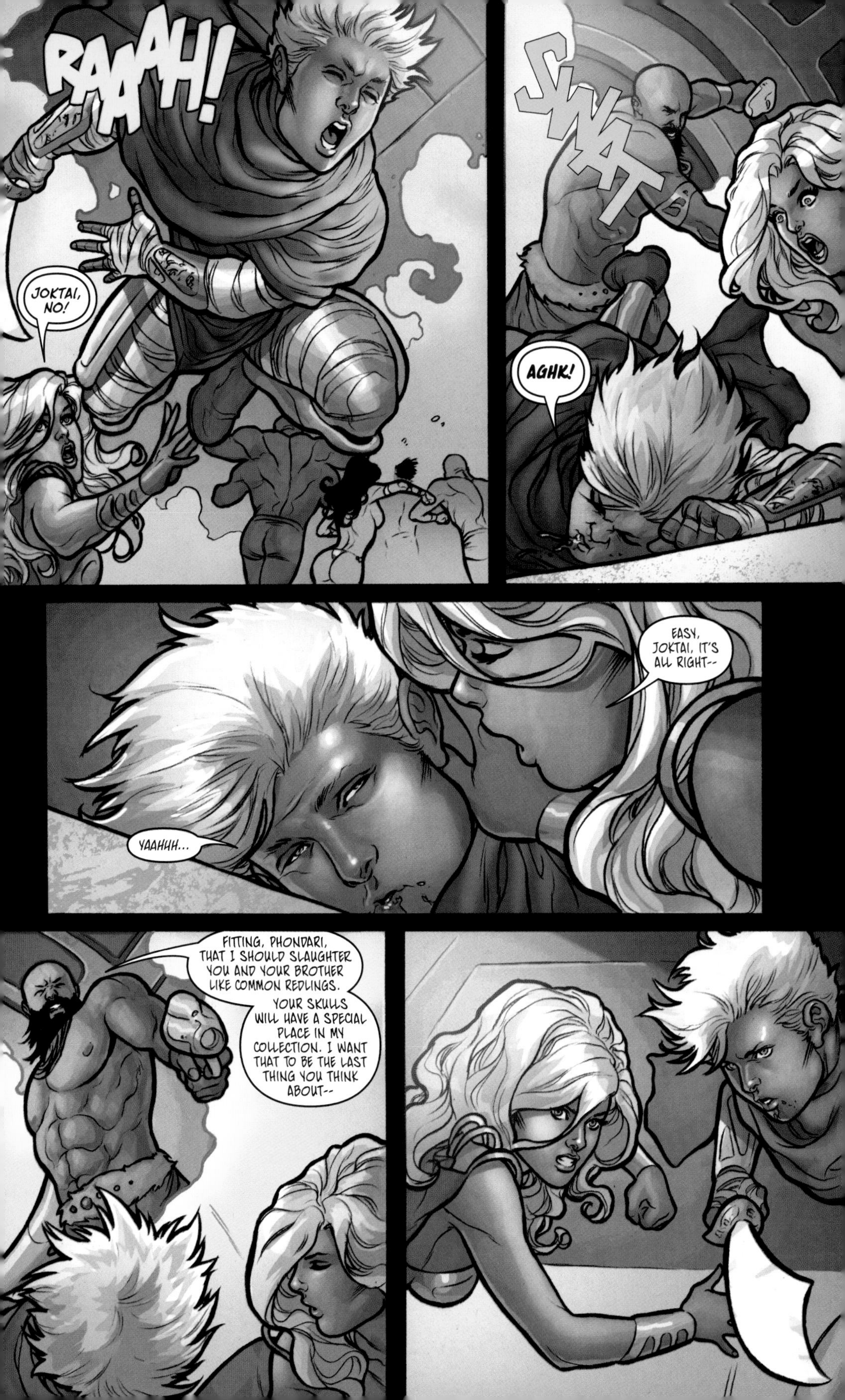
RAAAH!
JOKTAI, NO!
SWAT
AGHK!
EASY, JOKTAI, IT'S ALL RIGHT--
YAAHUH...
FITTING, PHONDARI, THAT I SHOULD SLAUGHTER YOU AND YOUR BROTHER LIKE COMMON REDLINGS.
YOUR SKULLS WILL HAVE A SPECIAL PLACE IN MY COLLECTION. I WANT THAT TO BE THE LAST THING YOU THINK ABOUT--

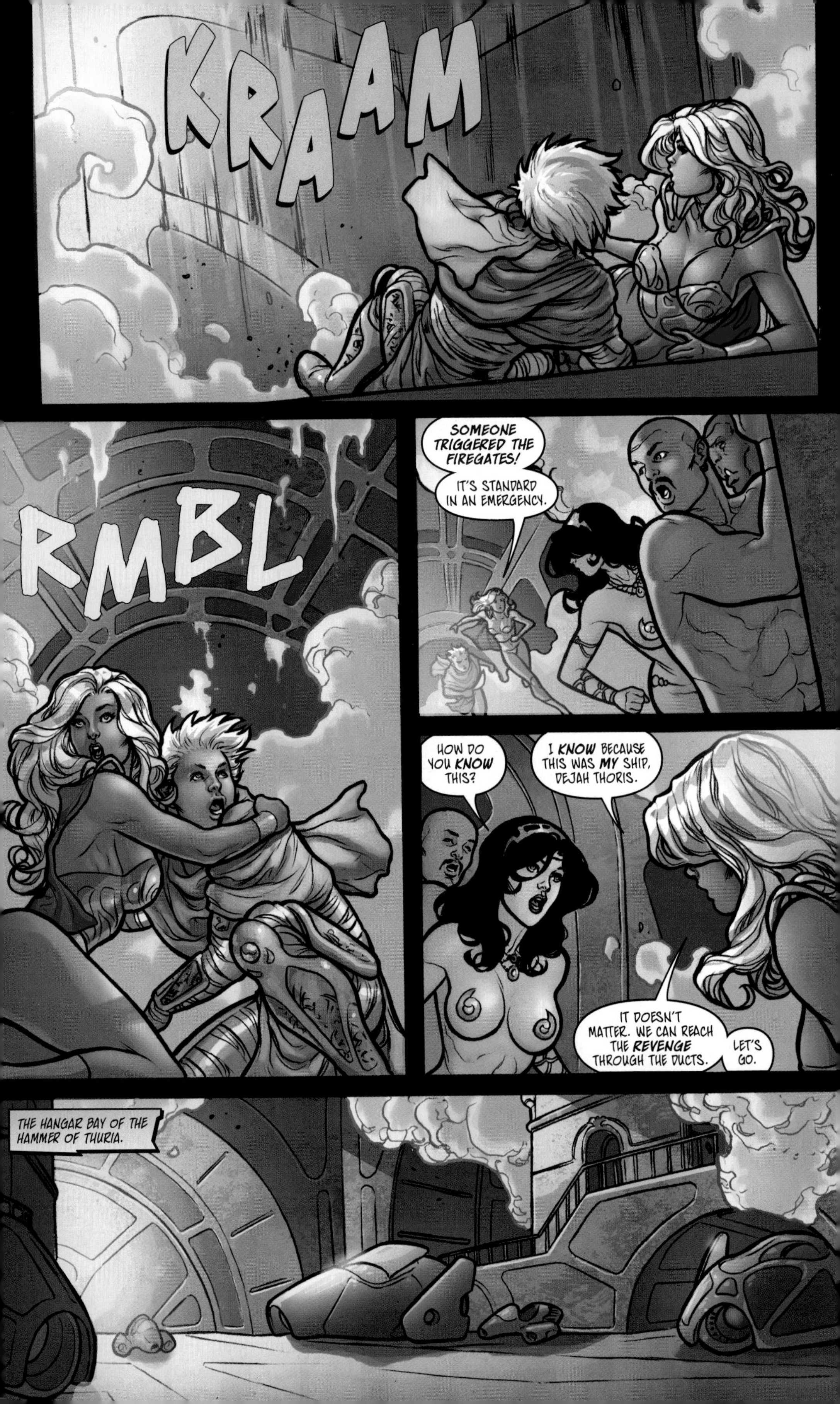
KRAAM
RMBL
SOMEONE TRIGGERED THE FIREGATES!
IT'S STANDARD IN AN EMERGENCY.
HOW DO YOU KNOW THIS?
I KNOW BECAUSE THIS WAS MY SHIP, DEJAH THORIS.
IT DOESN'T MATTER. WE CAN REACH THE REVENGE THROUGH THE DUCTS.
LET'S GO.
THE HANGAR BAY OF THE HAMMER OF THURIA.

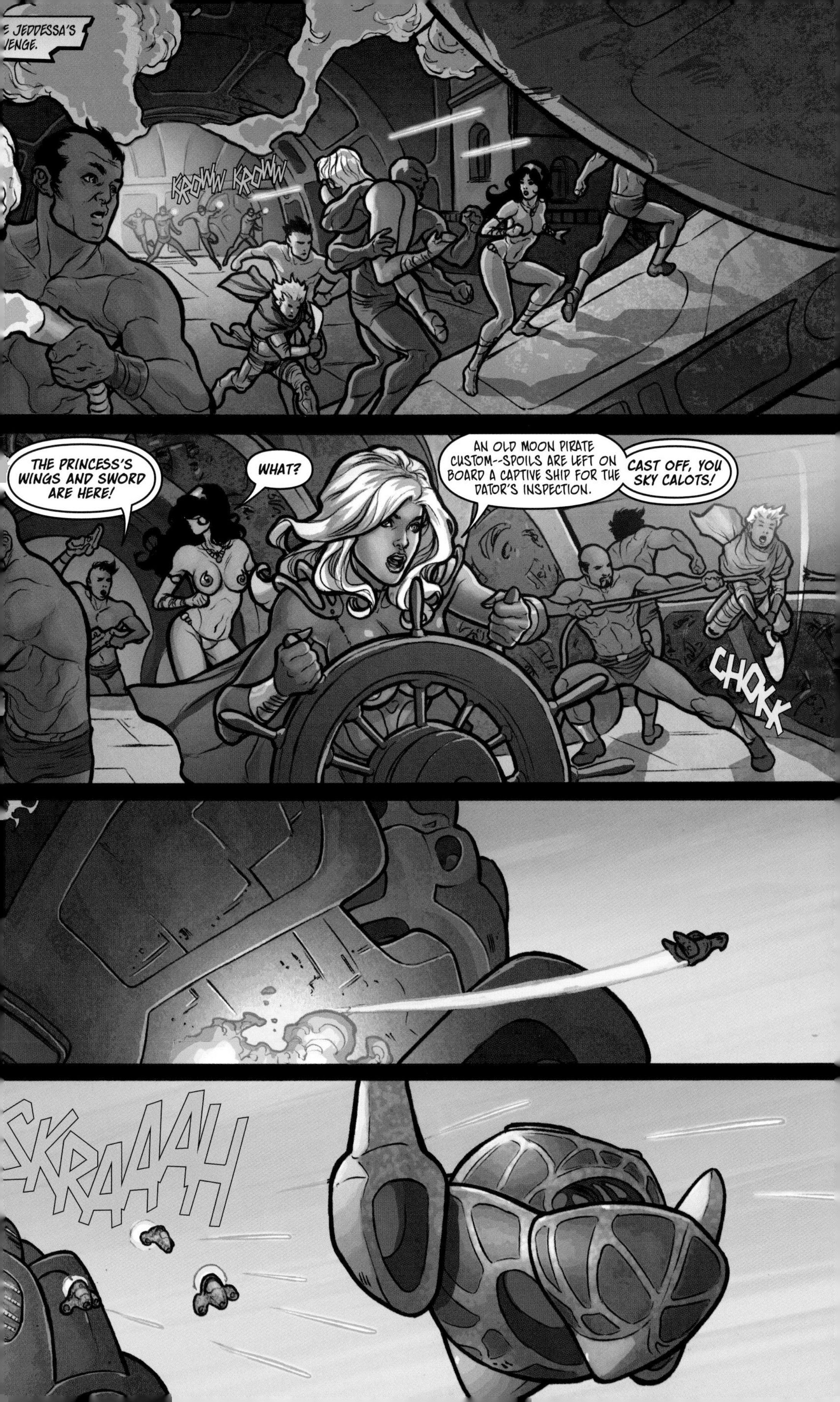
E JEDDESSA'S
VENGE.
KROWW KROWW
THE PRINCESS'S WINGS AND SWORD ARE HERE!
WHAT?
AN OLD MOON PIRATE CUSTOM--SPOILS ARE LEFT ON BOARD A CAPTIVE SHIP FOR THE DATOR'S INSPECTION.
CAST OFF, YOU SKY CALOTS!
CHOKK
SKRAAAH

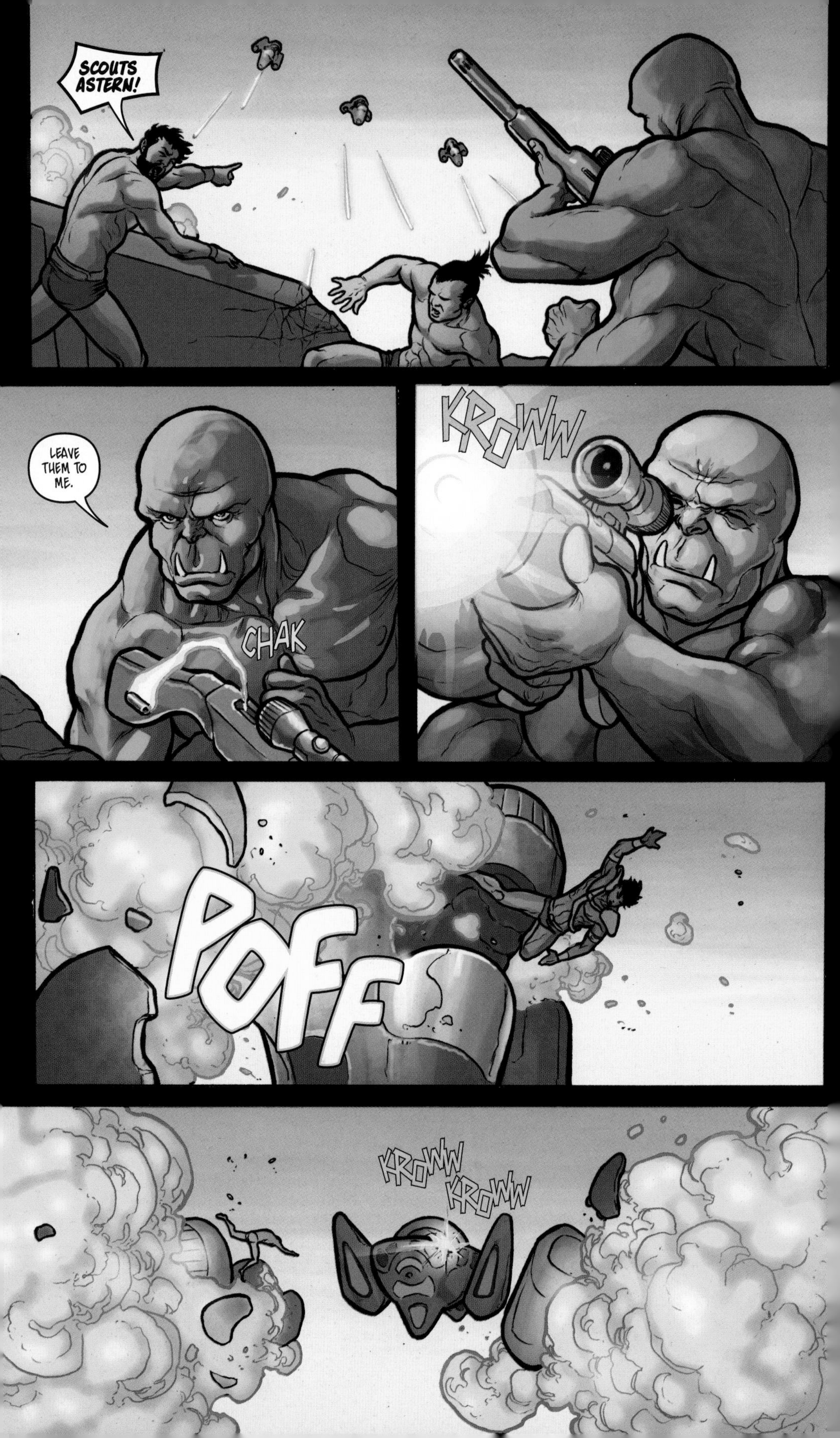
SCOUTS ASTERN!
LEAVE THEM TO ME.
CHAK
KROWW
POFF
KROWW
KROWW

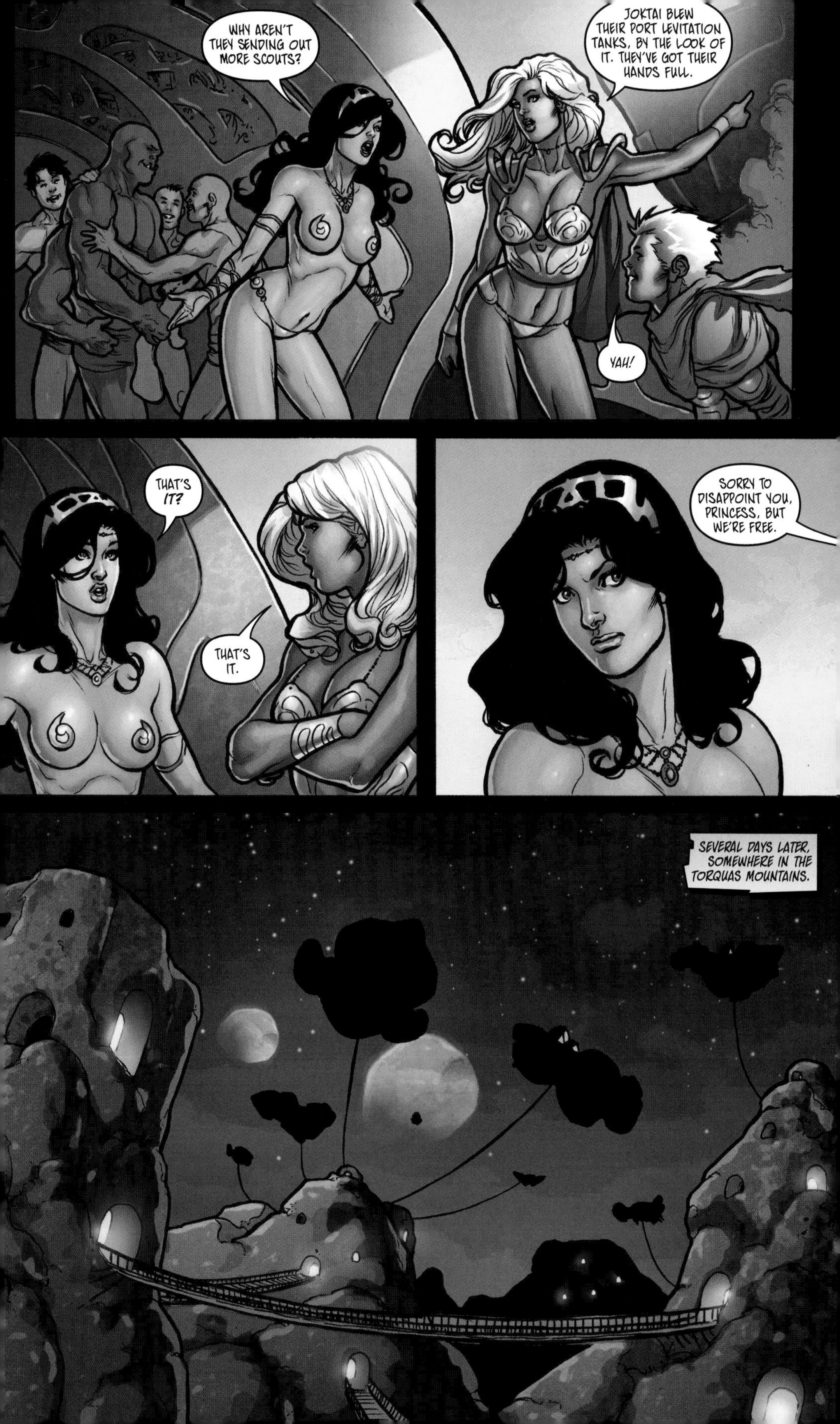
WHY AREN'T THEY SENDING OUT MORE SCOUTS?
JOKTAI BLEW THEIR PORT LEVITATION TANKS, BY THE LOOK OF IT. THEY'VE GOT THEIR HANDS FULL.
YAH!
THAT'S IT?
THAT'S IT.
SORRY TO DISAPPOINT YOU, PRINCESS, BUT WE'RE FREE.
SEVERAL DAYS LATER, SOMEWHERE IN THE TORQUAS MOUNTAINS.

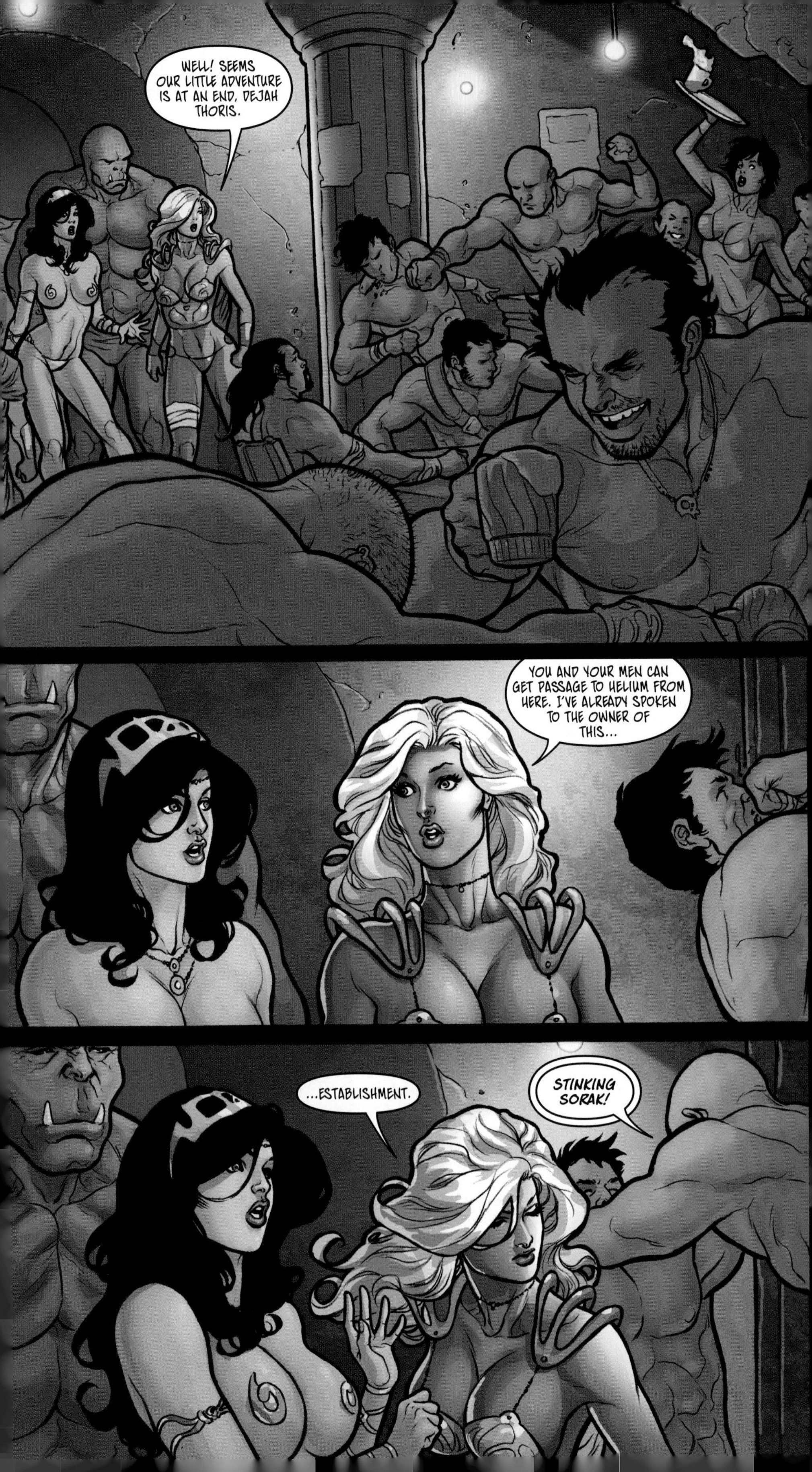
WELL! SEEMS OUR LITTLE ADVENTURE IS AT AN END, DEJAH THORIS.
YOU AND YOUR MEN CAN GET PASSAGE TO HELIUM FROM HERE. I'VE ALREADY SPOKEN TO THE OWNER OF THIS...
...ESTABLISHMENT.
STINKING SORAK!

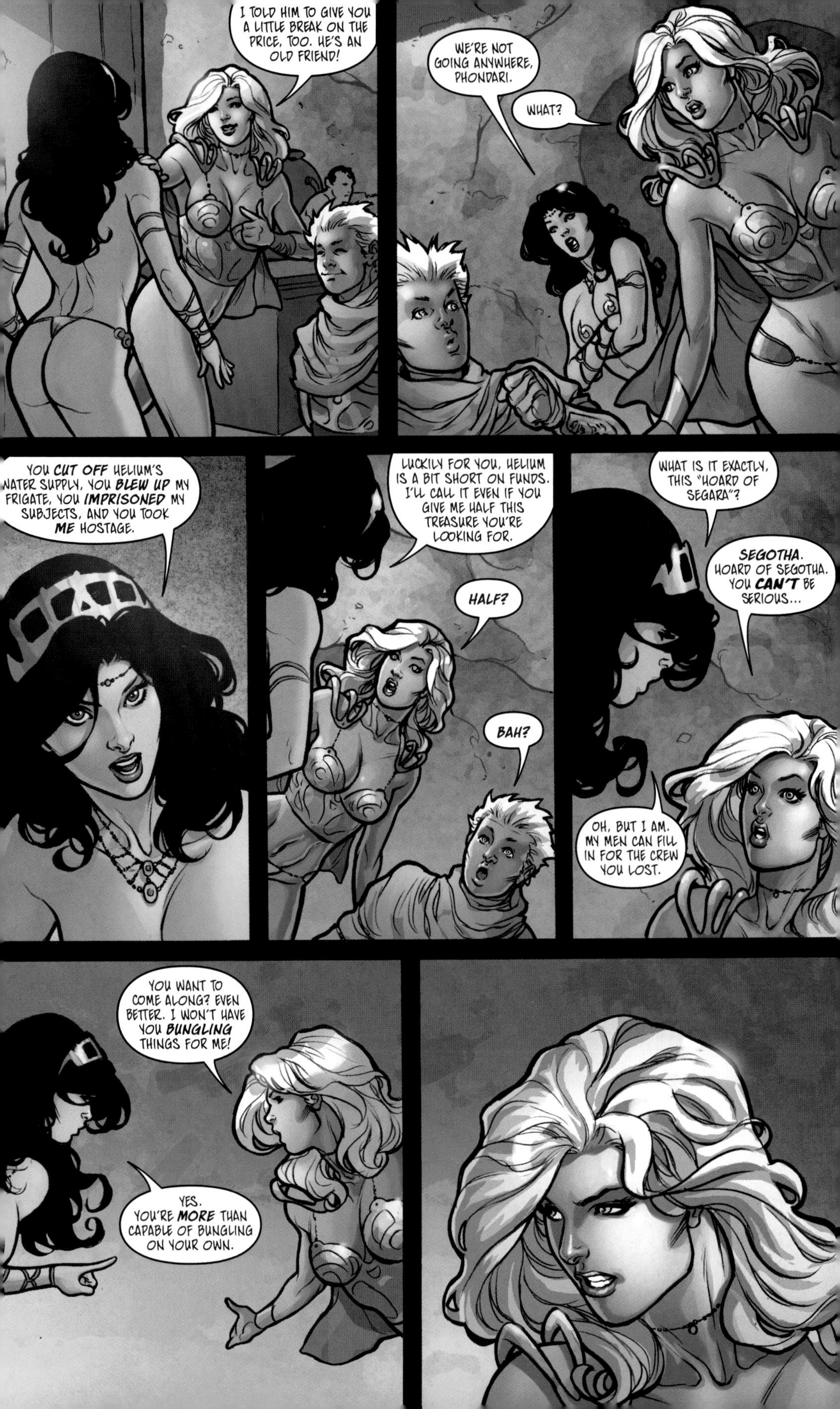
I TOLD HIM TO GIVE YOU A LITTLE BREAK ON THE PRICE, TOO. HE'S AN OLD FRIEND!
WE'RE NOT GOING ANYWHERE, PHONDARI.
WHAT?
YOU CUT OFF HELIUM'S WATER SUPPLY, YOU BLEW UP MY FRIGATE, YOU IMPRISONED MY SUBJECTS, AND YOU TOOK ME HOSTAGE.
LUCKILY FOR YOU, HELIUM IS A BIT SHORT ON FUNDS. I'LL CALL IT EVEN IF YOU GIVE ME HALF THIS TREASURE YOU'RE LOOKING FOR.
HALF?
BAH?
WHAT IS IT EXACTLY, THIS "HOARD OF SEGARA"?
SEGOTHA. HOARD OF SEGOTHA. YOU CAN'T BE SERIOUS...
OH, BUT I AM. MY MEN CAN FILL IN FOR THE CREW YOU LOST.
YOU WANT TO COME ALONG? EVEN BETTER. I WON'T HAVE YOU BUNGLING THINGS FOR ME!
YES. YOU'RE MORE THAN CAPABLE OF BUNGLING ON YOUR OWN.

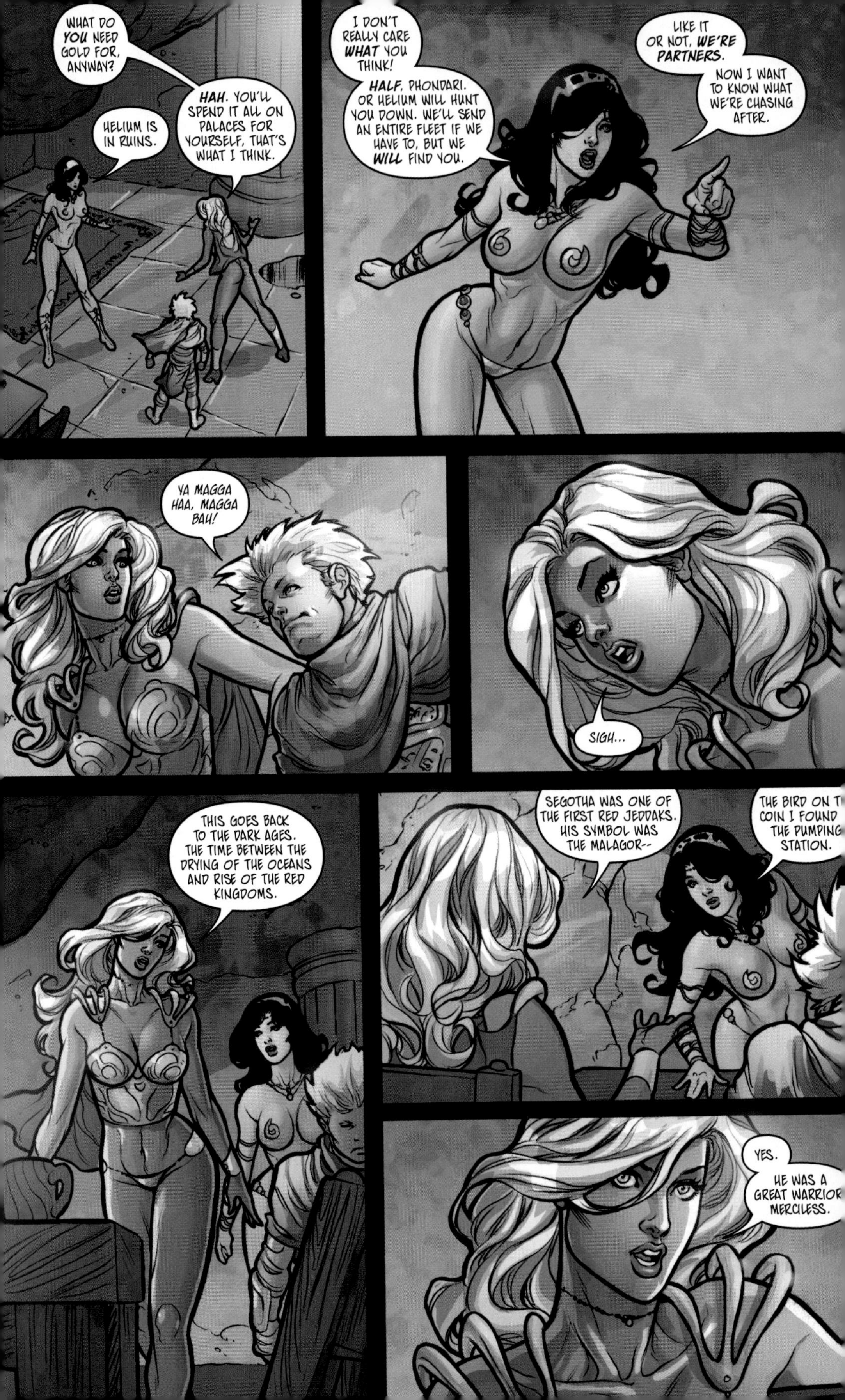

WHAT DO YOU NEED GOLD FOR, ANYWAY?
HELIUM IS IN RUINS.
HAH. YOU'LL SPEND IT ALL ON PALACES FOR YOURSELF, THAT'S WHAT I THINK.
I DON'T REALLY CARE WHAT YOU THINK!
HALF, PHONDARI. OR HELIUM WILL HUNT YOU DOWN. WE'LL SEND AN ENTIRE FLEET IF WE HAVE TO, BUT WE WILL FIND YOU.
LIKE IT OR NOT, WE'RE PARTNERS.
NOW I WANT TO KNOW WHAT WE'RE CHASING AFTER.
YA MAGGA HAA, MAGGA BAH!
SIGH...
THIS GOES BACK TO THE DARK AGES. THE TIME BETWEEN THE DRYING OF THE OCEANS AND RISE OF THE RED KINGDOMS.
SEGOTHA WAS ONE OF THE FIRST RED JEDDAKS. HIS SYMBOL WAS THE MALAGOR--
THE BIRD ON T COIN I FOUND THE PUMPING STATION.
YES.
HE WAS A GREAT WARRIOR MERCILESS.

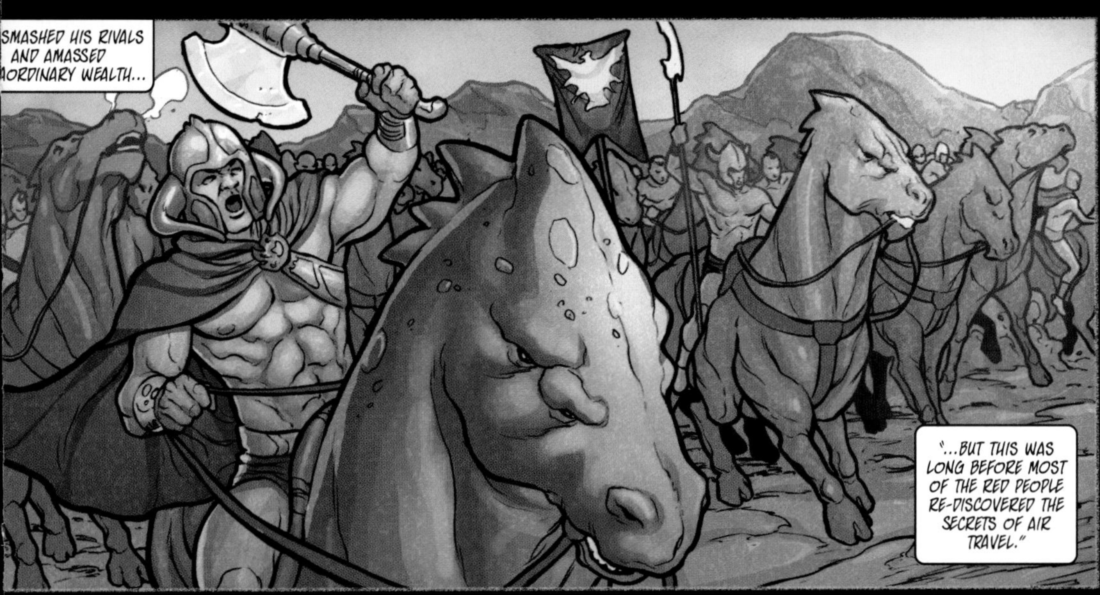

SMASHED HIS RIVALS AND AMASSED ...ORDINARY WEALTH...
"...BUT THIS WAS LONG BEFORE MOST OF THE RED PEOPLE RE-DISCOVERED THE SECRETS OF AIR TRAVEL."

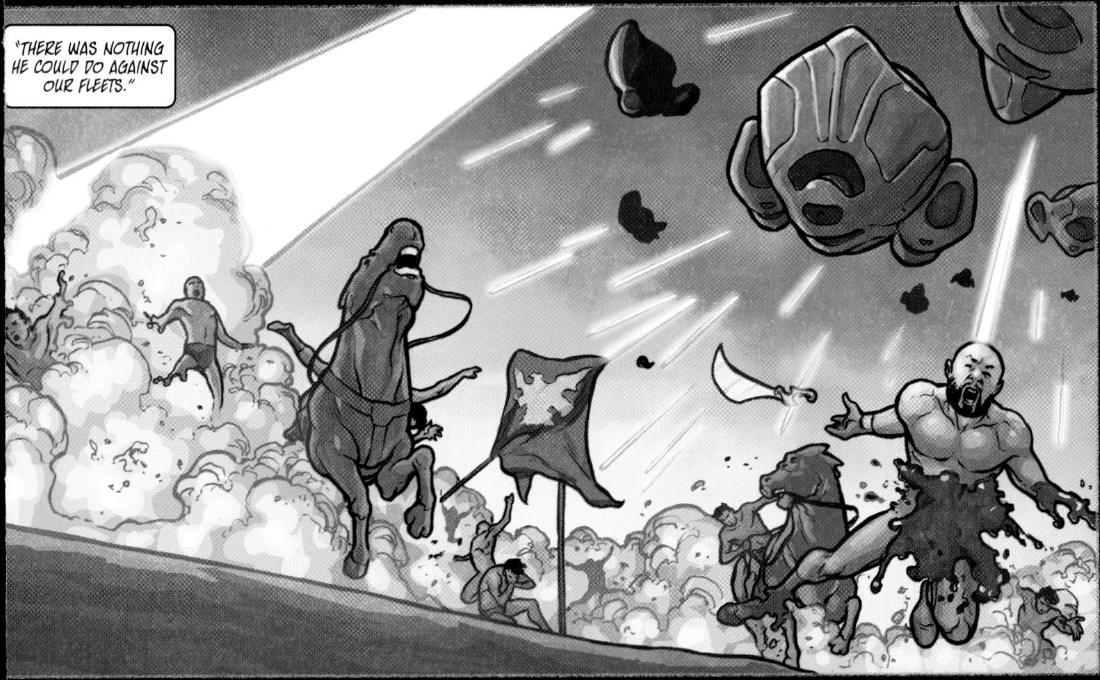

"THERE WAS NOTHING HE COULD DO AGAINST OUR FLEETS."

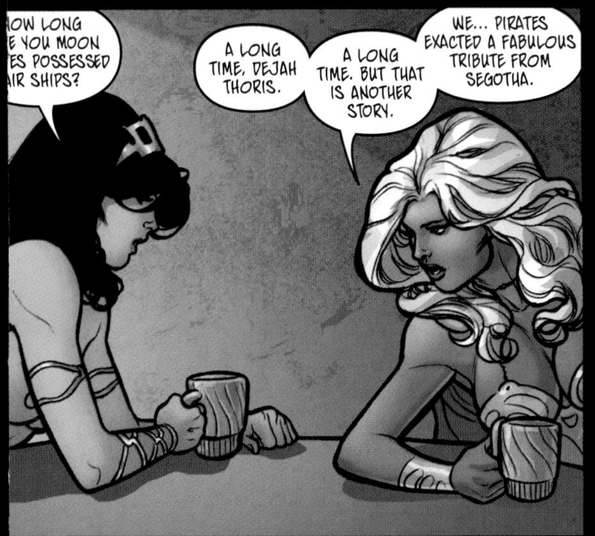

...OW LONG ...E YOU MOON ...ES POSSESSED ...AIR SHIPS?
A LONG TIME, DEJAH THORIS.
A LONG TIME. BUT THAT IS ANOTHER STORY.
WE... PIRATES EXACTED A FABULOUS TRIBUTE FROM SEGOTHA.

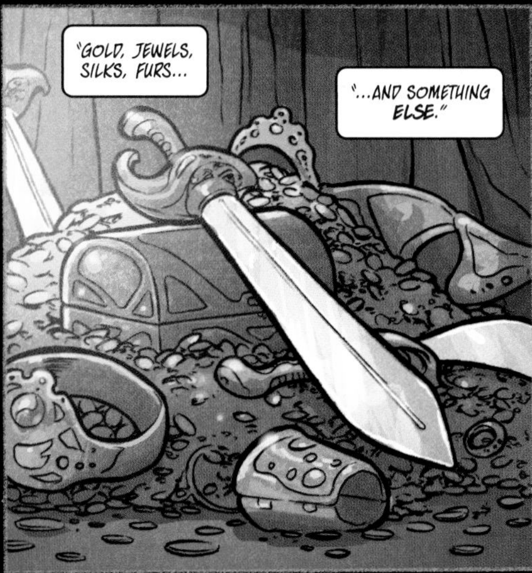

"GOLD, JEWELS, SILKS, FURS...
"...AND SOMETHING ELSE."

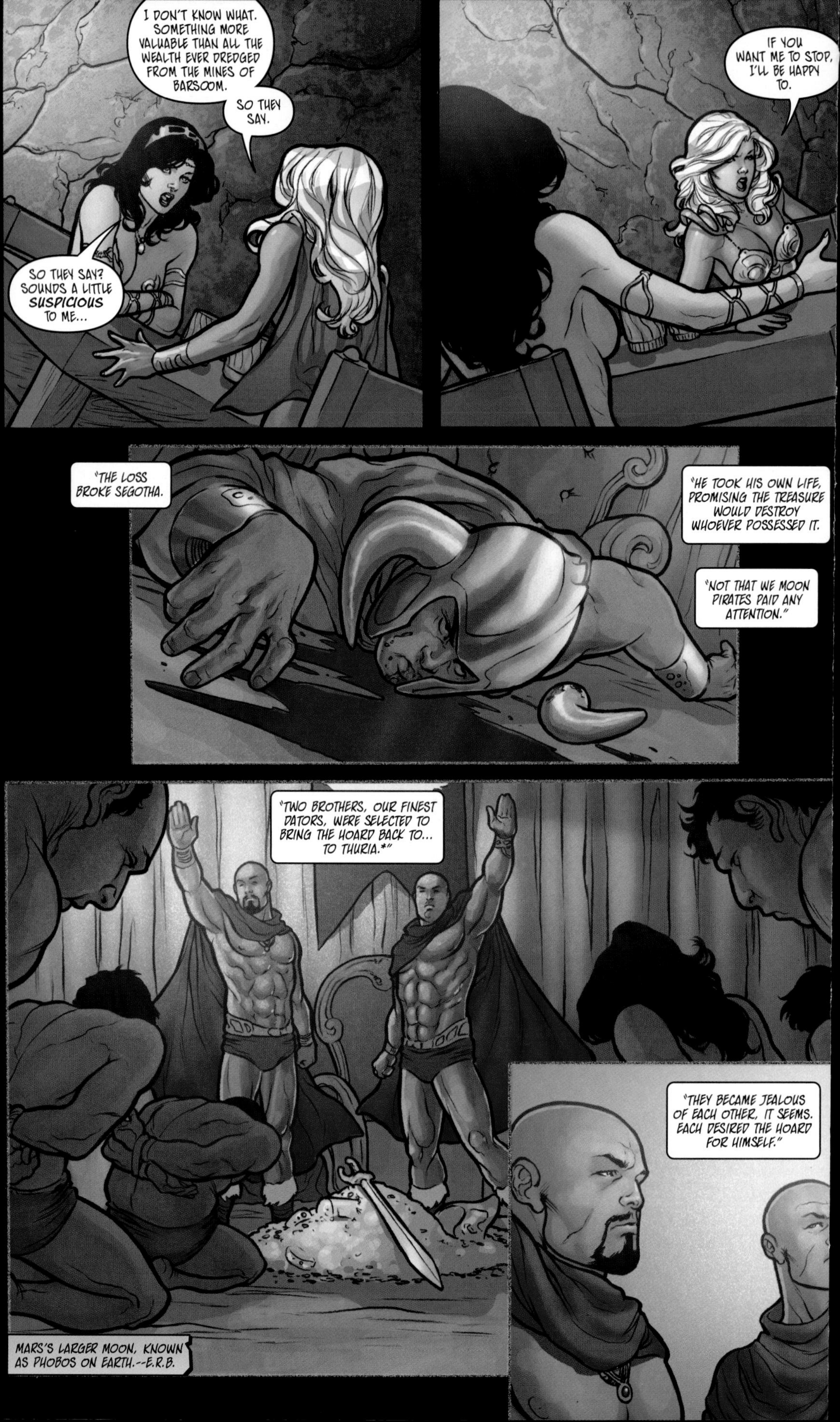

I DON'T KNOW WHAT. SOMETHING MORE VALUABLE THAN ALL THE WEALTH EVER DREDGED FROM THE MINES OF BARSOOM.
SO THEY SAY.
SO THEY SAY? SOUNDS A LITTLE SUSPICIOUS TO ME...
IF YOU WANT ME TO STOP, I'LL BE HAPPY TO.
"THE LOSS BROKE SEGOTHA.
"HE TOOK HIS OWN LIFE, PROMISING THE TREASURE WOULD DESTROY WHOEVER POSSESSED IT.
"NOT THAT WE MOON PIRATES PAID ANY ATTENTION."
"TWO BROTHERS, OUR FINEST DATORS, WERE SELECTED TO BRING THE HOARD BACK TO... TO THURIA.*"
*MARS'S LARGER MOON, KNOWN AS PHOBOS ON EARTH.--E.R.B.
"THEY BECAME JEALOUS OF EACH OTHER, IT SEEMS. EACH DESIRED THE HOARD FOR HIMSELF."

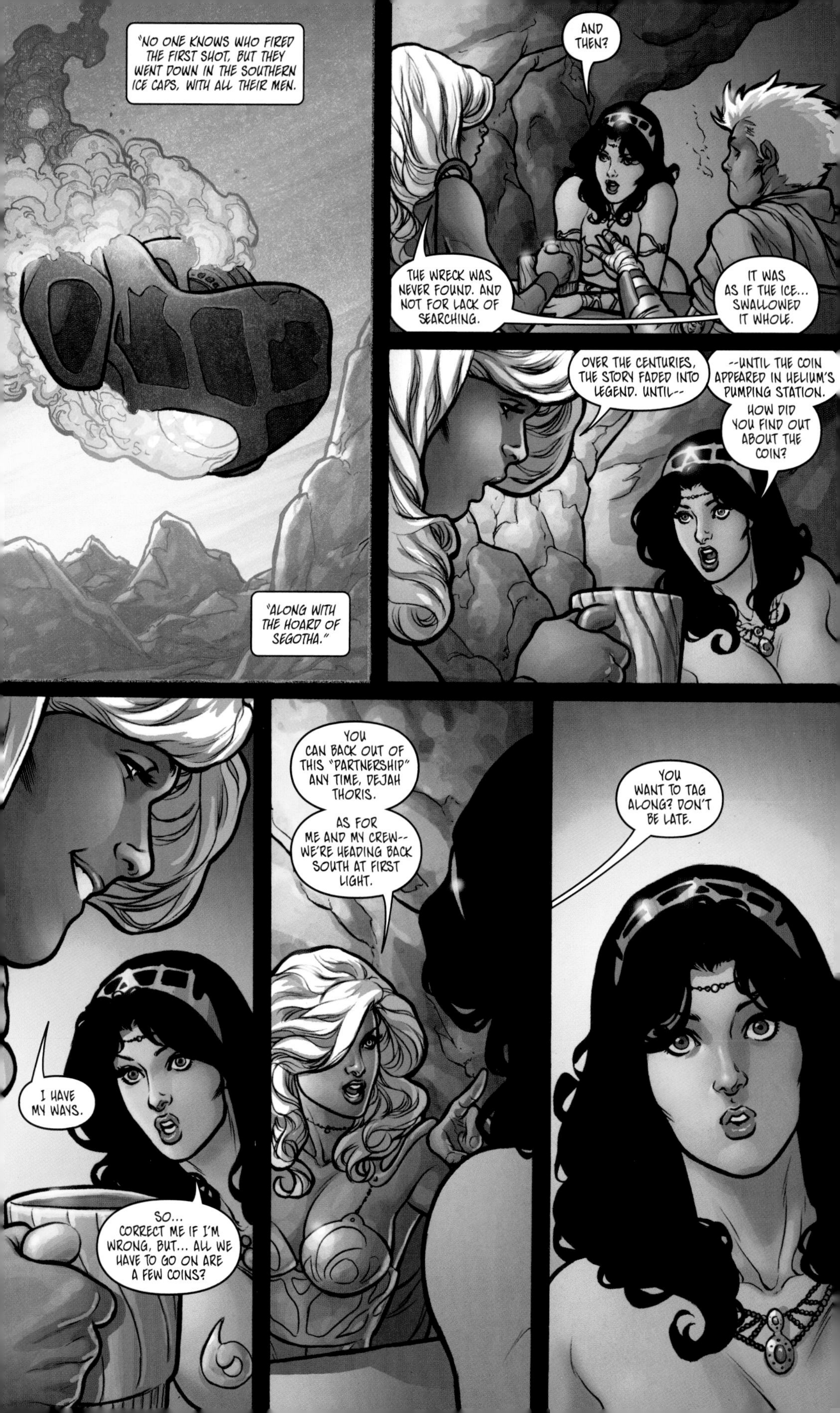
"NO ONE KNOWS WHO FIRED THE FIRST SHOT, BUT THEY WENT DOWN IN THE SOUTHERN ICE CAPS, WITH ALL THEIR MEN.
"ALONG WITH THE HOARD OF SEGOTHA."
AND THEN?
THE WRECK WAS NEVER FOUND. AND NOT FOR LACK OF SEARCHING.
IT WAS AS IF THE ICE... SWALLOWED IT WHOLE.
OVER THE CENTURIES, THE STORY FADED INTO LEGEND. UNTIL--
--UNTIL THE COIN APPEARED IN HELIUM'S PUMPING STATION.
HOW DID YOU FIND OUT ABOUT THE COIN?
I HAVE MY WAYS.
SO... CORRECT ME IF I'M WRONG, BUT... ALL WE HAVE TO GO ON ARE A FEW COINS?
YOU CAN BACK OUT OF THIS "PARTNERSHIP" ANY TIME, DEJAH THORIS.
AS FOR ME AND MY CREW-- WE'RE HEADING BACK SOUTH AT FIRST LIGHT.
YOU WANT TO TAG ALONG? DON'T BE LATE.

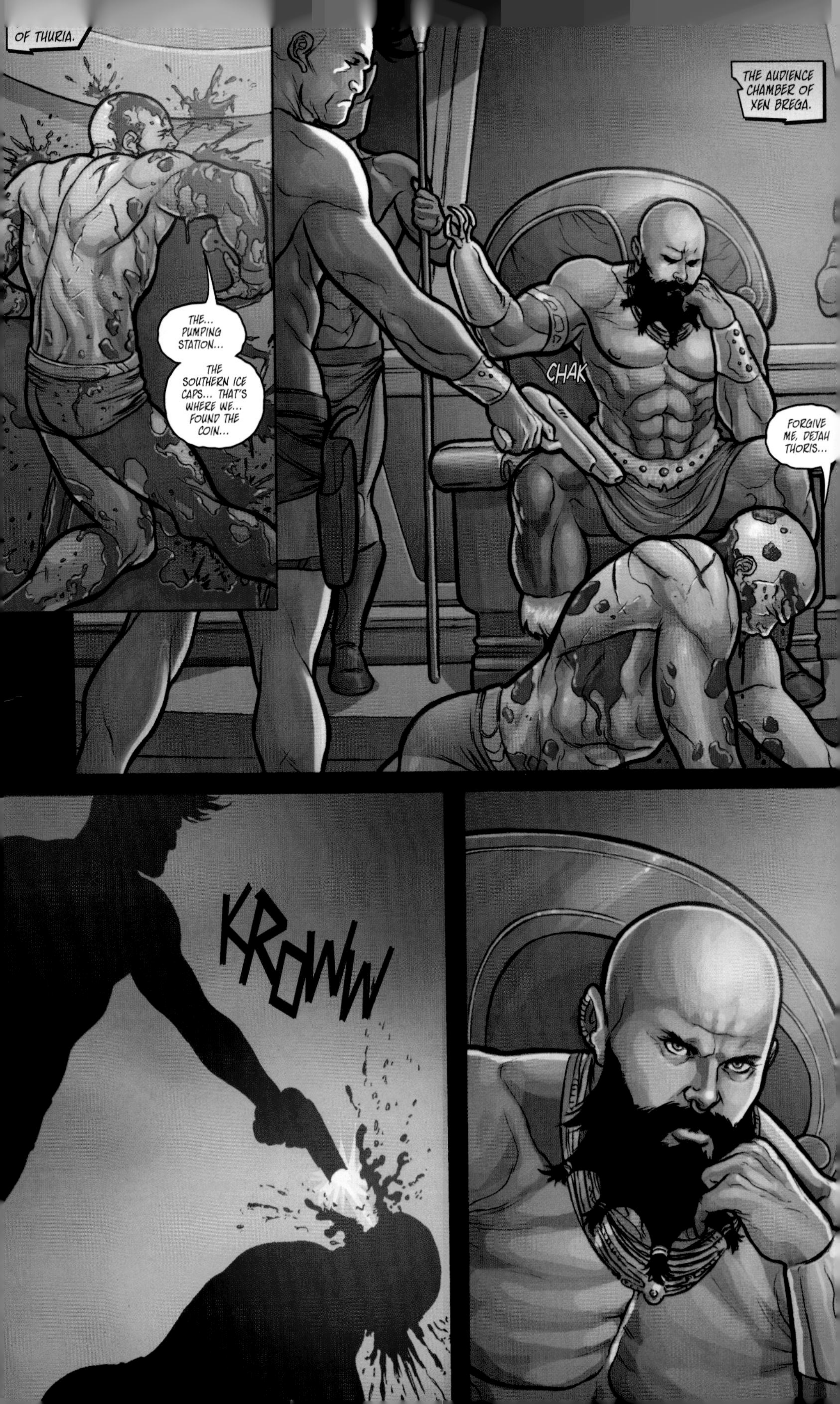
OF THURIA.
THE... PUMPING STATION...
THE SOUTHERN ICE CAPS... THAT'S WHERE WE... FOUND THE COIN...
THE AUDIENCE CHAMBER OF XEN BREGA.
CHAK
FORGIVE ME, DEJAH THORIS...
KROWW

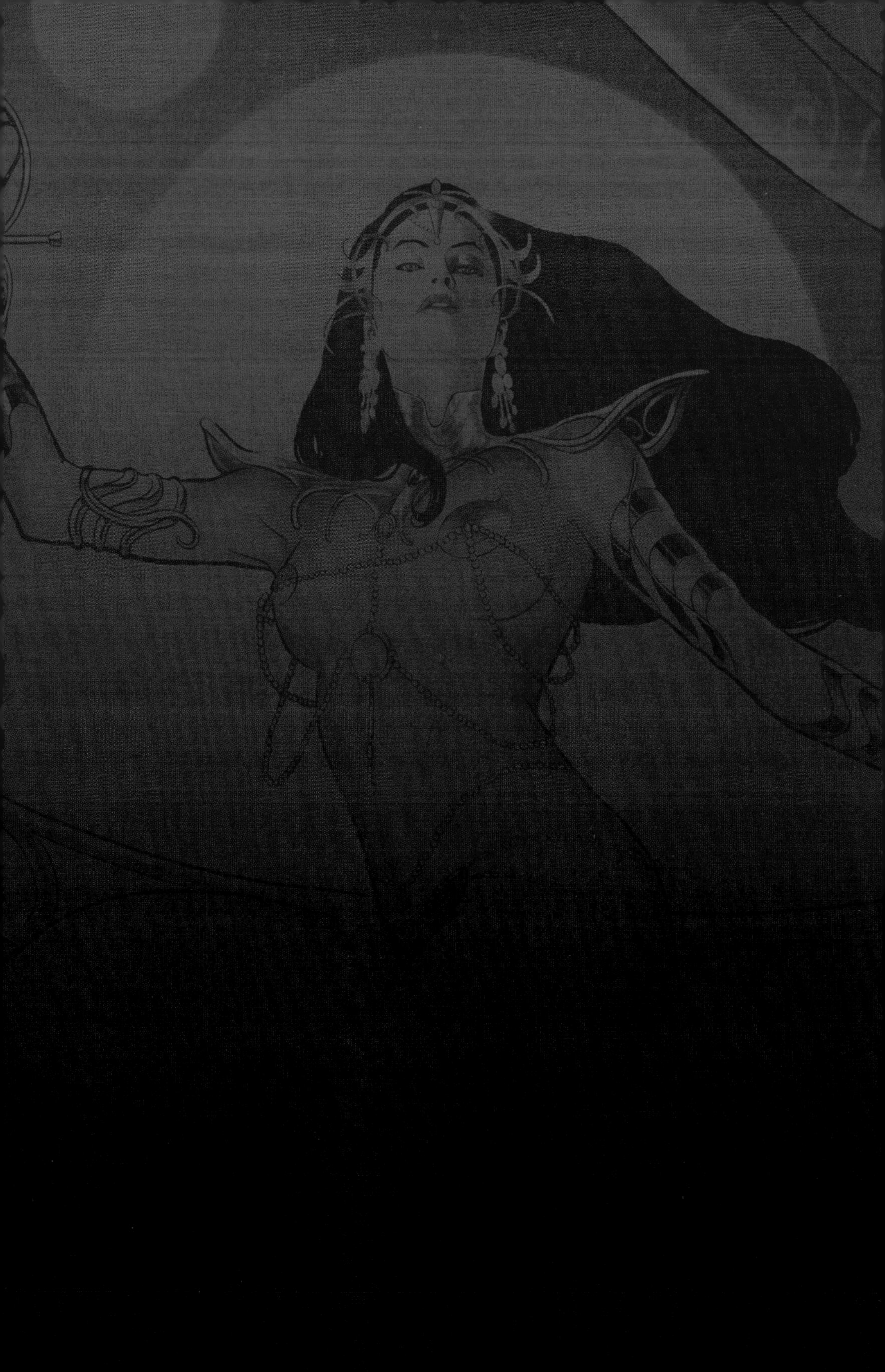

# ISSUE NINE
# PRICELESS

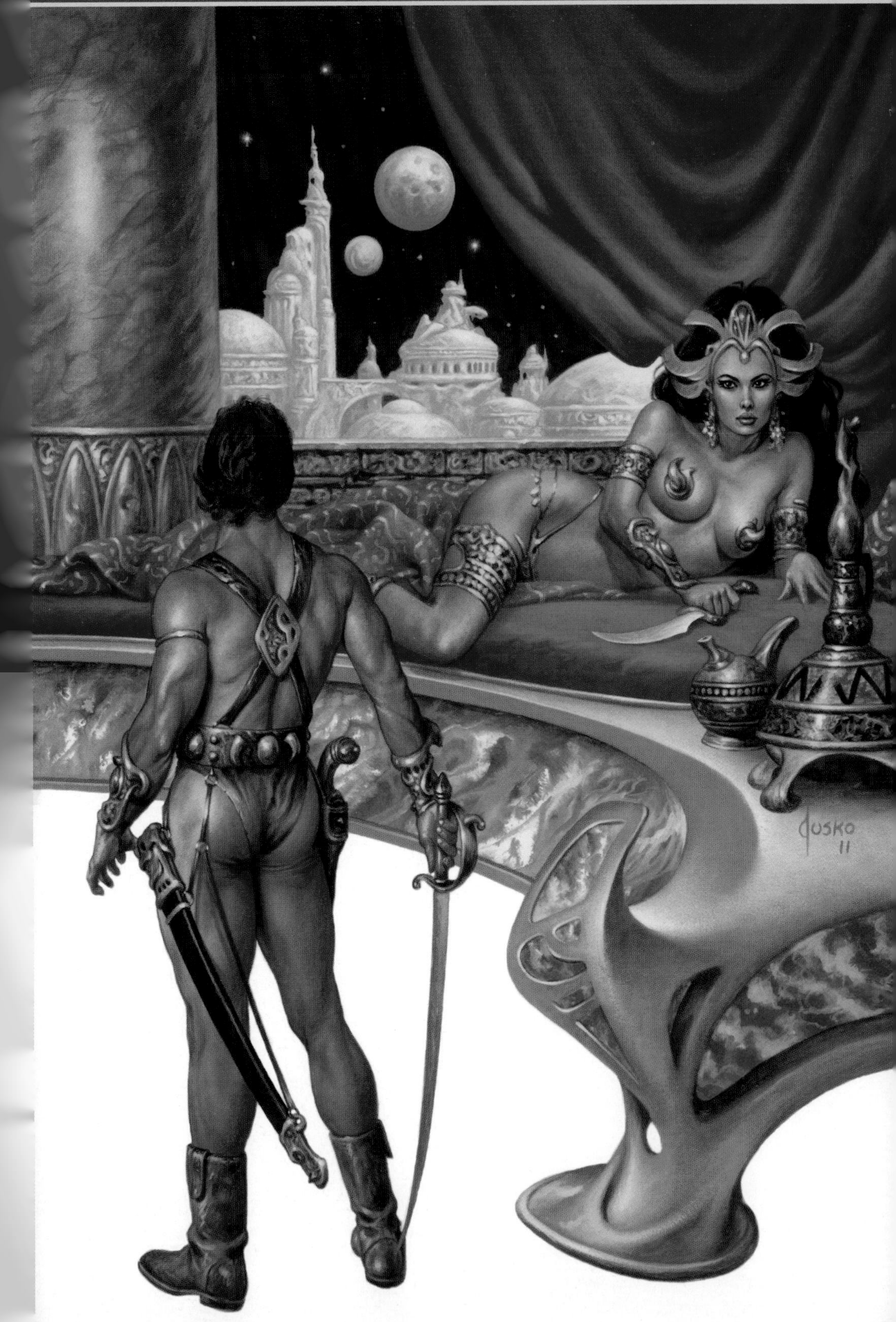
JUSKO
11

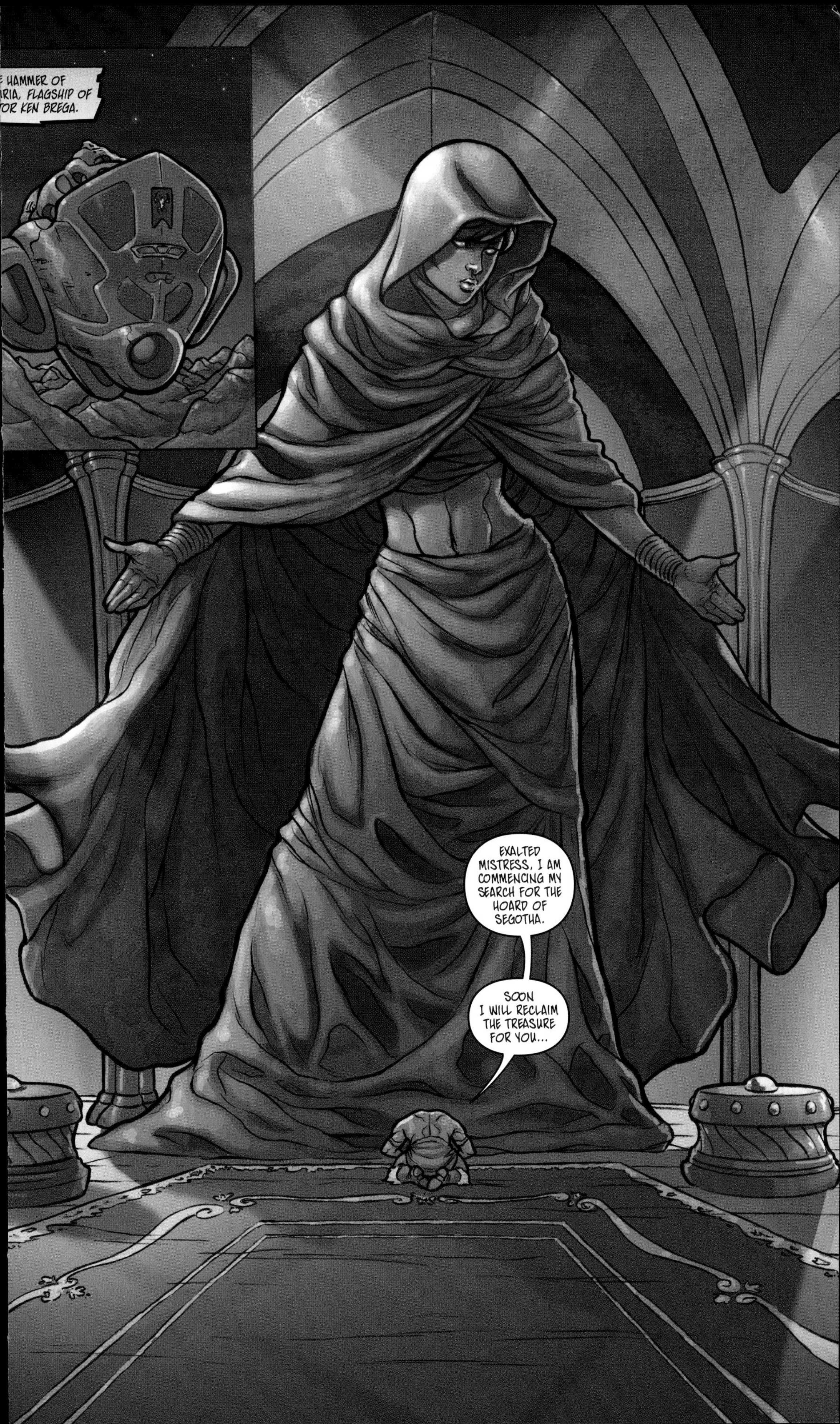
E HAMMER OF
RIA, FLAGSHIP OF
TOR KEN BREGA.
EXALTED MISTRESS, I AM COMMENCING MY SEARCH FOR THE HOARD OF SEGOTHA.
SOON I WILL RECLAIM THE TREASURE FOR YOU...

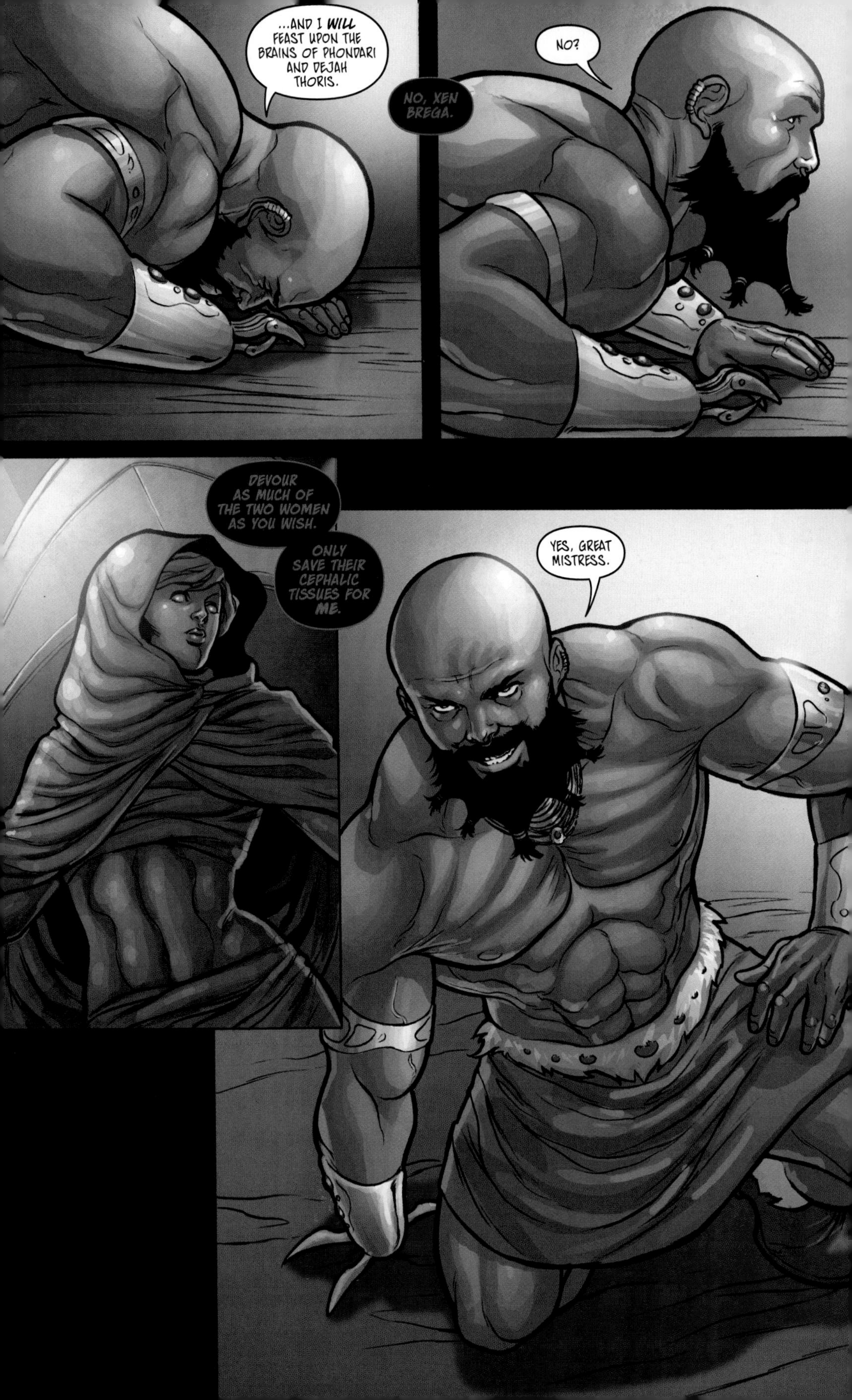
...AND I WILL FEAST UPON THE BRAINS OF PHONDARI AND DEJAH THORIS.
NO, XEN BREGA.
NO?
DEVOUR AS MUCH OF THE TWO WOMEN AS YOU WISH.
ONLY SAVE THEIR CEPHALIC TISSUES FOR ME.
YES, GREAT MISTRESS.

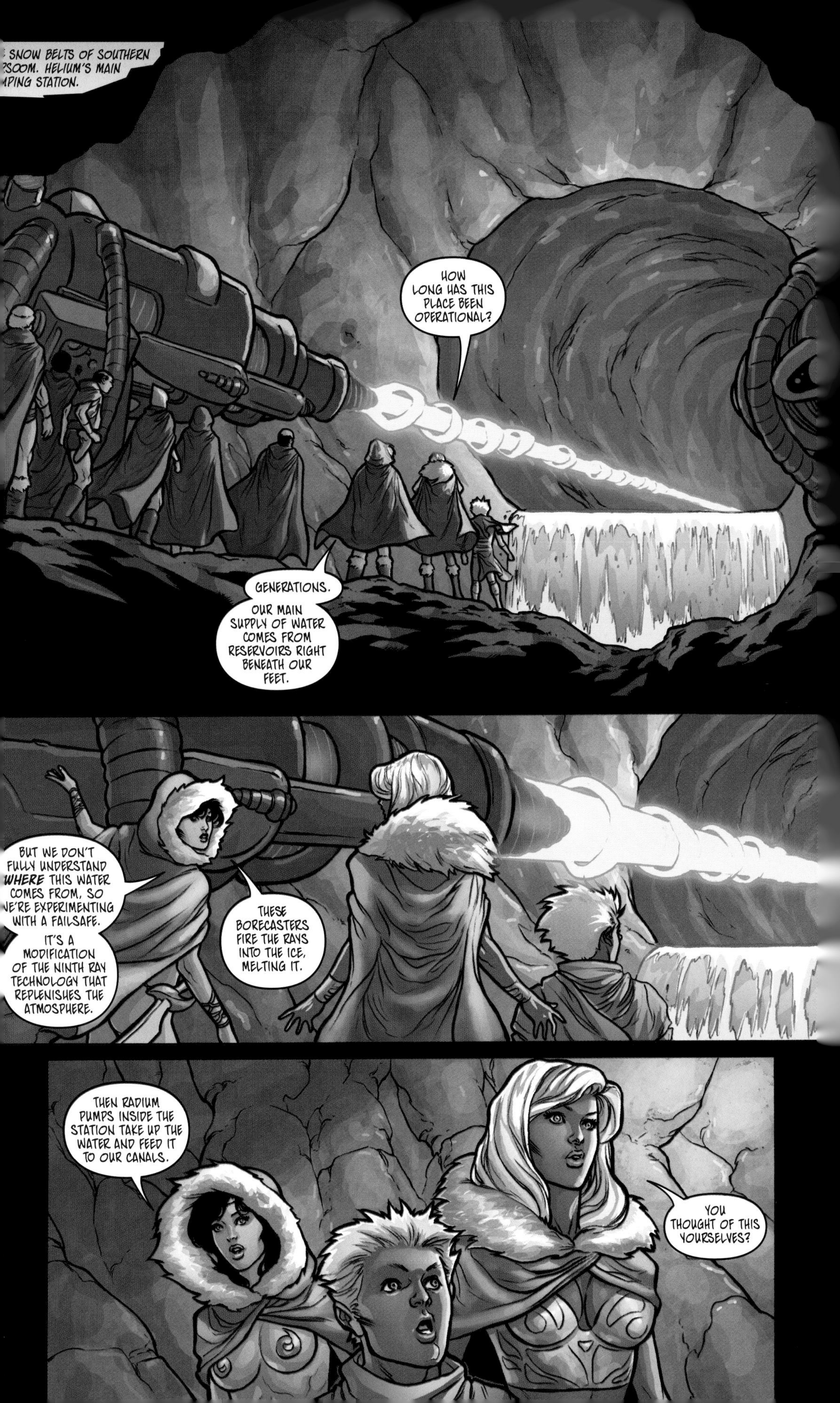

SNOW BELTS OF SOUTHERN
RSOOM. HELIUM'S MAIN
MPING STATION.
HOW LONG HAS THIS PLACE BEEN OPERATIONAL?
GENERATIONS.
OUR MAIN SUPPLY OF WATER COMES FROM RESERVOIRS RIGHT BENEATH OUR FEET.
BUT WE DON'T FULLY UNDERSTAND WHERE THIS WATER COMES FROM, SO WE'RE EXPERIMENTING WITH A FAILSAFE.
IT'S A MODIFICATION OF THE NINTH RAY TECHNOLOGY THAT REPLENISHES THE ATMOSPHERE.
THESE BORECASTERS FIRE THE RAYS INTO THE ICE, MELTING IT.
THEN RADIUM PUMPS INSIDE THE STATION TAKE UP THE WATER AND FEED IT TO OUR CANALS.
YOU THOUGHT OF THIS YOURSELVES?

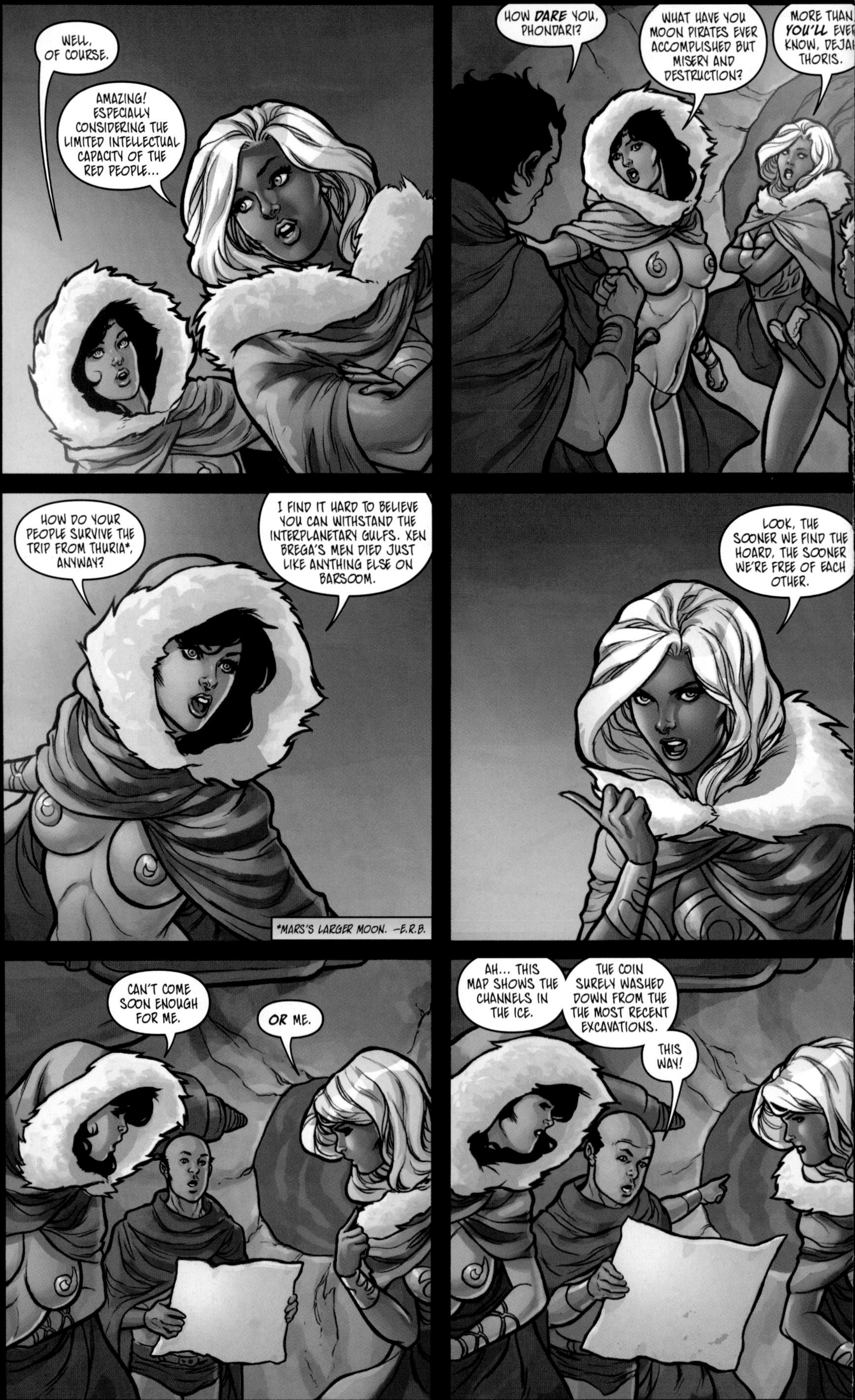

WELL, OF COURSE.
AMAZING! ESPECIALLY CONSIDERING THE LIMITED INTELLECTUAL CAPACITY OF THE RED PEOPLE...
HOW DARE YOU, PHONDARI?
WHAT HAVE YOU MOON PIRATES EVER ACCOMPLISHED BUT MISERY AND DESTRUCTION?
MORE THAN YOU'LL EVER KNOW, DEJAH THORIS.
HOW DO YOUR PEOPLE SURVIVE THE TRIP FROM THURIA*, ANYWAY?
I FIND IT HARD TO BELIEVE YOU CAN WITHSTAND THE INTERPLANETARY GULFS. XEN BREGA'S MEN DIED JUST LIKE ANYTHING ELSE ON BARSOOM.
*MARS'S LARGER MOON. —E.R.B.
LOOK, THE SOONER WE FIND THE HOARD, THE SOONER WE'RE FREE OF EACH OTHER.
CAN'T COME SOON ENOUGH FOR ME.
OR ME.
AH... THIS MAP SHOWS THE CHANNELS IN THE ICE.
THE COIN SURELY WASHED DOWN FROM THE THE MOST RECENT EXCAVATIONS.
THIS WAY!

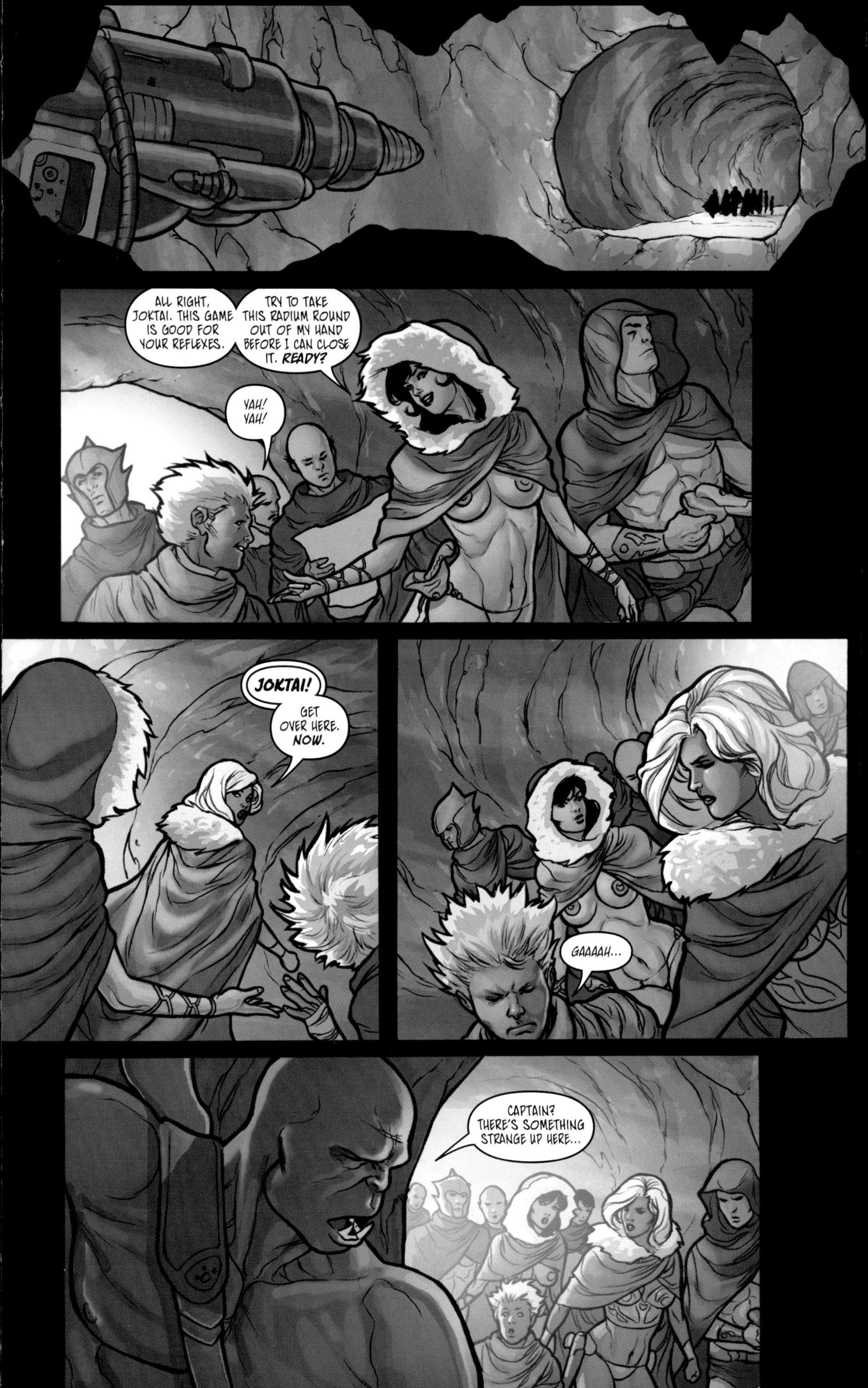
ALL RIGHT, JOKTAI. THIS GAME IS GOOD FOR YOUR REFLEXES.
TRY TO TAKE THIS RADIUM ROUND OUT OF MY HAND BEFORE I CAN CLOSE IT. READY?
YAH! YAH!
JOKTAI!
GET OVER HERE. NOW.
GAAAAH...
CAPTAIN? THERE'S SOMETHING STRANGE UP HERE...

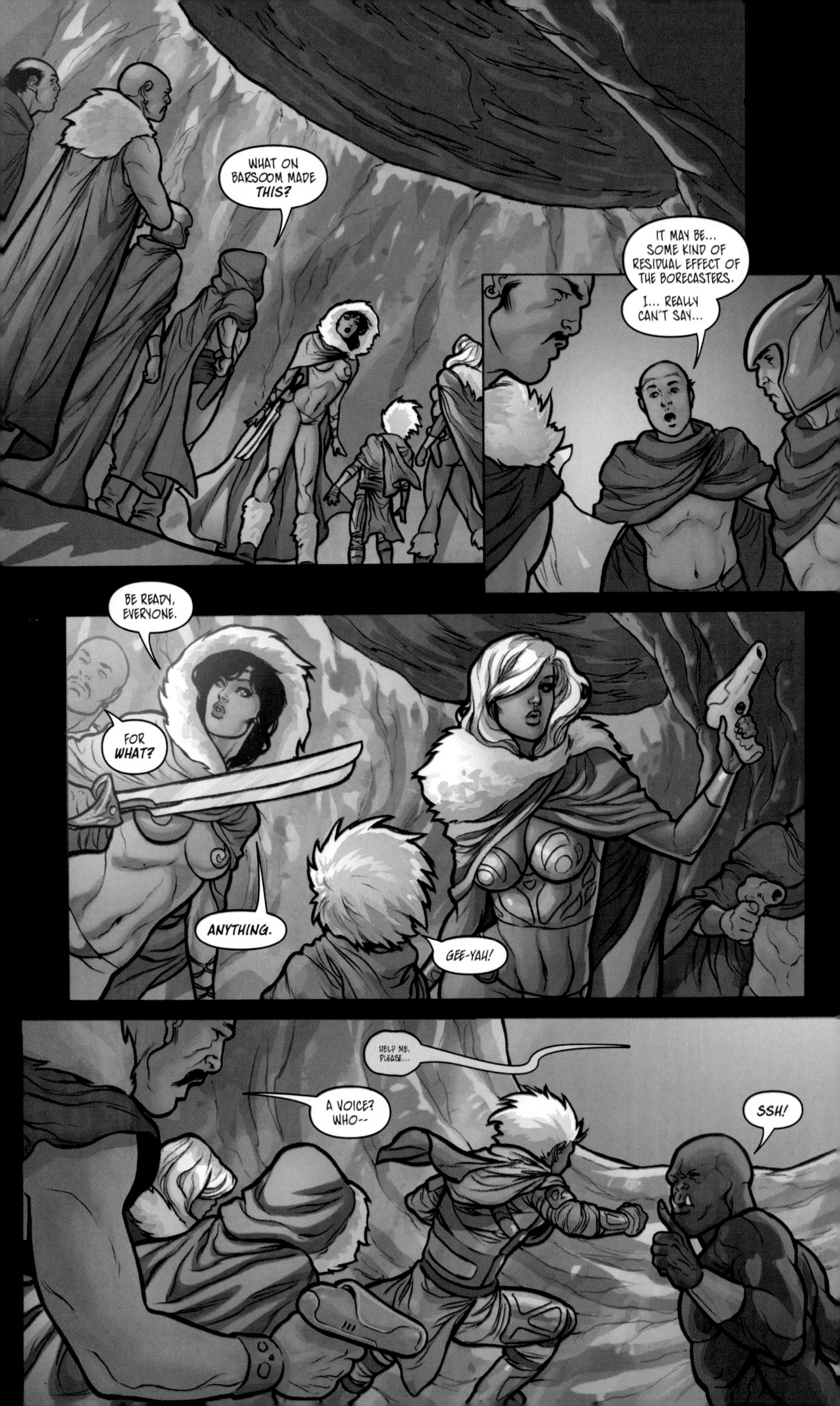
WHAT ON BARSOOM MADE THIS?
IT MAY BE... SOME KIND OF RESIDUAL EFFECT OF THE BORECASTERS.
I... REALLY CAN'T SAY...
BE READY, EVERYONE.
FOR WHAT?
ANYTHING.
GEE-YAH!
HELP ME, PLEASE...
A VOICE? WHO--
SSH!

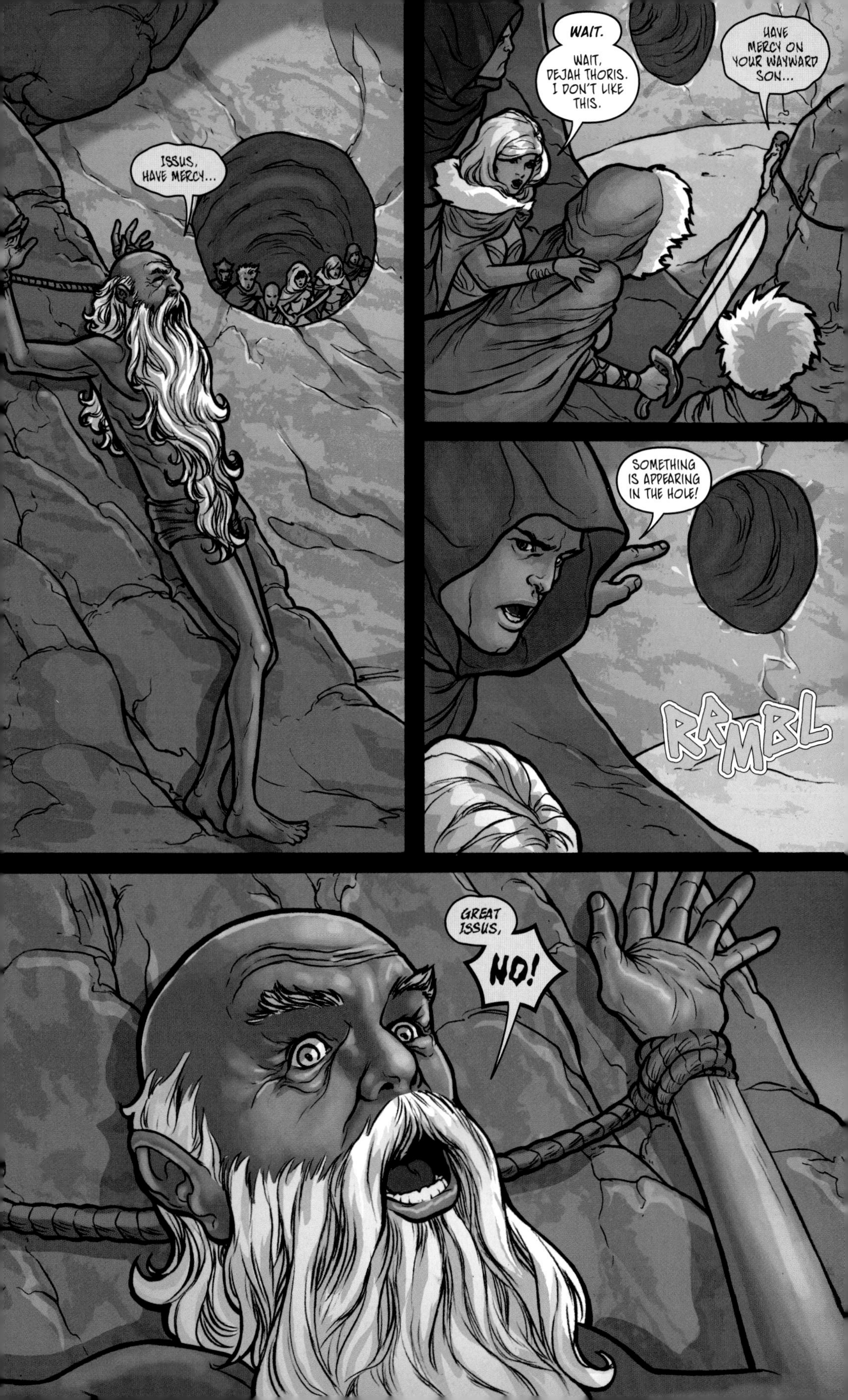
ISSUS, HAVE MERCY...
WAIT.
WAIT, DEJAH THORIS. I DON'T LIKE THIS.
HAVE MERCY ON YOUR WAYWARD SON...
SOMETHING IS APPEARING IN THE HOLE!
RRMBL
GREAT ISSUS,
NO!

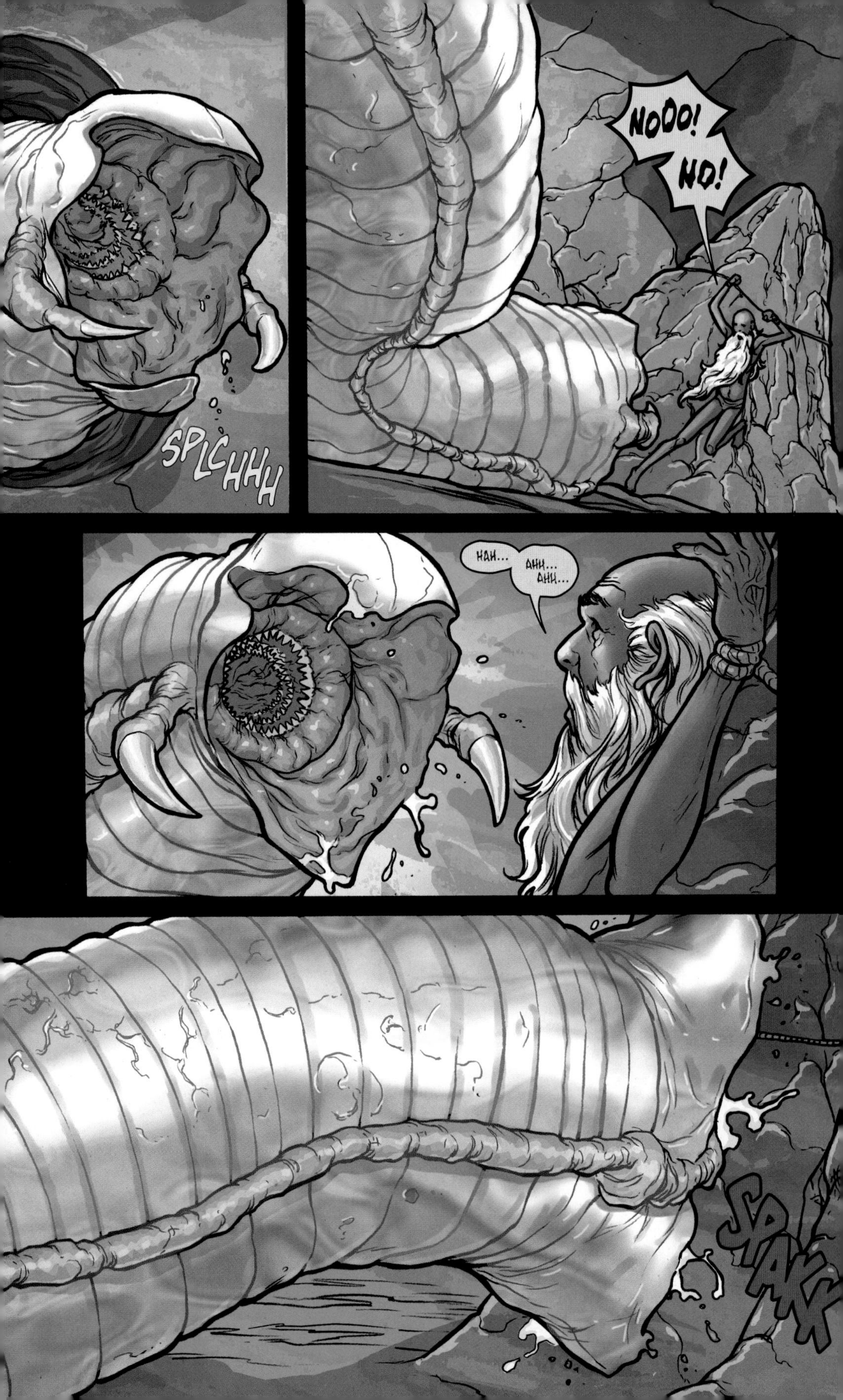
SPLCHHH
NOOO!
NO!
HAH...
AHH... AHH...
SPAKK

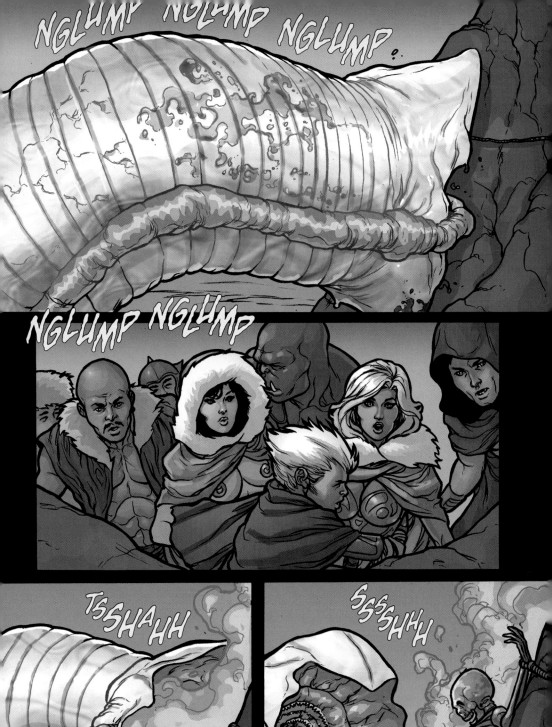

NGLUMP NGLUMP NGLUMP

NGLUMP NGLUMP

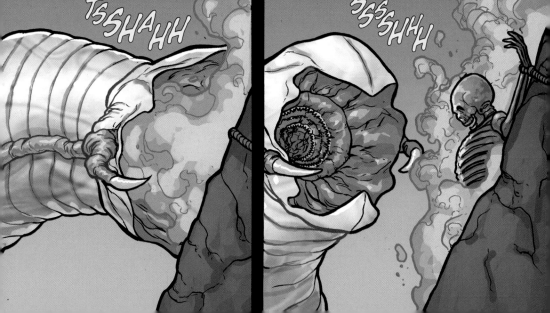

TSSHAHH

SSSSHHH

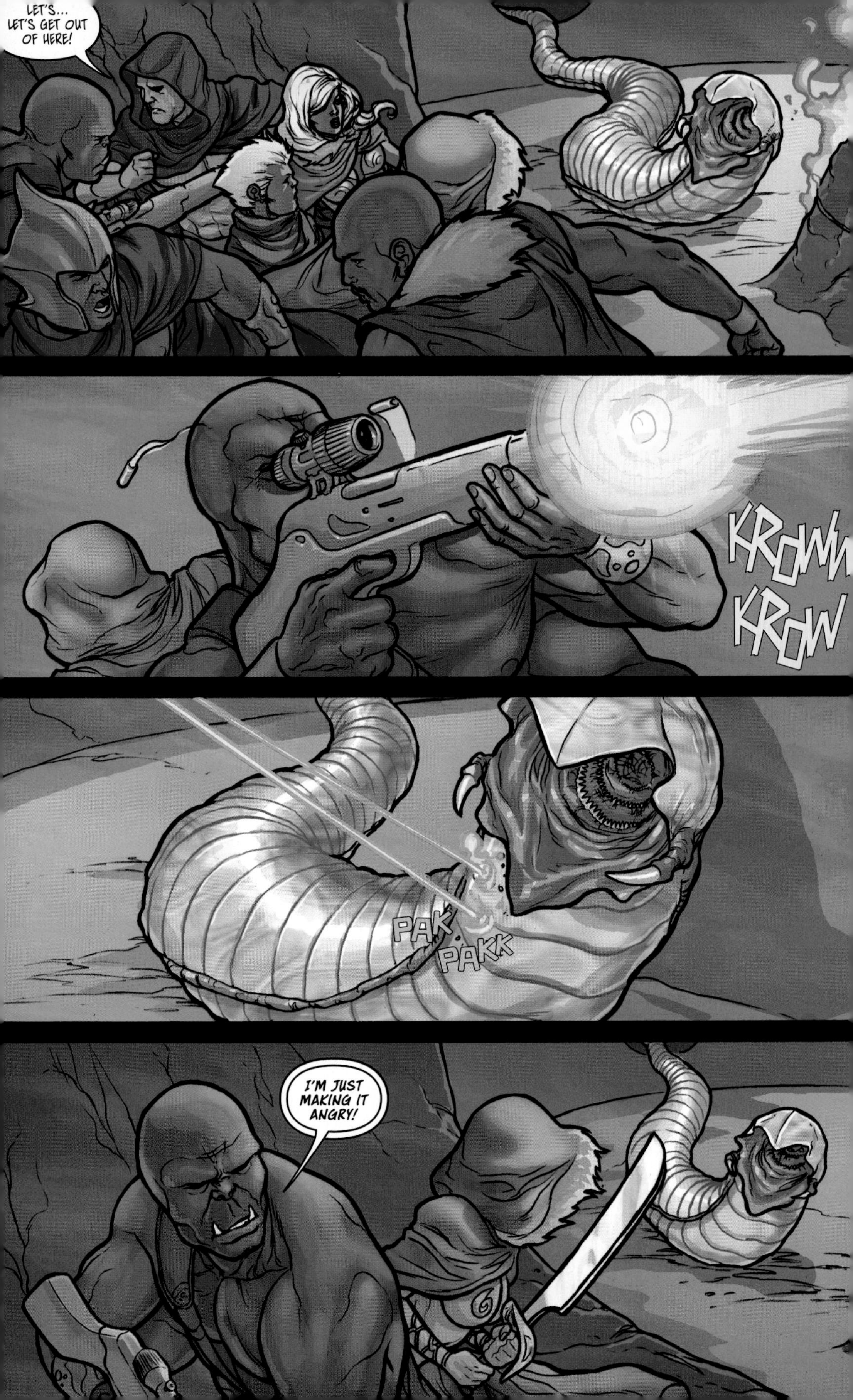
LET'S... LET'S GET OUT OF HERE!
KROWW KROW
PAK PAKK
I'M JUST MAKING IT ANGRY!

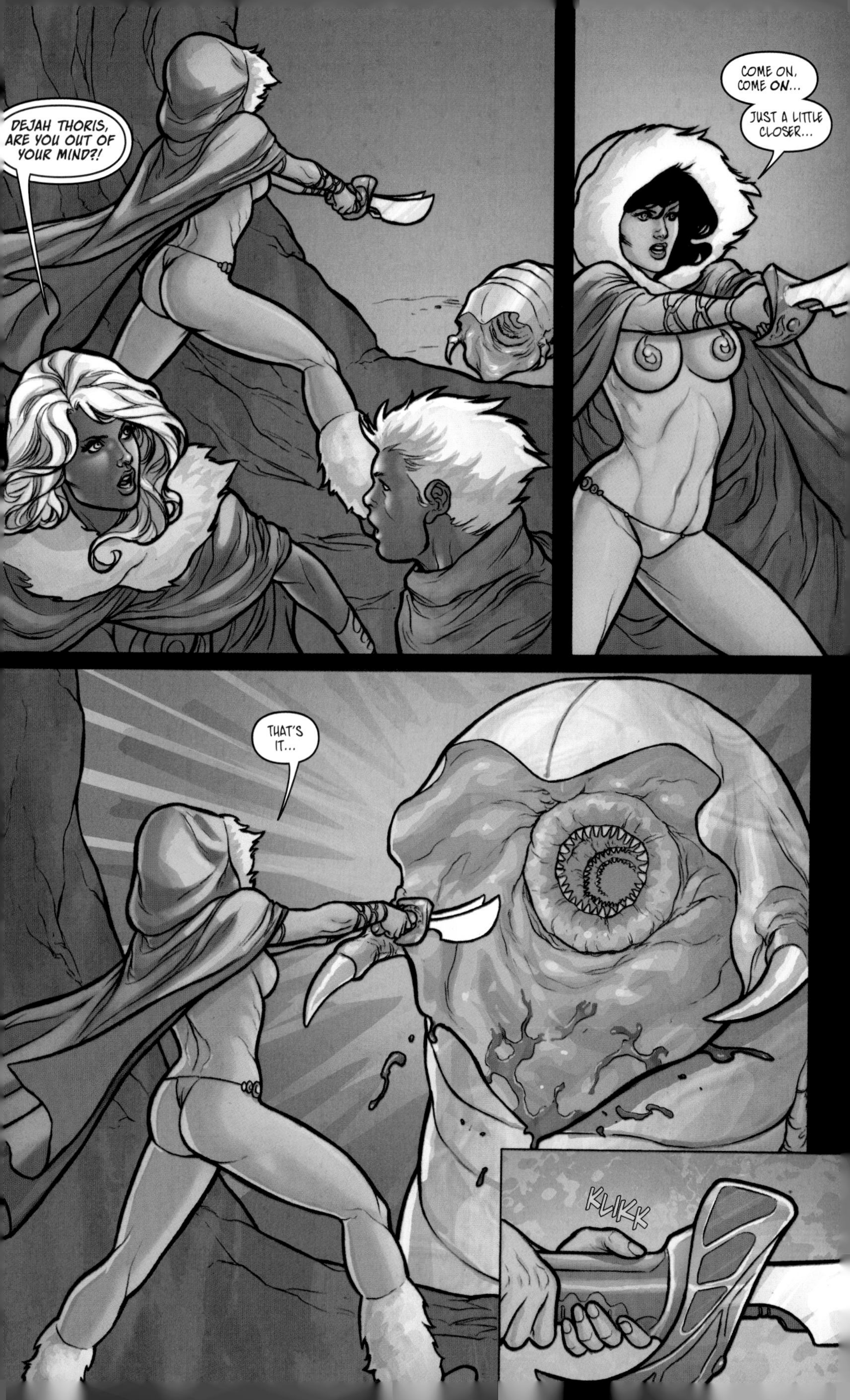
DEJAH THORIS, ARE YOU OUT OF YOUR MIND?!
COME ON, COME ON...
JUST A LITTLE CLOSER...
THAT'S IT...
KLIKK

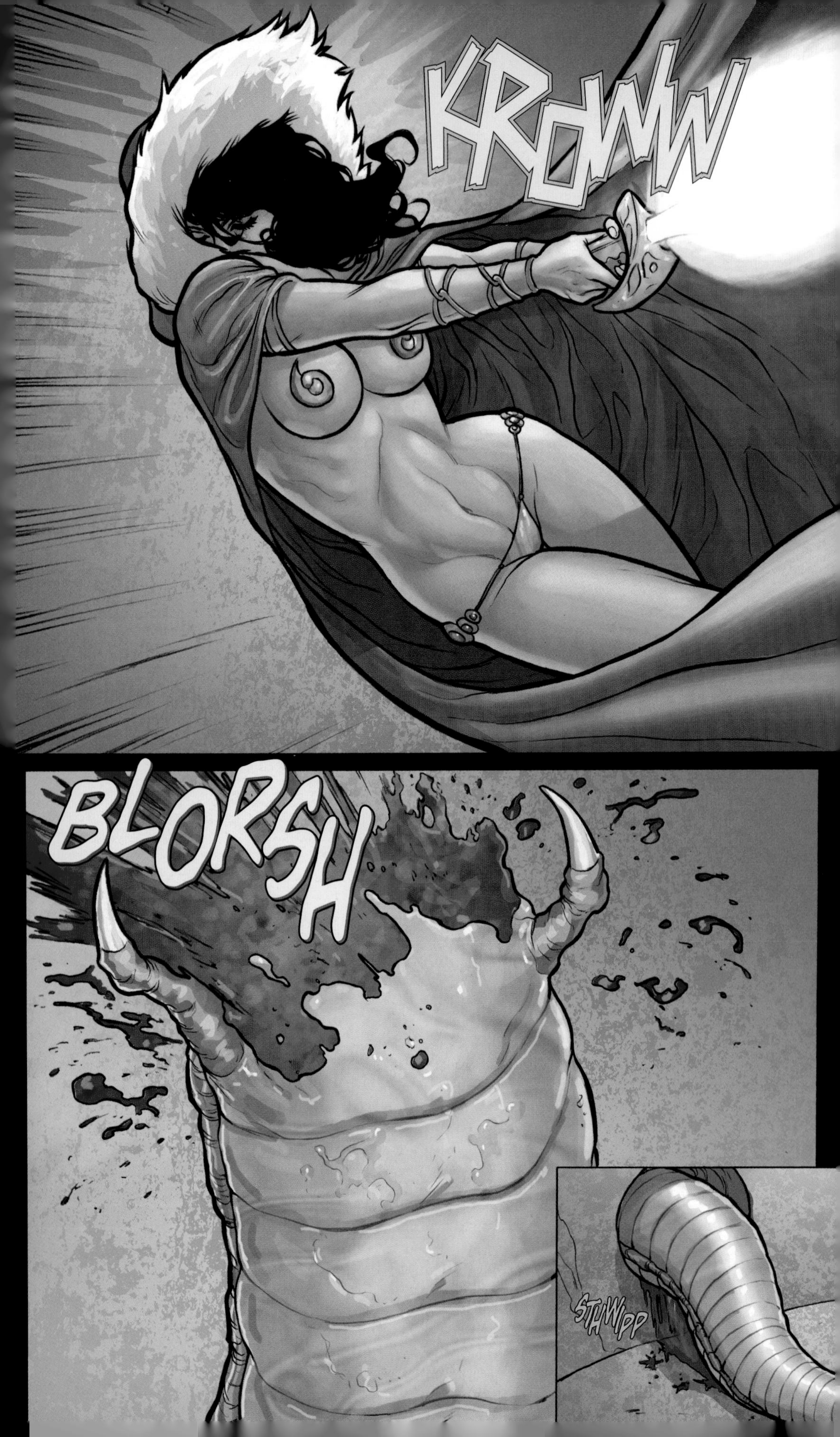
KROWW
BLORSH
STHWIPP

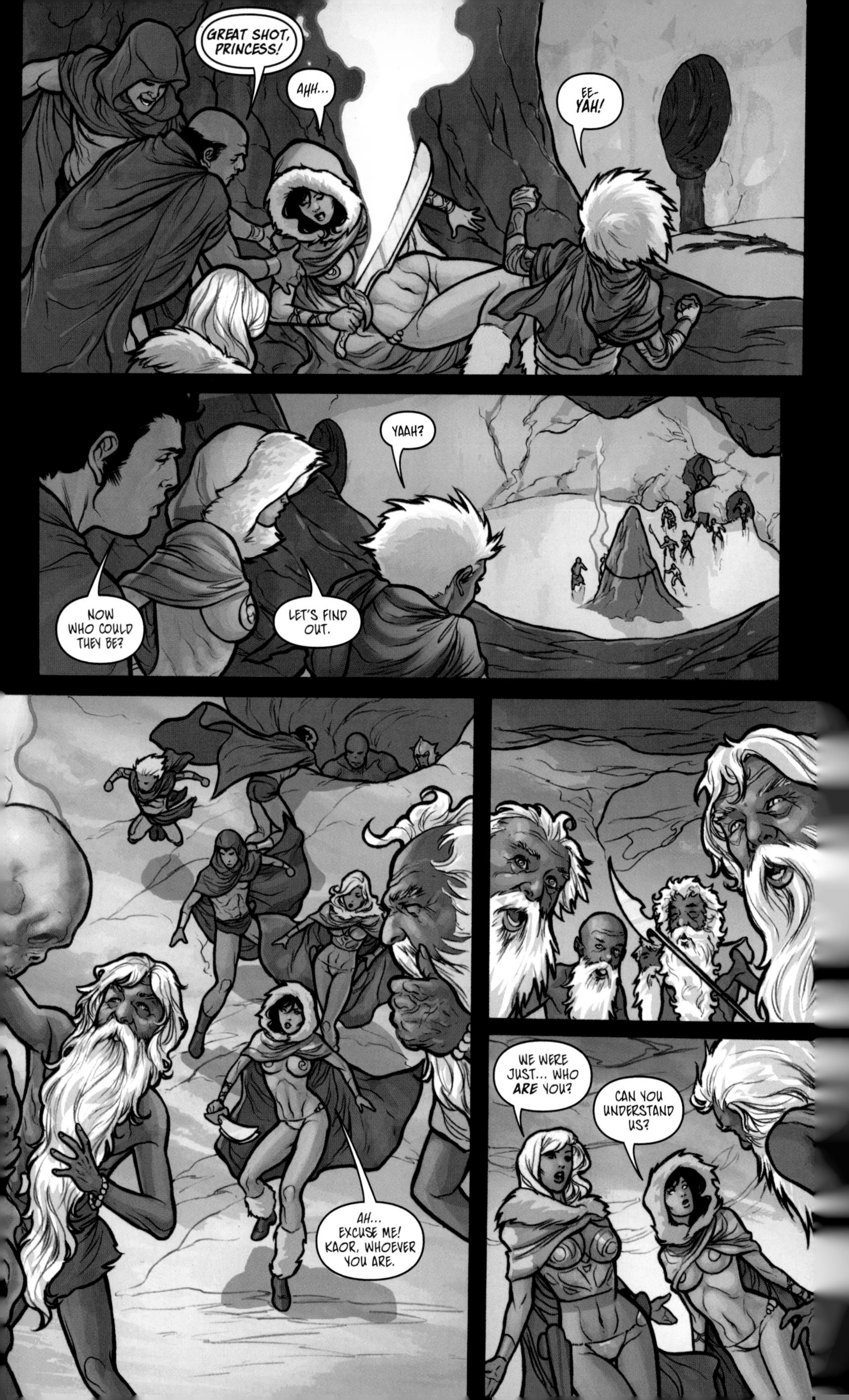
GREAT SHOT, PRINCESS!
AHH...
EE-YAH!
YAAH?
NOW WHO COULD THEY BE?
LET'S FIND OUT.
AH... EXCUSE ME! KAOR, WHOEVER YOU ARE.
WE WERE JUST... WHO ARE YOU?
CAN YOU UNDERSTAND US?

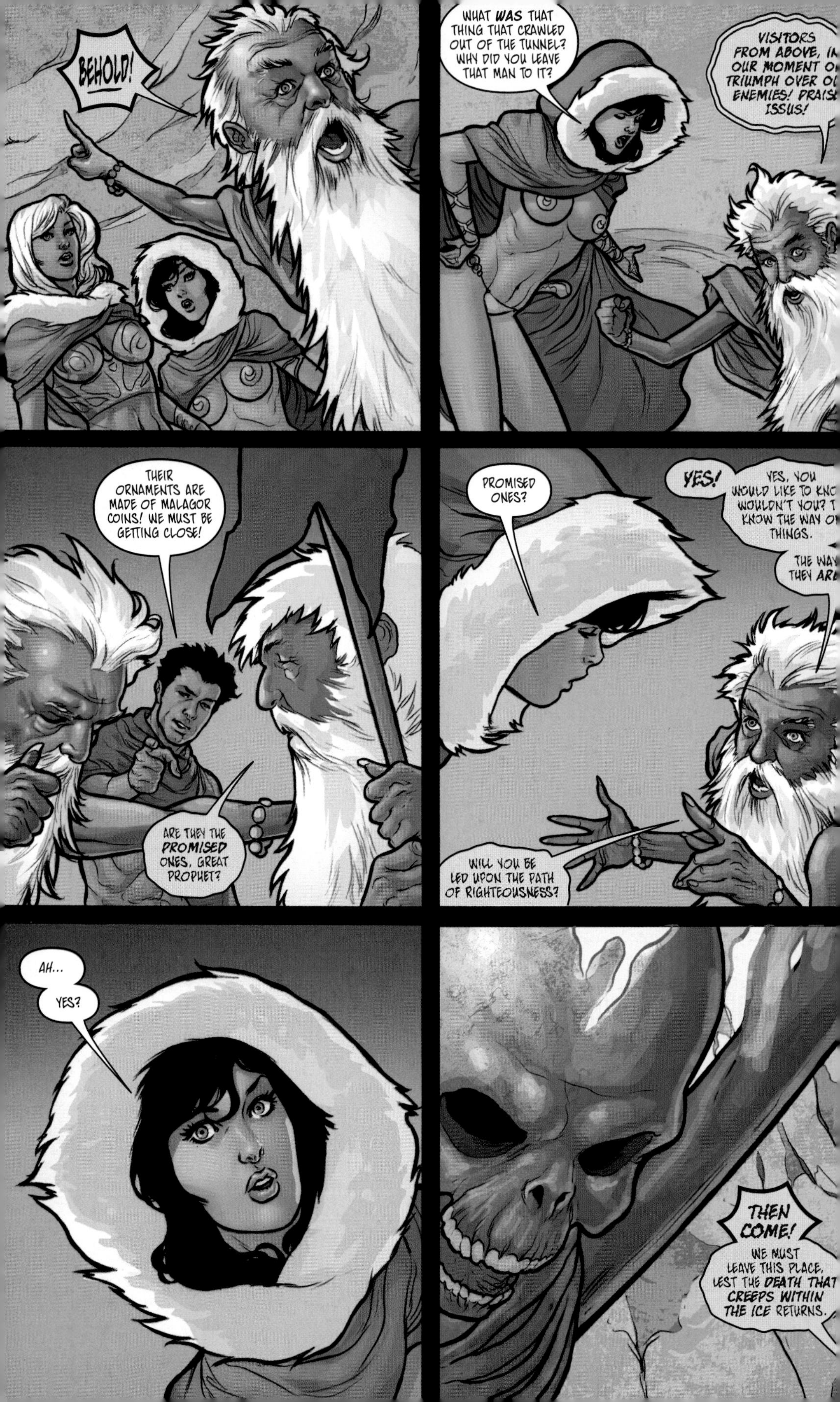
BEHOLD!
WHAT WAS THAT THING THAT CRAWLED OUT OF THE TUNNEL? WHY DID YOU LEAVE THAT MAN TO IT?
VISITORS FROM ABOVE, IN OUR MOMENT OF TRIUMPH OVER OUR ENEMIES! PRAISE ISSUS!
THEIR ORNAMENTS ARE MADE OF MALAGOR COINS! WE MUST BE GETTING CLOSE!
ARE THEY THE PROMISED ONES, GREAT PROPHET?
PROMISED ONES?
YES!
YES, YOU WOULD LIKE TO KNOW, WOULDN'T YOU? I KNOW THE WAY OF THINGS.
THE WAY THEY ARE.
WILL YOU BE LED UPON THE PATH OF RIGHTEOUSNESS?
AH...
YES?
THEN COME!
WE MUST LEAVE THIS PLACE, LEST THE DEATH THAT CREEPS WITHIN THE ICE RETURNS.

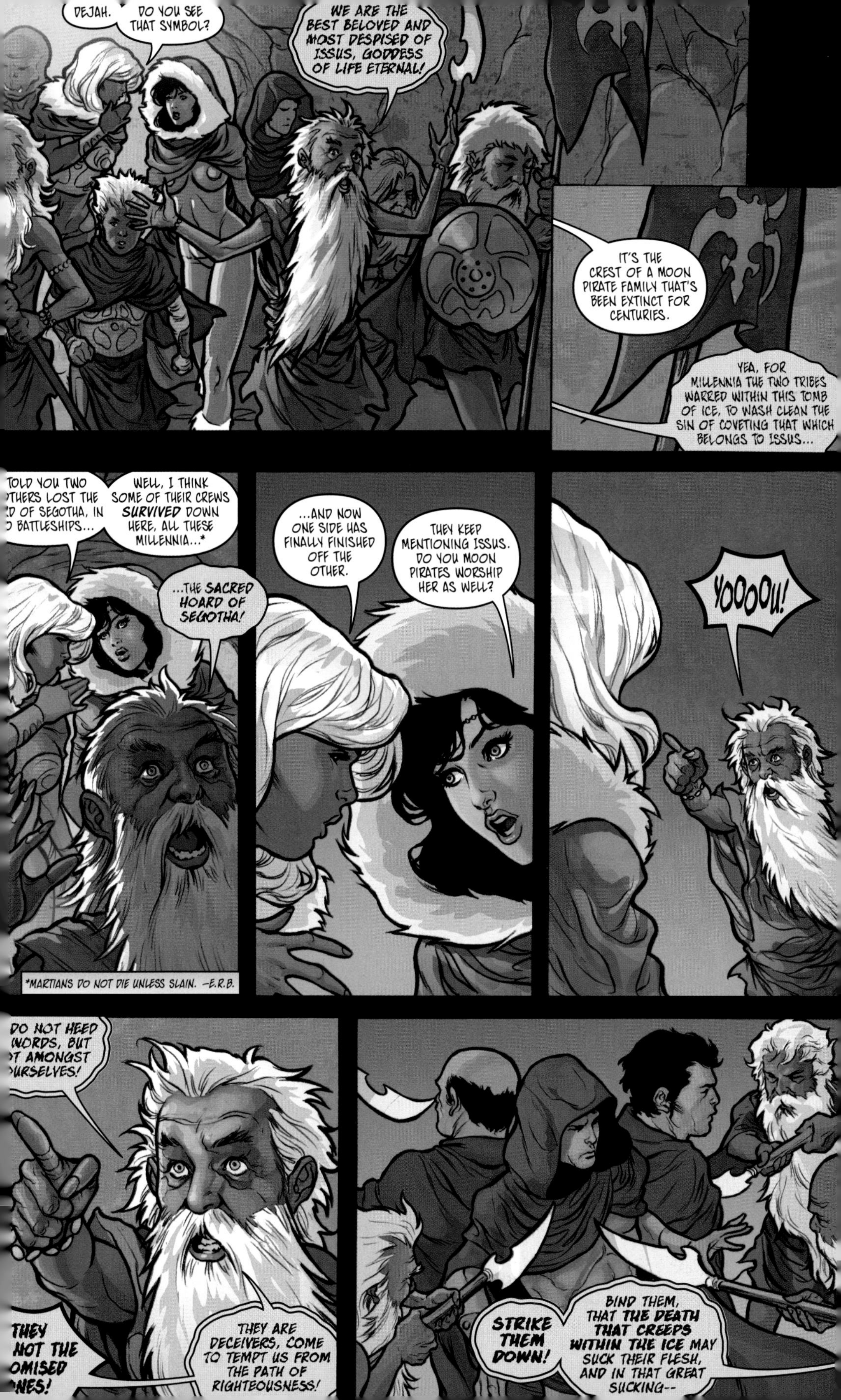

DEJAH.
DO YOU SEE THAT SYMBOL?
WE ARE THE BEST BELOVED AND MOST DESPISED OF ISSUS, GODDESS OF LIFE ETERNAL!
IT'S THE CREST OF A MOON PIRATE FAMILY THAT'S BEEN EXTINCT FOR CENTURIES.
YEA, FOR MILLENNIA THE TWO TRIBES WARRED WITHIN THIS TOMB OF ICE, TO WASH CLEAN THE SIN OF COVETING THAT WHICH BELONGS TO ISSUS...
WELL, I THINK SOME OF THEIR CREWS SURVIVED DOWN HERE, ALL THESE MILLENNIA...*
...THE SACRED HOARD OF SEGOTHA!
*MARTIANS DO NOT DIE UNLESS SLAIN. —E.R.B.
...AND NOW ONE SIDE HAS FINALLY FINISHED OFF THE OTHER.
THEY KEEP MENTIONING ISSUS. DO YOU MOON PIRATES WORSHIP HER AS WELL?
YOOOOU!
THEY ARE DECEIVERS, COME TO TEMPT US FROM THE PATH OF RIGHTEOUSNESS!
STRIKE THEM DOWN!
BIND THEM, THAT THE DEATH THAT CREEPS WITHIN THE ICE MAY SUCK THEIR FLESH, AND IN THAT GREAT SUCKING--

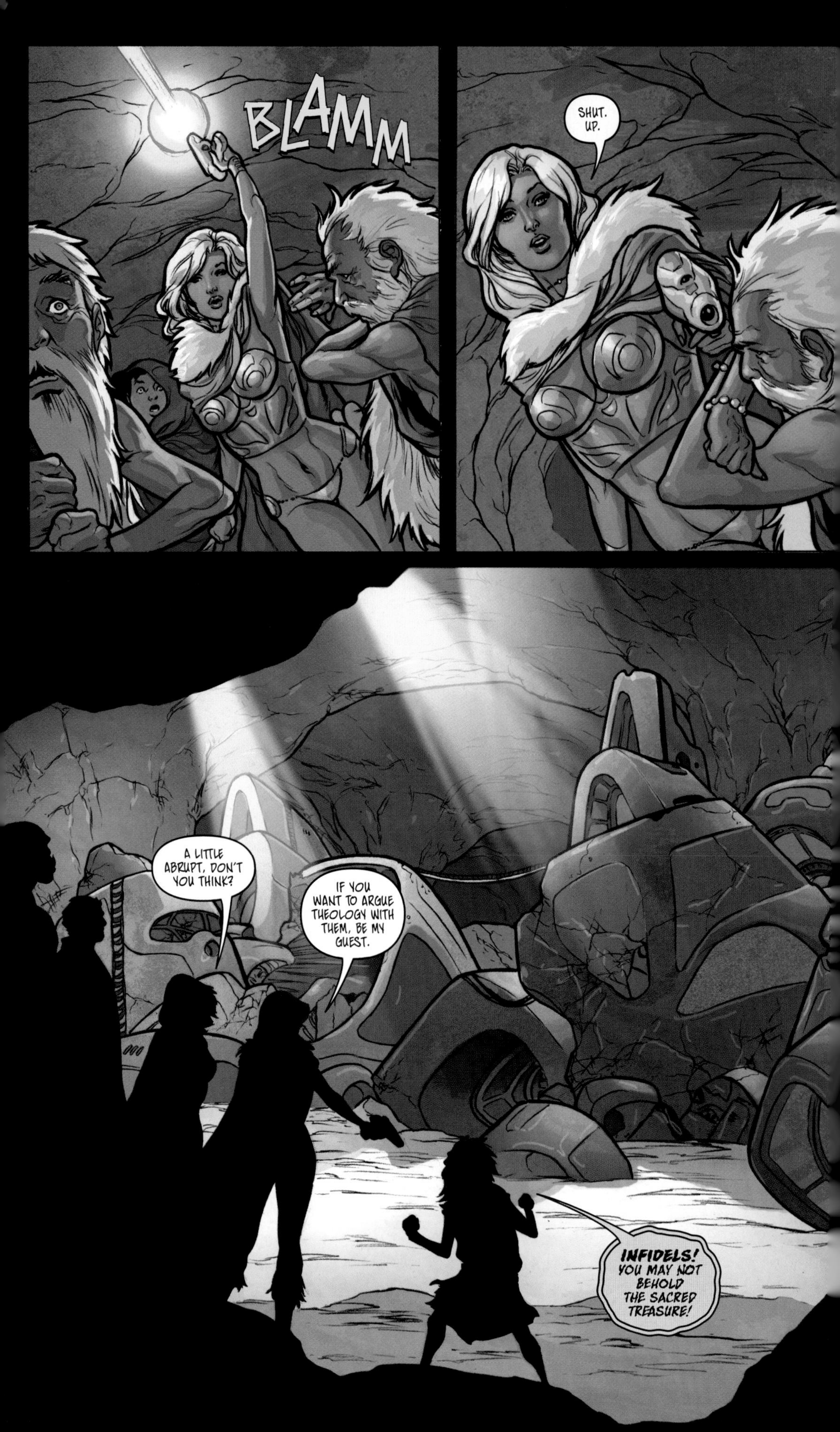
BLAMM
SHUT. UP.
A LITTLE ABRUPT, DON'T YOU THINK?
IF YOU WANT TO ARGUE THEOLOGY WITH THEM, BE MY GUEST.
INFIDELS! YOU MAY NOT BEHOLD THE SACRED TREASURE!

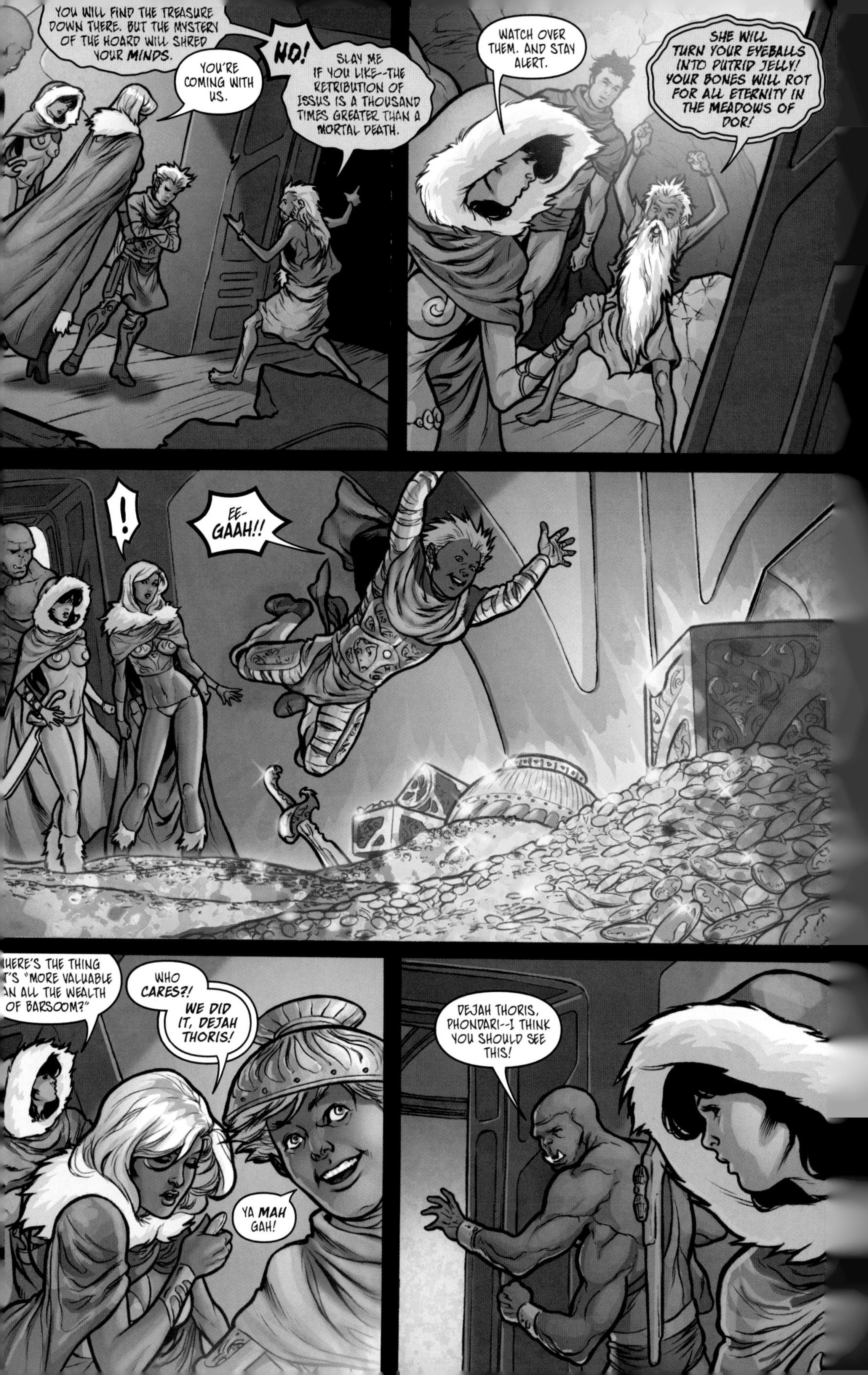
YOU WILL FIND THE TREASURE DOWN THERE. BUT THE MYSTERY OF THE HOARD WILL SHRED YOUR MINDS.
YOU'RE COMING WITH US.
NO!
SLAY ME IF YOU LIKE--THE RETRIBUTION OF ISSUS IS A THOUSAND TIMES GREATER THAN A MORTAL DEATH.
WATCH OVER THEM. AND STAY ALERT.
SHE WILL TURN YOUR EYEBALLS INTO PUTRID JELLY! YOUR BONES WILL ROT FOR ALL ETERNITY IN THE MEADOWS OF DOR!
!
EE-GAAH!!
HERE'S THE THING T'S "MORE VALUABLE AN ALL THE WEALTH OF BARSOOM?"
WHO CARES?! WE DID IT, DEJAH THORIS!
YA MAH GAH!
DEJAH THORIS, PHONDARI--I THINK YOU SHOULD SEE THIS!

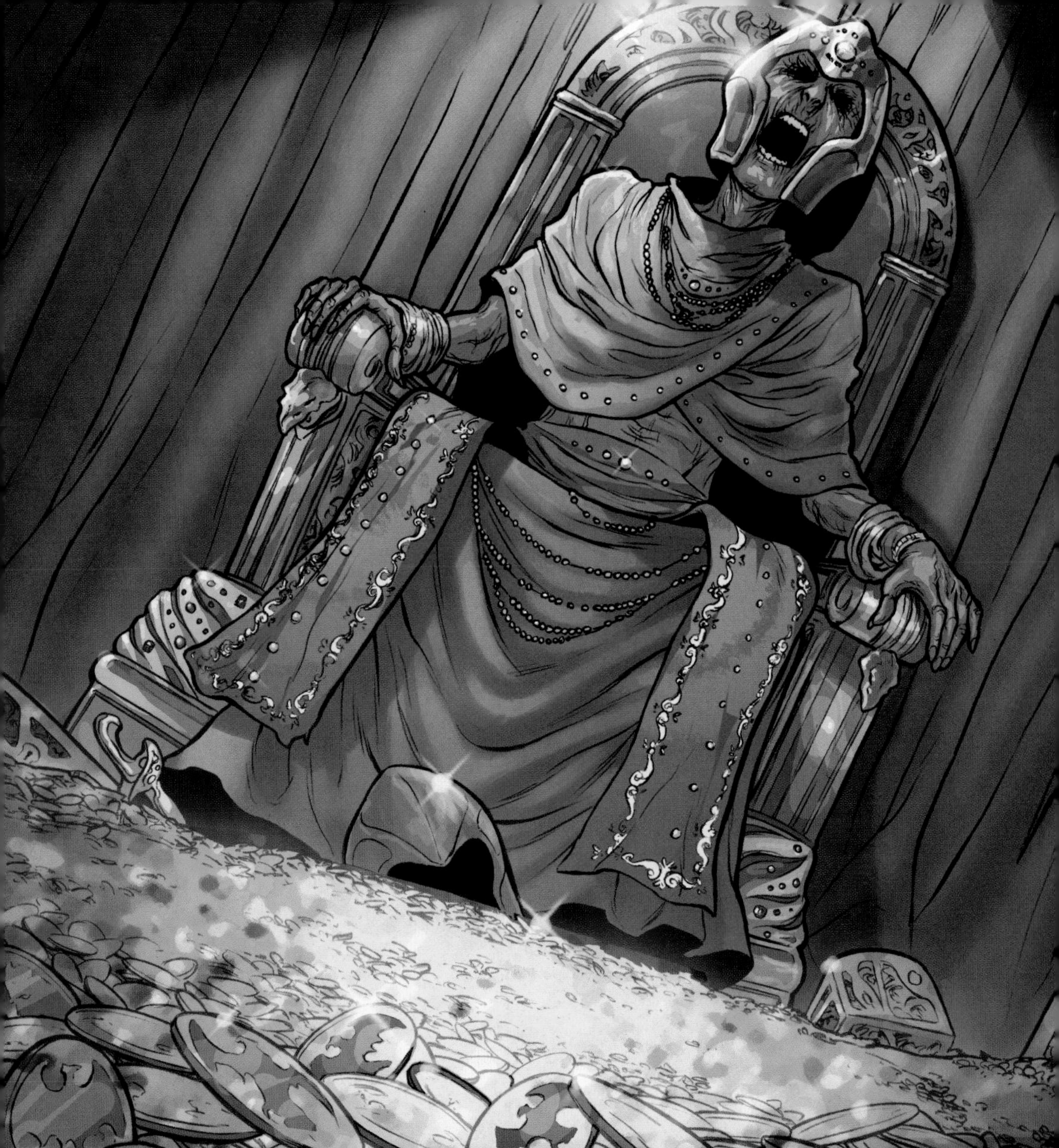

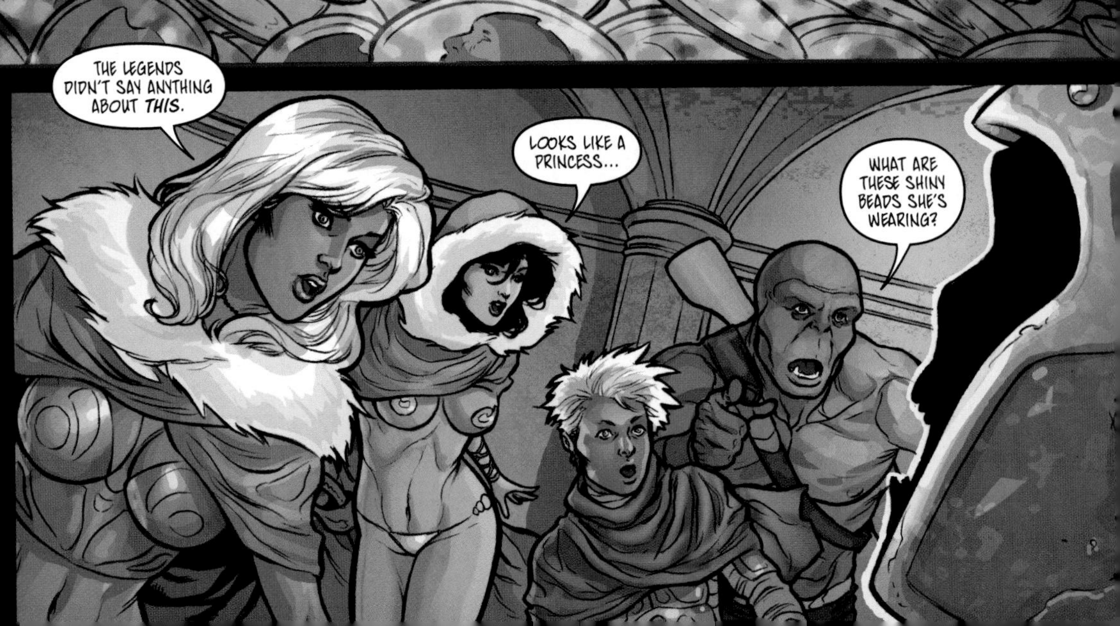
THE LEGENDS DIDN'T SAY ANYTHING ABOUT *THIS*.
LOOKS LIKE A PRINCESS...
WHAT ARE THESE SHINY BEADS SHE'S WEARING?

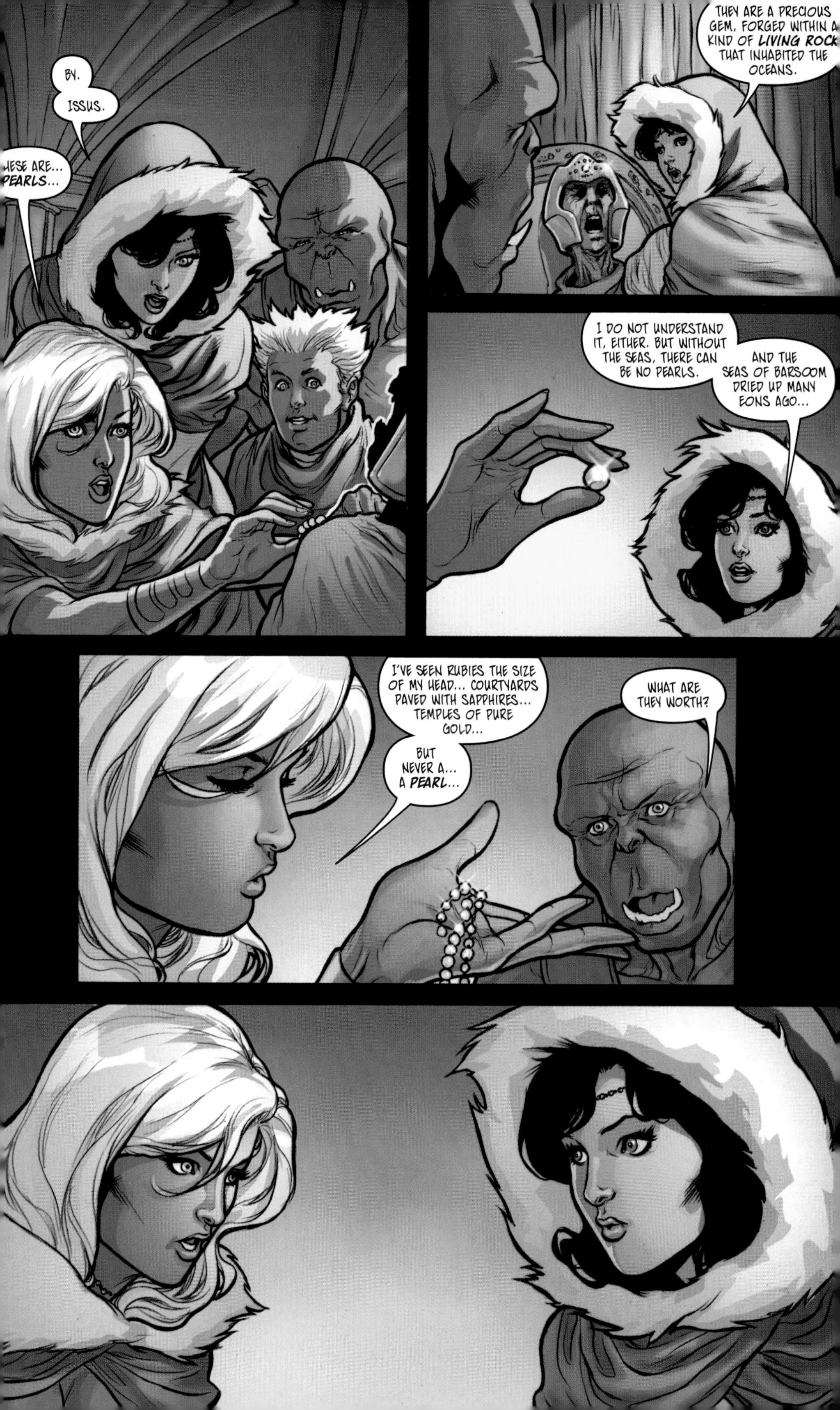

HESE ARE... PEARLS...
BY.
ISSUS.
THEY ARE A PRECIOUS GEM, FORGED WITHIN A KIND OF LIVING ROCK THAT INHABITED THE OCEANS.
I DO NOT UNDERSTAND IT, EITHER. BUT WITHOUT THE SEAS, THERE CAN BE NO PEARLS.
AND THE SEAS OF BARSOOM DRIED UP MANY EONS AGO...
I'VE SEEN RUBIES THE SIZE OF MY HEAD... COURTYARDS PAVED WITH SAPPHIRES... TEMPLES OF PURE GOLD...
BUT NEVER A... A PEARL...
WHAT ARE THEY WORTH?

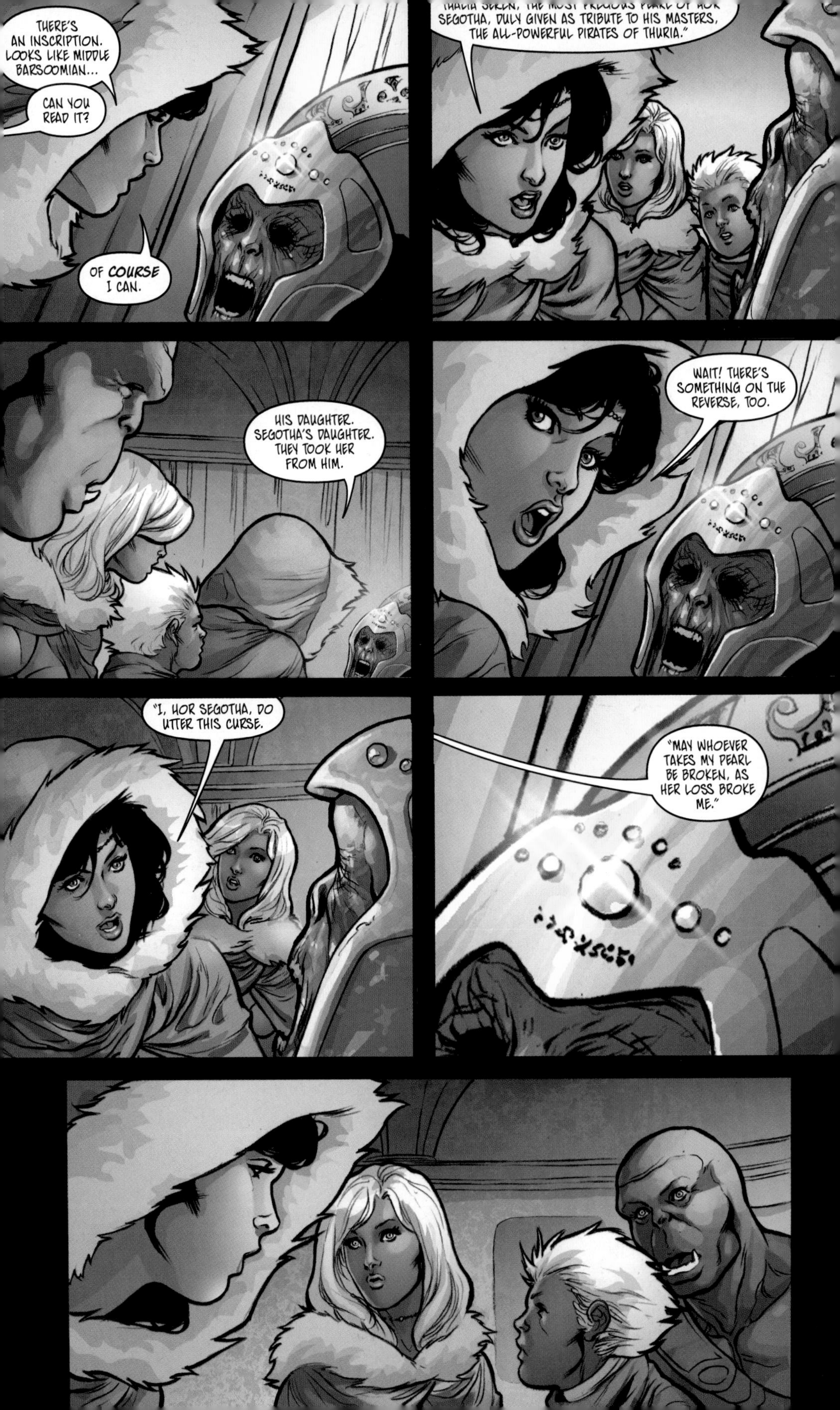

THERE'S AN INSCRIPTION. LOOKS LIKE MIDDLE BARSOOMIAN...
CAN YOU READ IT?
OF COURSE I CAN.
SEGOTHA, DULY GIVEN AS TRIBUTE TO HIS MASTERS, THE ALL-POWERFUL PIRATES OF THURIA."
HIS DAUGHTER. SEGOTHA'S DAUGHTER. THEY TOOK HER FROM HIM.
WAIT! THERE'S SOMETHING ON THE REVERSE, TOO.
"I, HOR SEGOTHA, DO UTTER THIS CURSE.
"MAY WHOEVER TAKES MY PEARL BE BROKEN, AS HER LOSS BROKE ME."

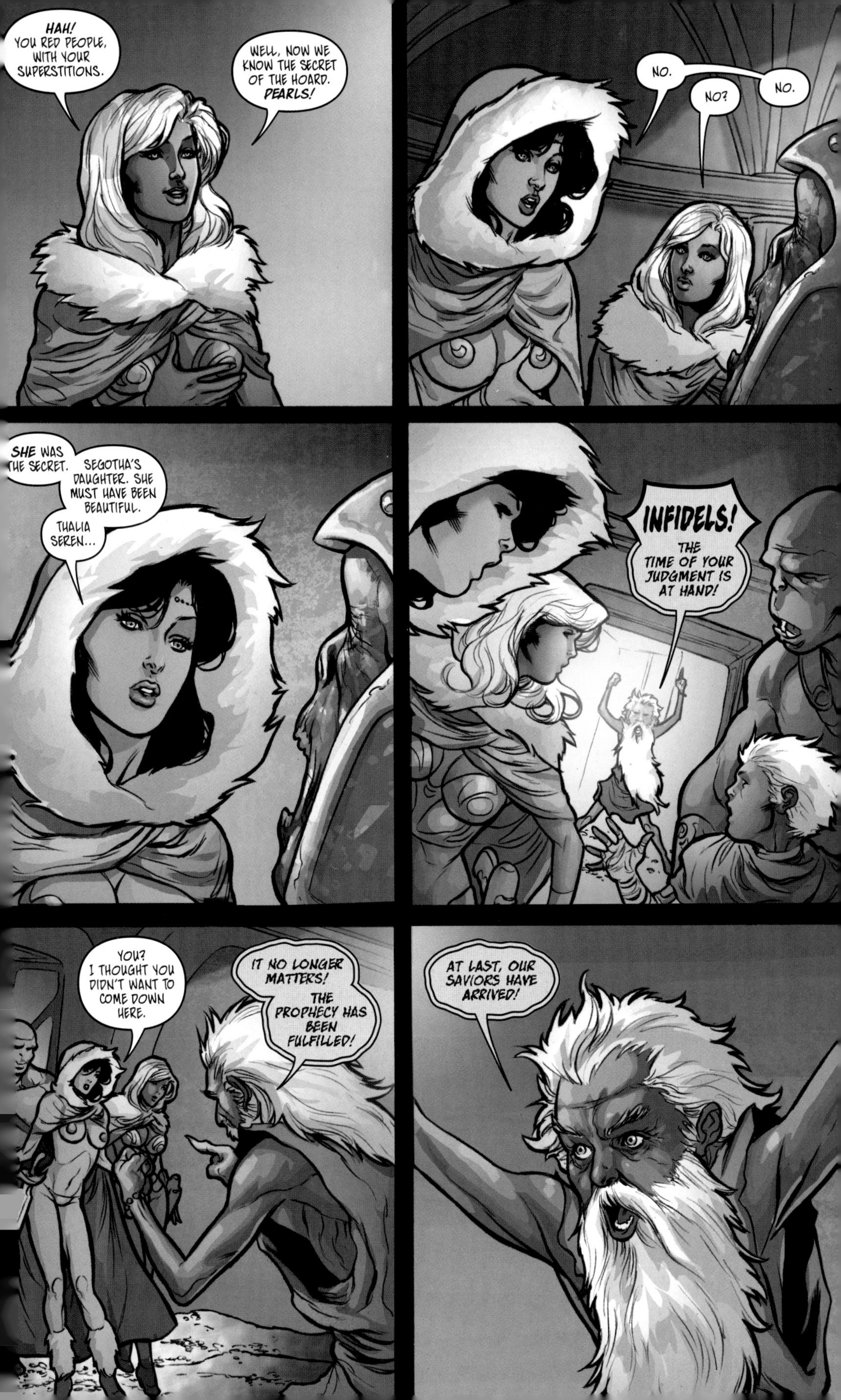

HAH! YOU RED PEOPLE, WITH YOUR SUPERSTITIONS.
WELL, NOW WE KNOW THE SECRET OF THE HOARD. PEARLS!
NO.
NO?
NO.
SHE WAS THE SECRET.
SEGOTHA'S DAUGHTER. SHE MUST HAVE BEEN BEAUTIFUL.
THALIA SEREN...
INFIDELS!
THE TIME OF YOUR JUDGMENT IS AT HAND!
YOU? I THOUGHT YOU DIDN'T WANT TO COME DOWN HERE.
IT NO LONGER MATTERS!
THE PROPHECY HAS BEEN FULFILLED!
AT LAST, OUR SAVIORS HAVE ARRIVED!

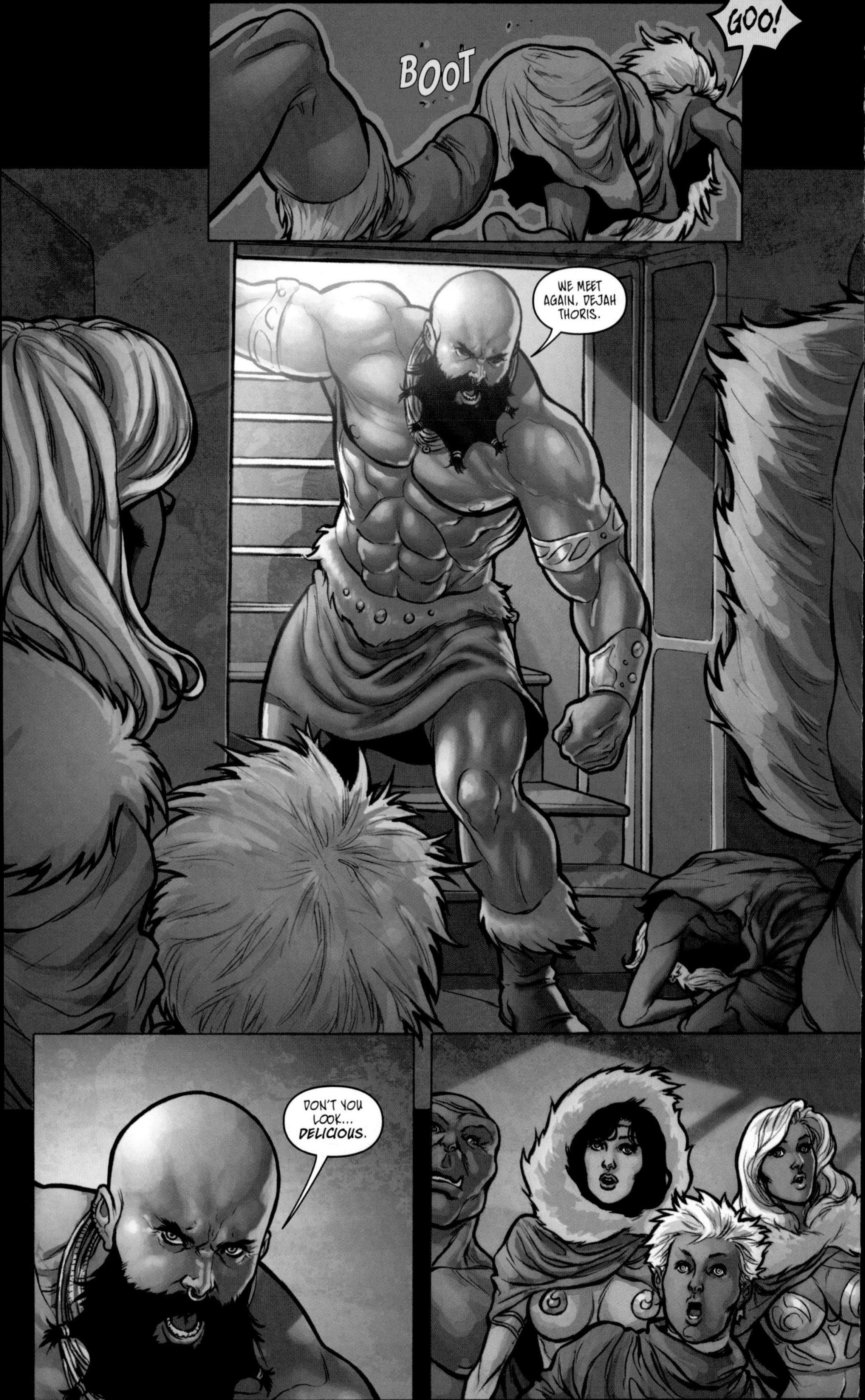
BOOT
GOO!
WE MEET AGAIN, DEJAH THORIS.
DON'T YOU LOOK... **DELICIOUS**.

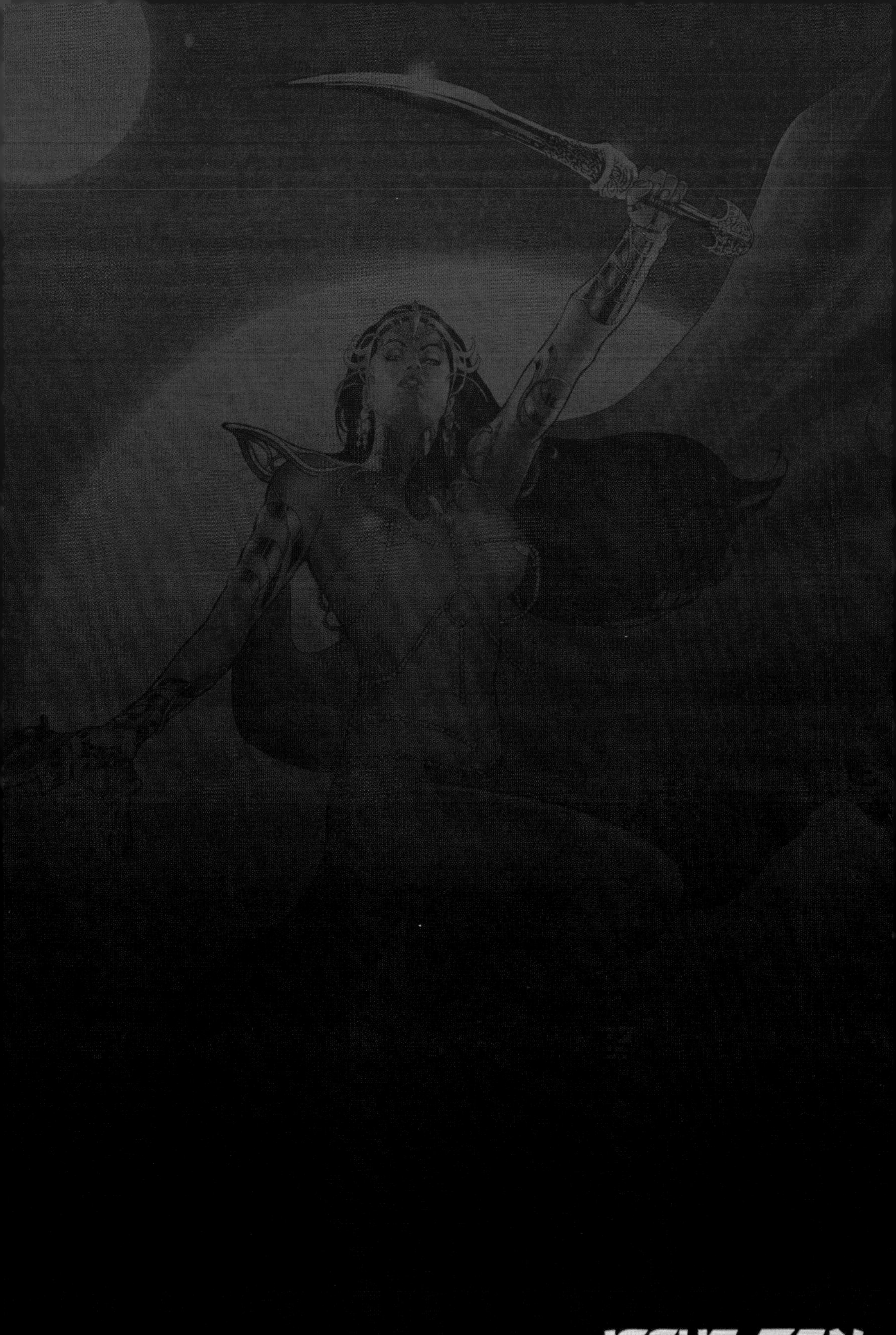

## ISSUE TEN

# THE DEATH THAT CREEPS WITHIN THE ICE

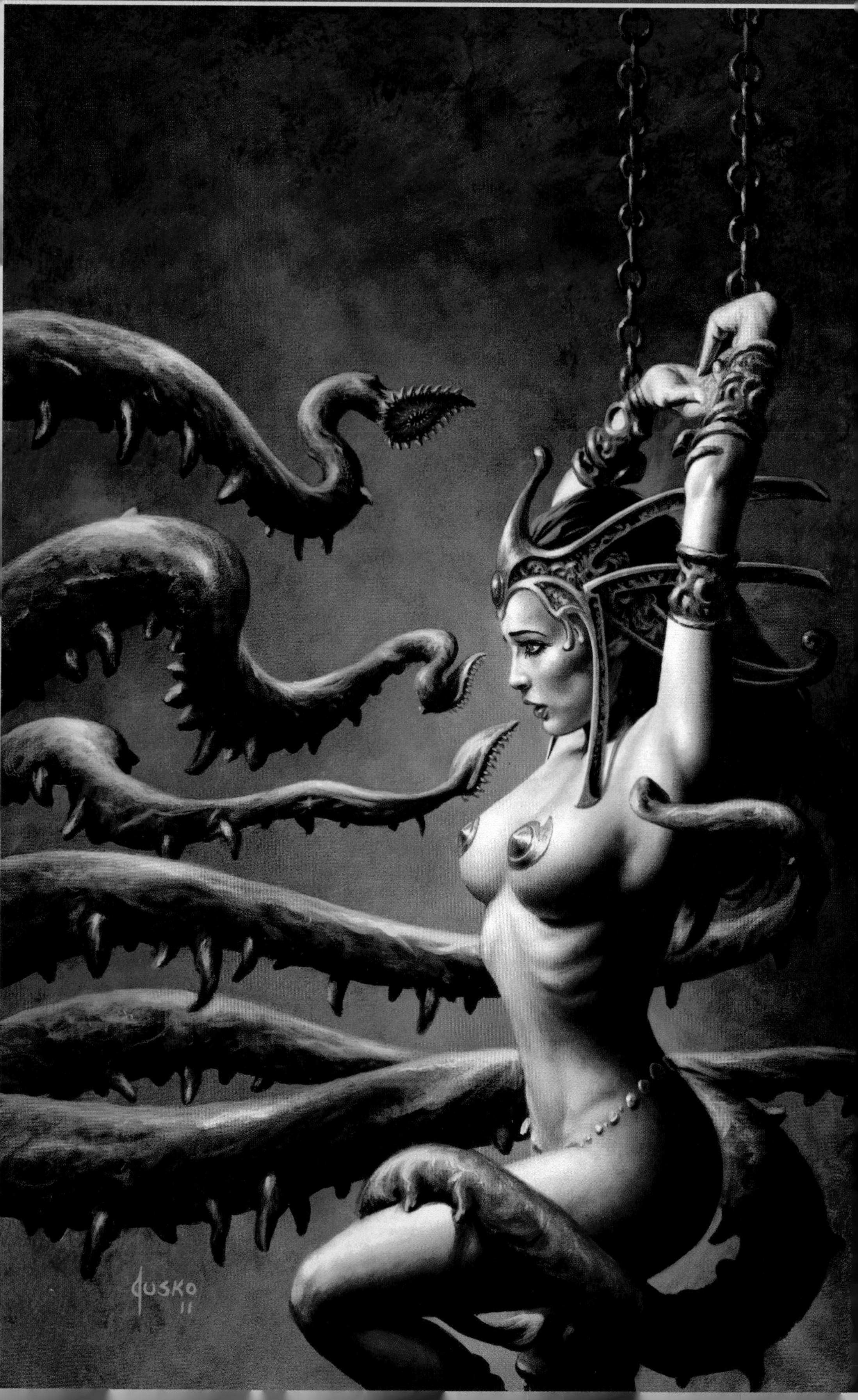
JUSKO
11

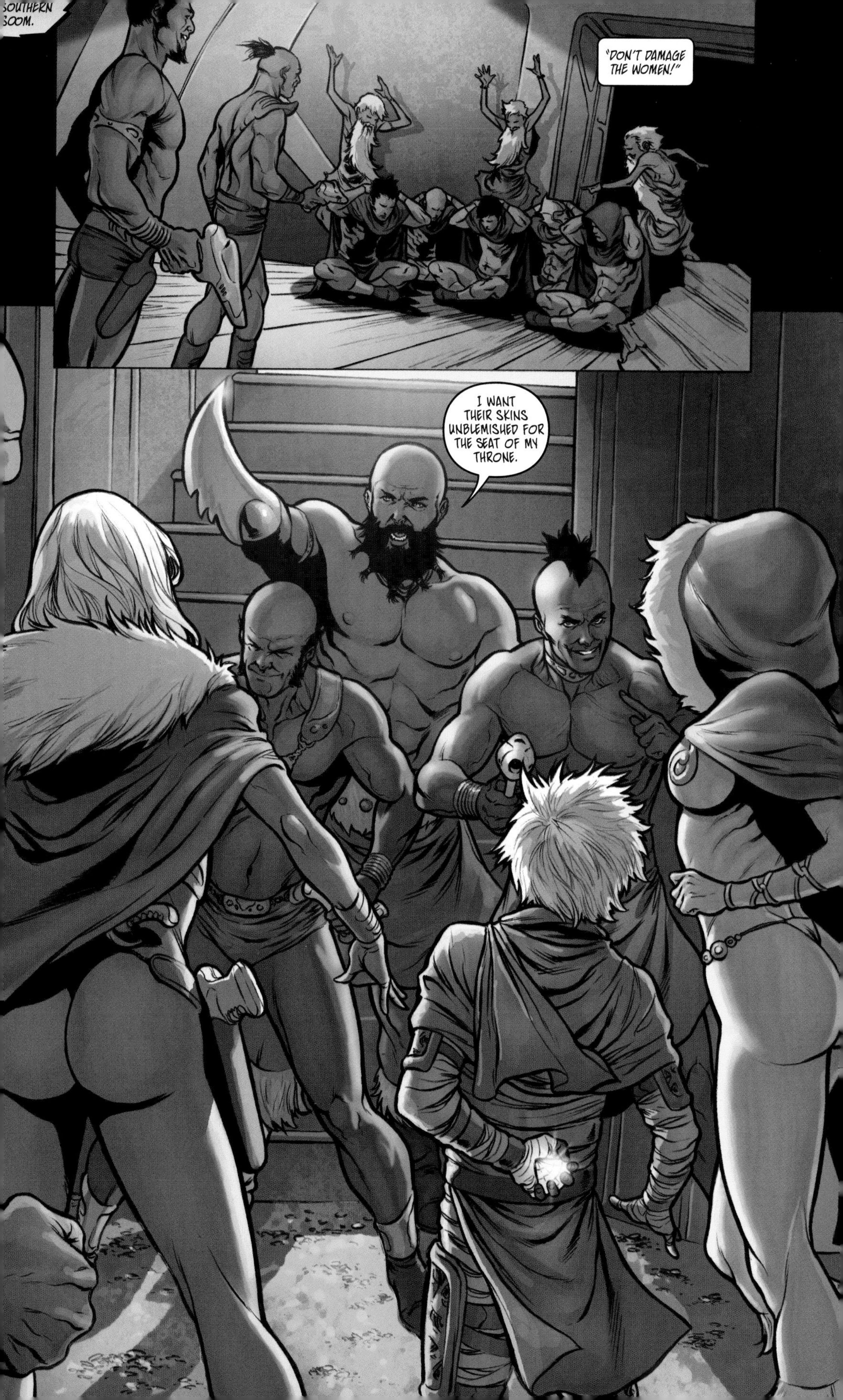
SOUTHERN
SOOM.
"DON'T DAMAGE THE WOMEN!"
I WANT THEIR SKINS UNBLEMISHED FOR THE SEAT OF MY THRONE.

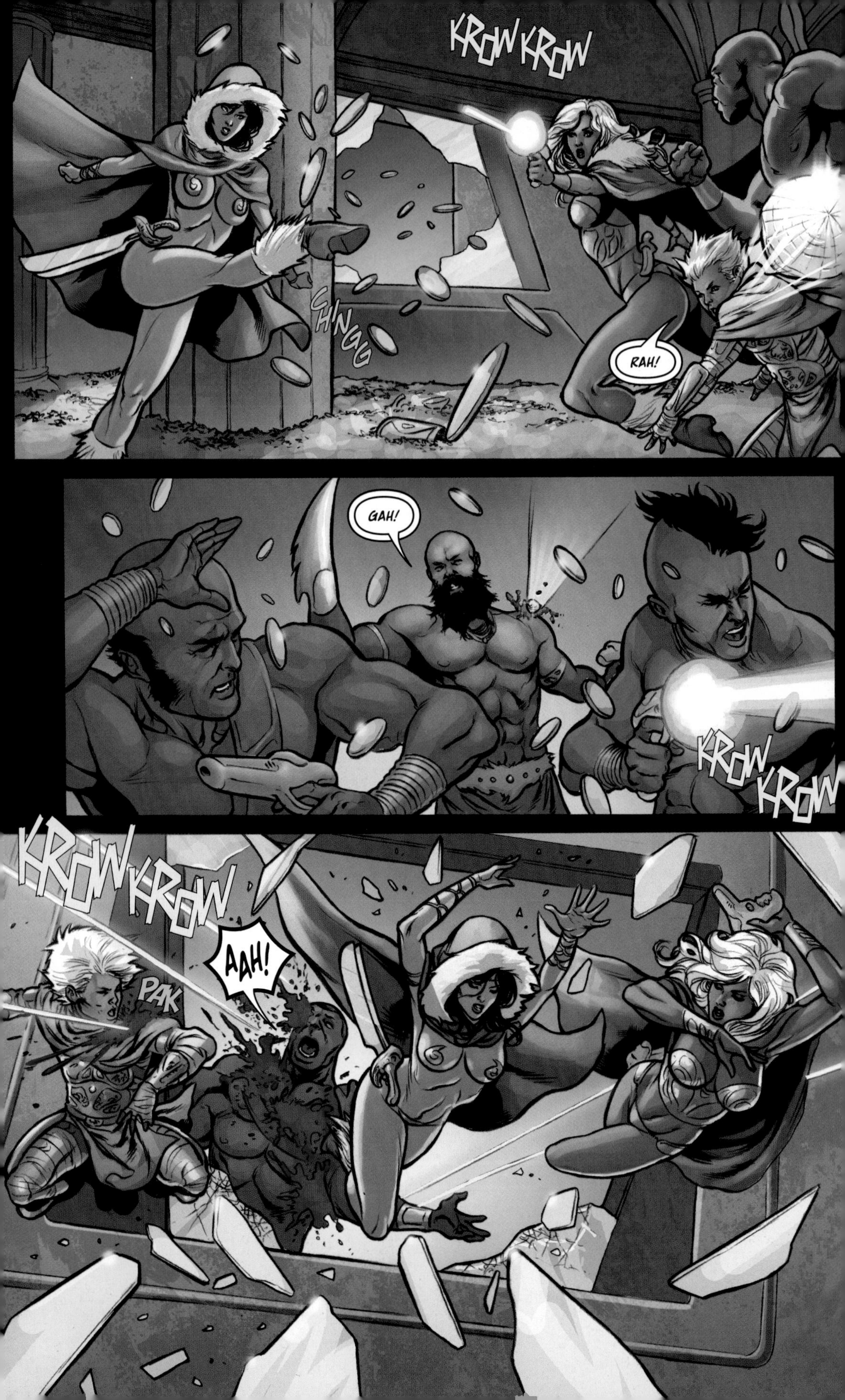
KROW KROW
CHINGG
RAH!
GAH!
KROW KROW
KROW KROW
AAH!
PAK

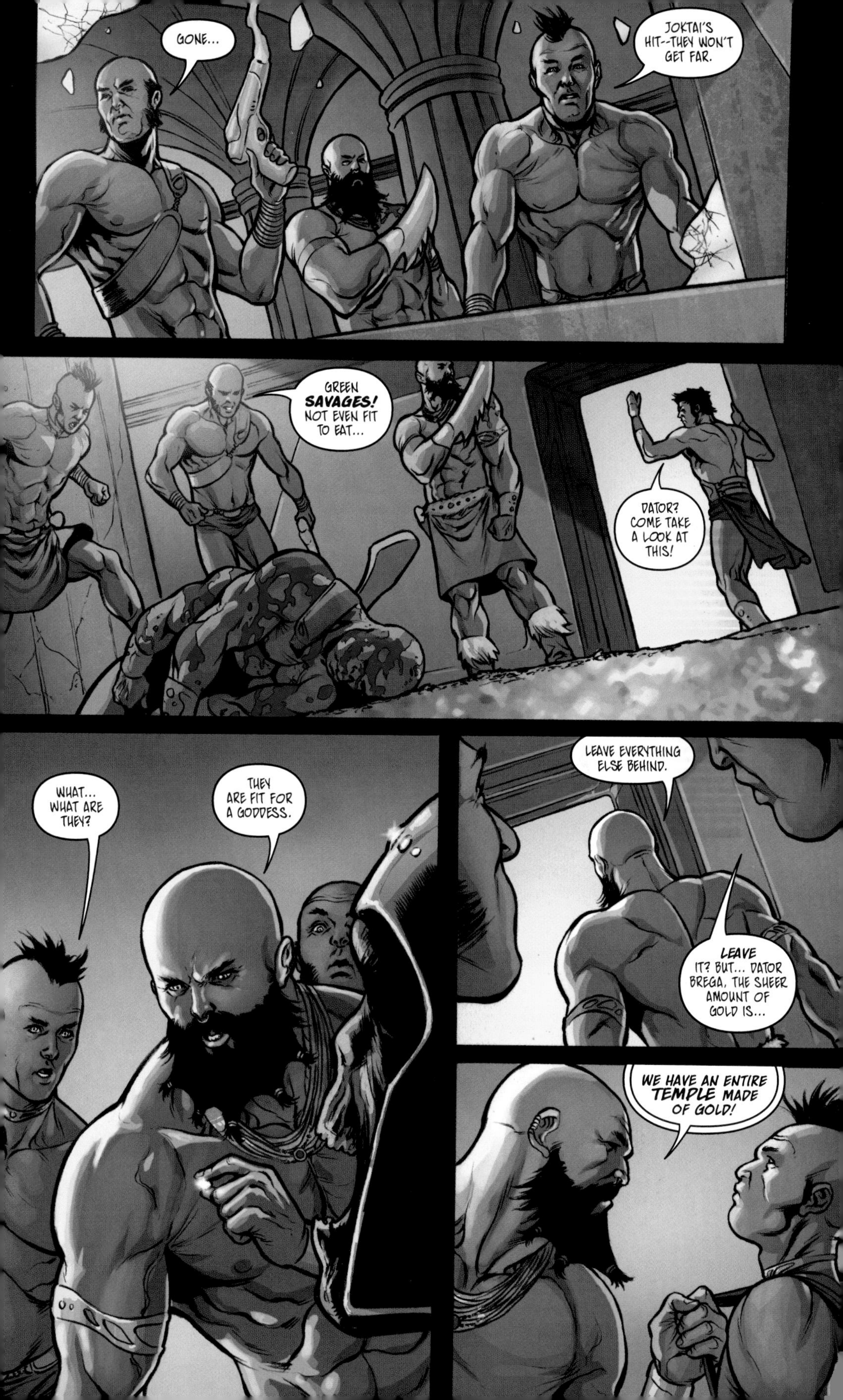
GONE...
JOKTAI'S HIT--THEY WON'T GET FAR.
GREEN SAVAGES! NOT EVEN FIT TO EAT...
DATOR? COME TAKE A LOOK AT THIS!
WHAT... WHAT ARE THEY?
THEY ARE FIT FOR A GODDESS.
LEAVE EVERYTHING ELSE BEHIND.
LEAVE IT? BUT... DATOR BREGA, THE SHEER AMOUNT OF GOLD IS...
WE HAVE AN ENTIRE TEMPLE MADE OF GOLD!

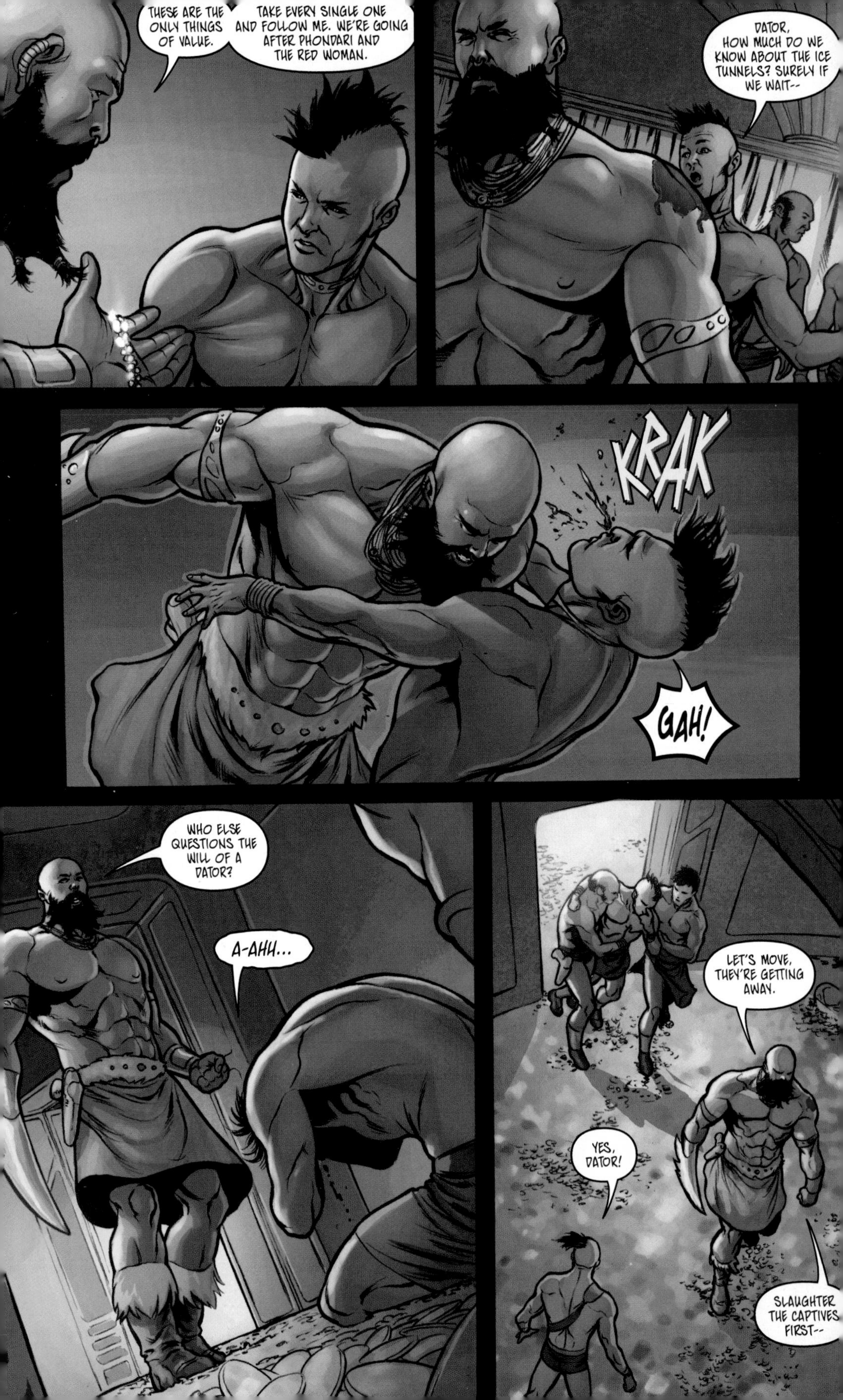
THESE ARE THE ONLY THINGS OF VALUE.
TAKE EVERY SINGLE ONE AND FOLLOW ME. WE'RE GOING AFTER PHONDARI AND THE RED WOMAN.
DATOR, HOW MUCH DO WE KNOW ABOUT THE ICE TUNNELS? SURELY IF WE WAIT--
KRAK
GAH!
WHO ELSE QUESTIONS THE WILL OF A DATOR?
A-AHH...
LET'S MOVE, THEY'RE GETTING AWAY.
YES, DATOR!
SLAUGHTER THE CAPTIVES FIRST--

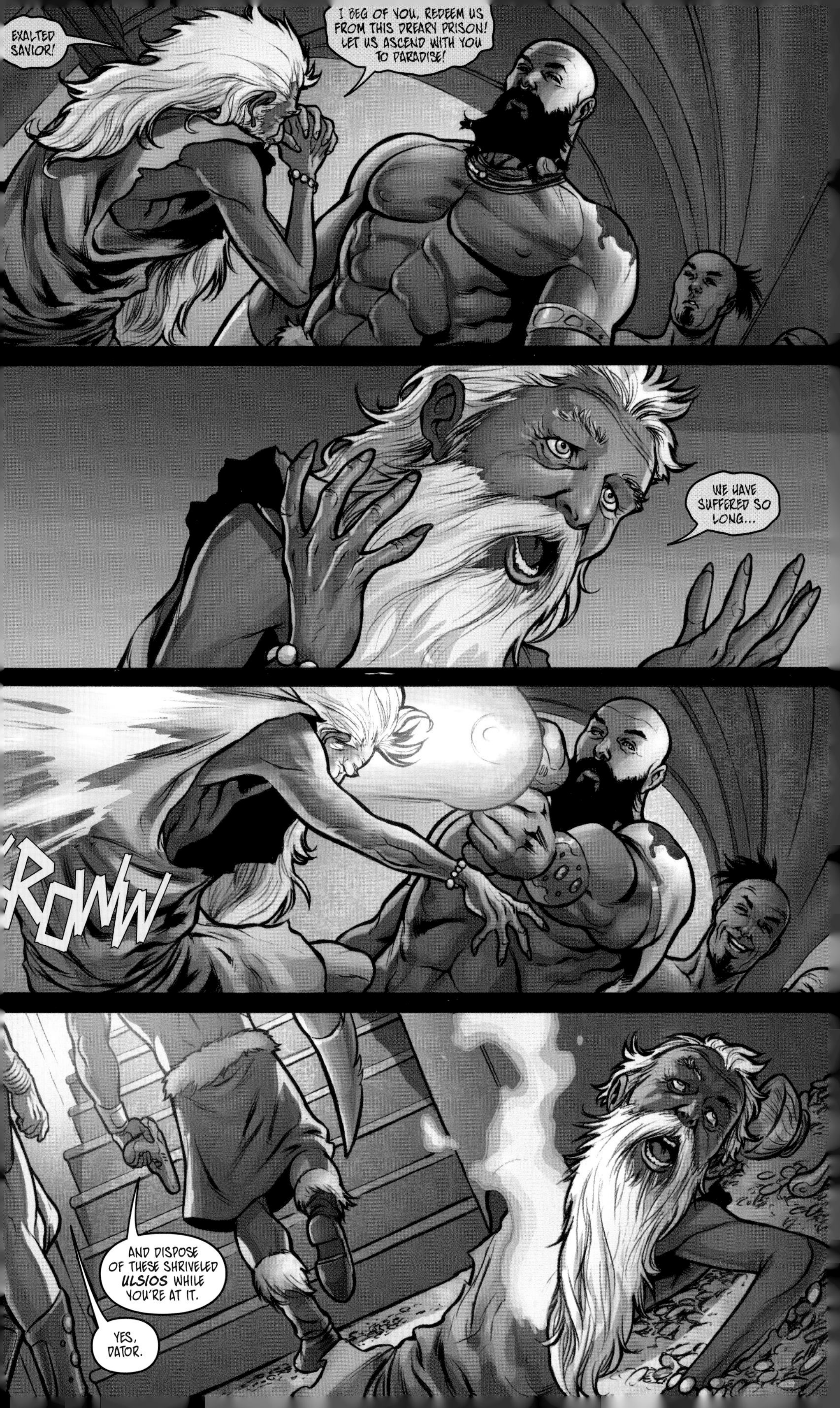
EXALTED SAVIOR!
I BEG OF YOU, REDEEM US FROM THIS DREARY PRISON! LET US ASCEND WITH YOU TO PARADISE!
WE HAVE SUFFERED SO LONG...
'RONNN
AND DISPOSE OF THESE SHRIVELED ULSIOS WHILE YOU'RE AT IT.
YES, DATOR.

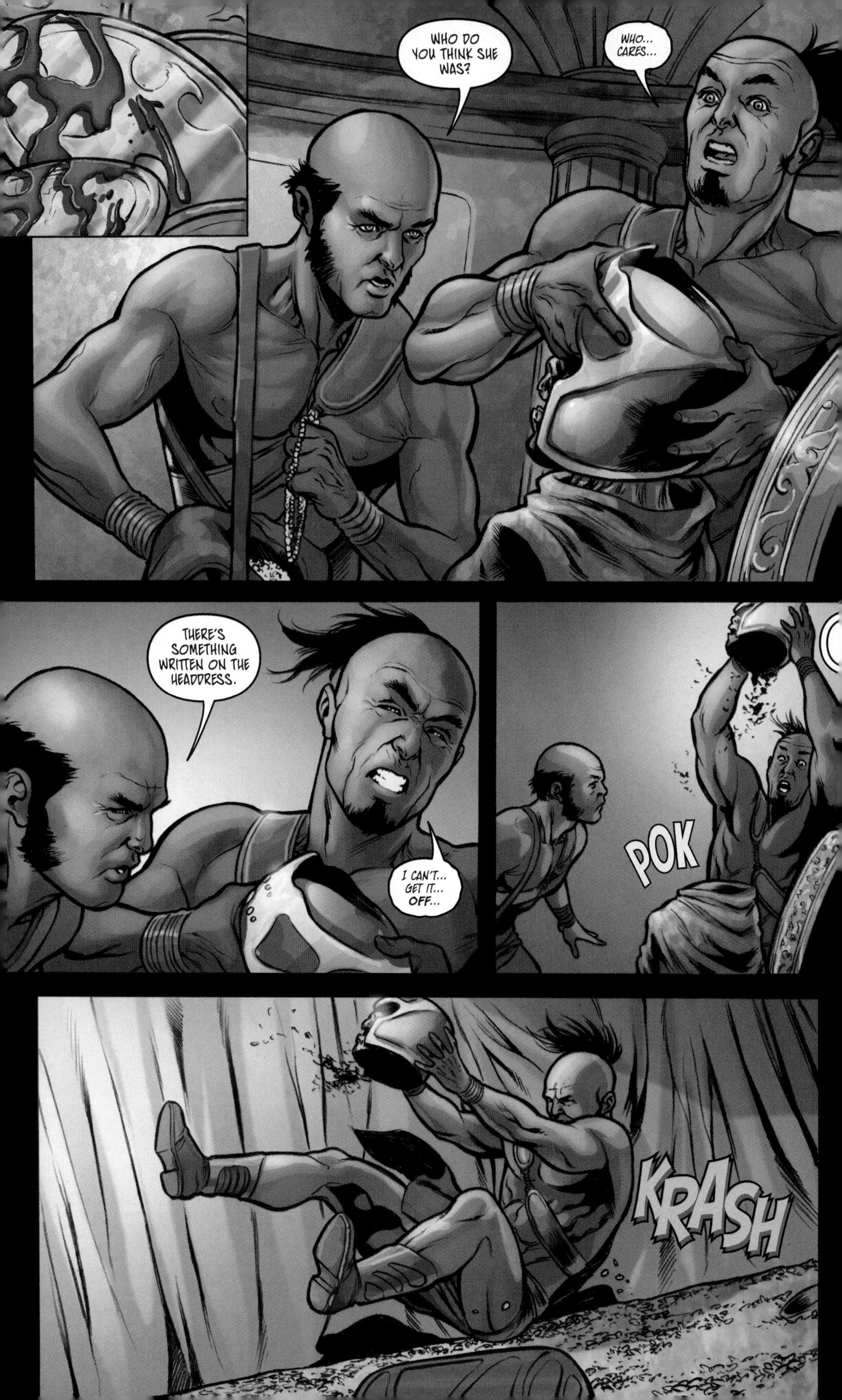
WHO DO YOU THINK SHE WAS?
WHO... CARES...
THERE'S SOMETHING WRITTEN ON THE HEADDRESS.
I CAN'T... GET IT... OFF...
POK
KRASH

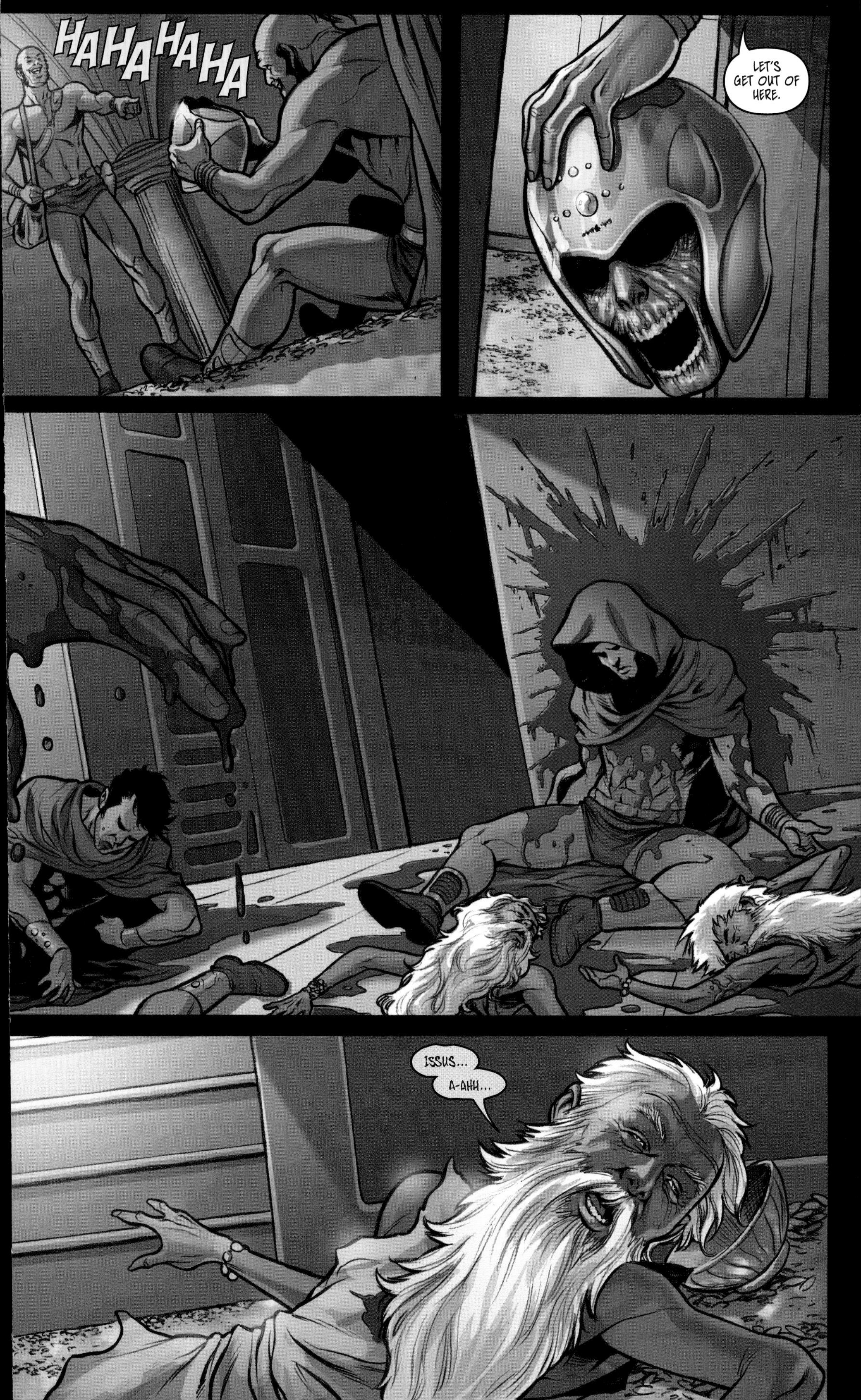
HAHAHAHA
LET'S GET OUT OF HERE.
ISSUS...
A-AHH...

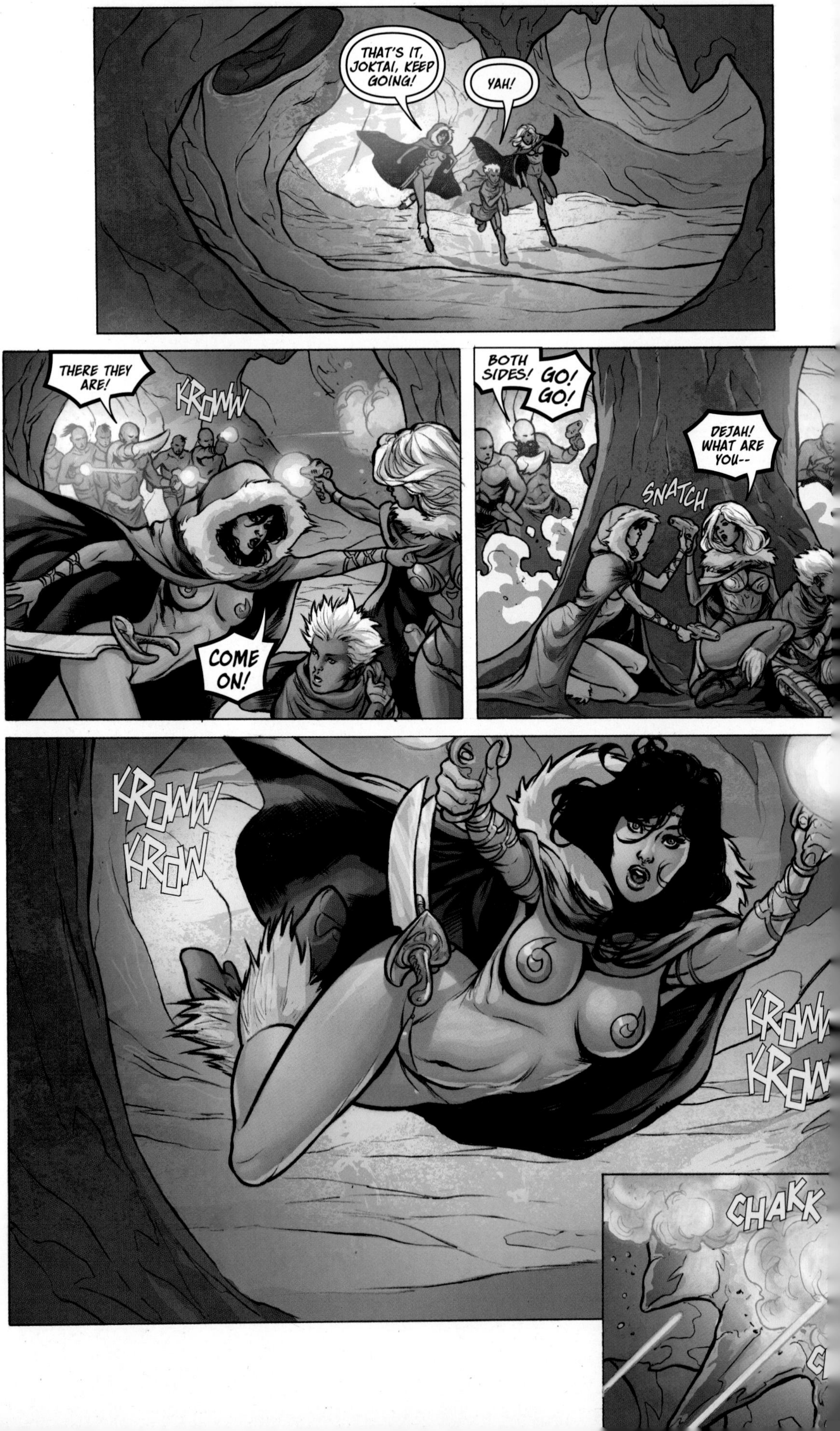
THAT'S IT, JOKTAI, KEEP GOING!
YAH!
THERE THEY ARE!
KROWW
COME ON!
BOTH SIDES!
GO! GO!
DEJAH! WHAT ARE YOU--
SNATCH
KROWW KROW
KROWW KROW
CHAKK

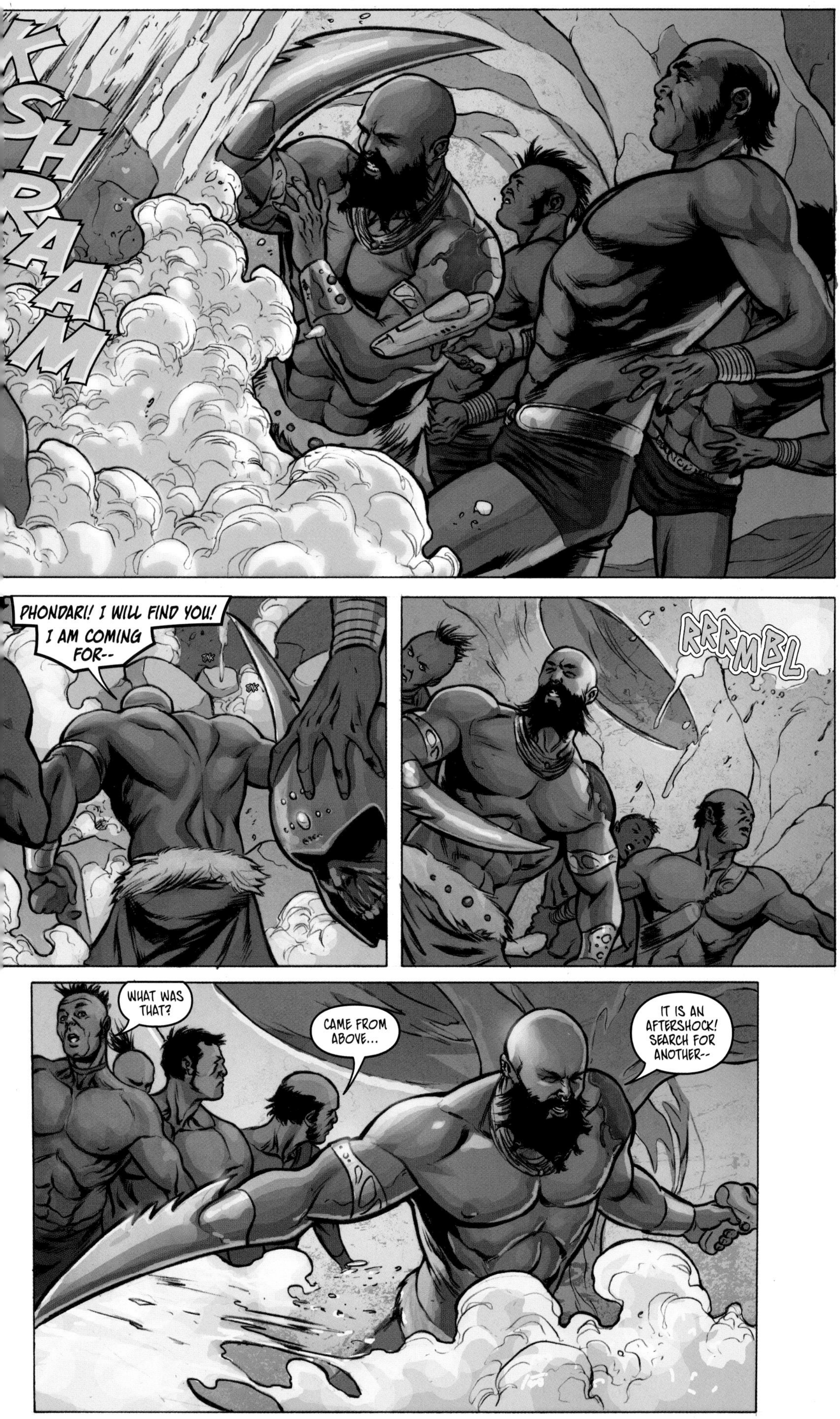
KSHRAAAM
PHONDARI! I WILL FIND YOU! I AM COMING FOR--
TINK
TINK
RRRMBL
WHAT WAS THAT?
CAME FROM ABOVE...
IT IS AN AFTERSHOCK! SEARCH FOR ANOTHER--

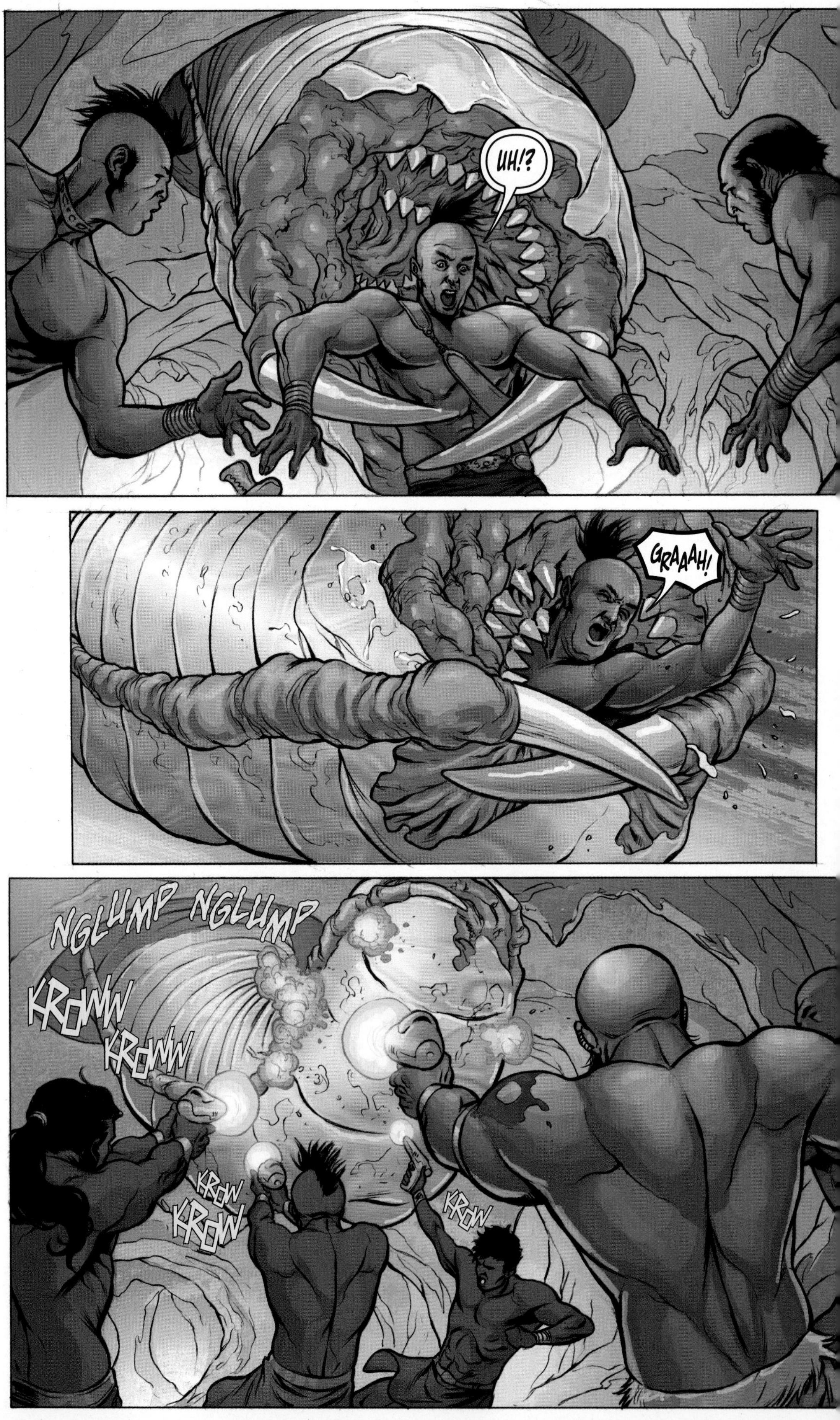
UH!?
GRAAAH!
NGLUMP NGLUMP
KROWW
KROWW
KROW
KROW
KROW

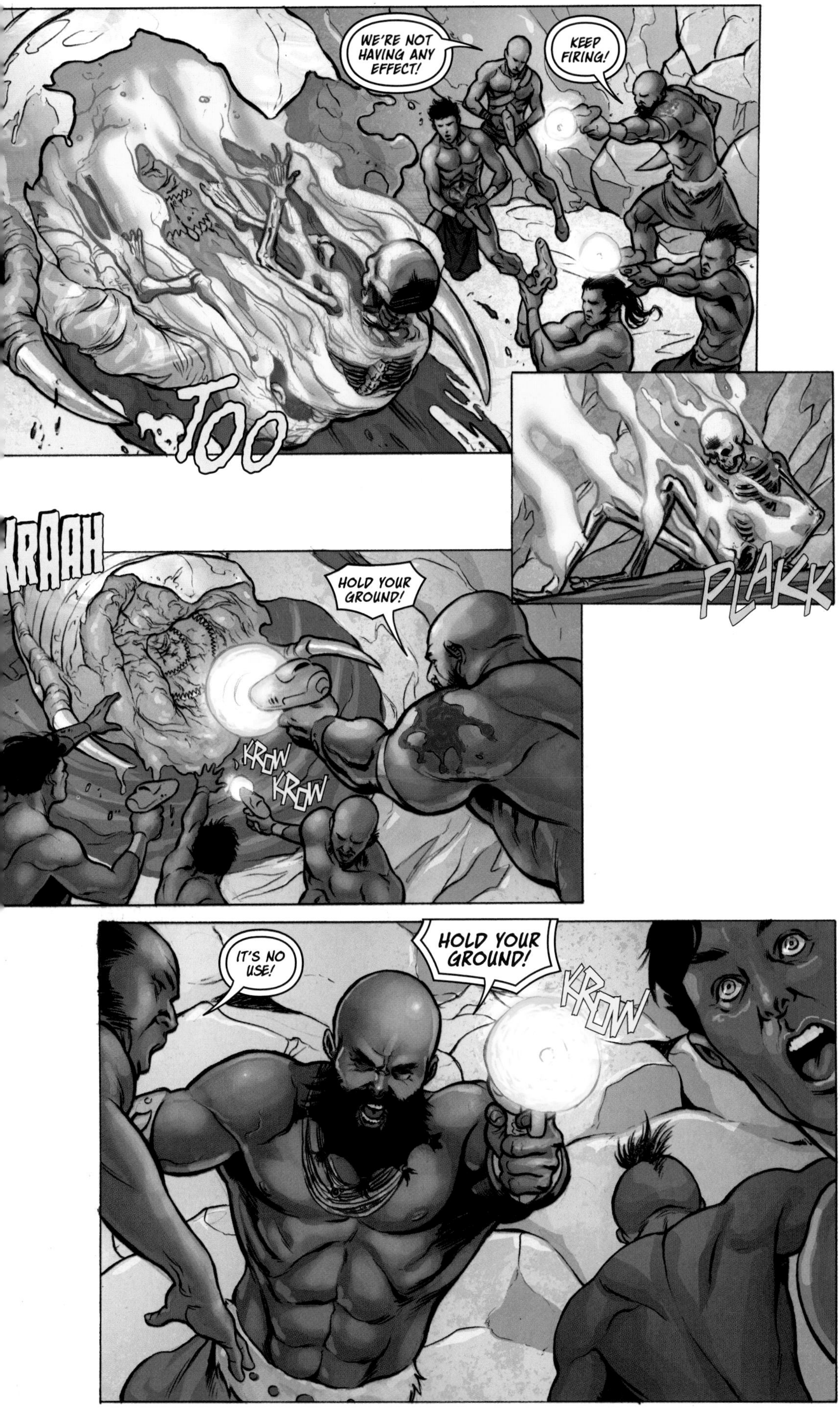
WE'RE NOT HAVING ANY EFFECT!
KEEP FIRING!
TOO
KRAAH
PLAKK
HOLD YOUR GROUND!
KROW
KROW
IT'S NO USE!
HOLD YOUR GROUND!
KROW

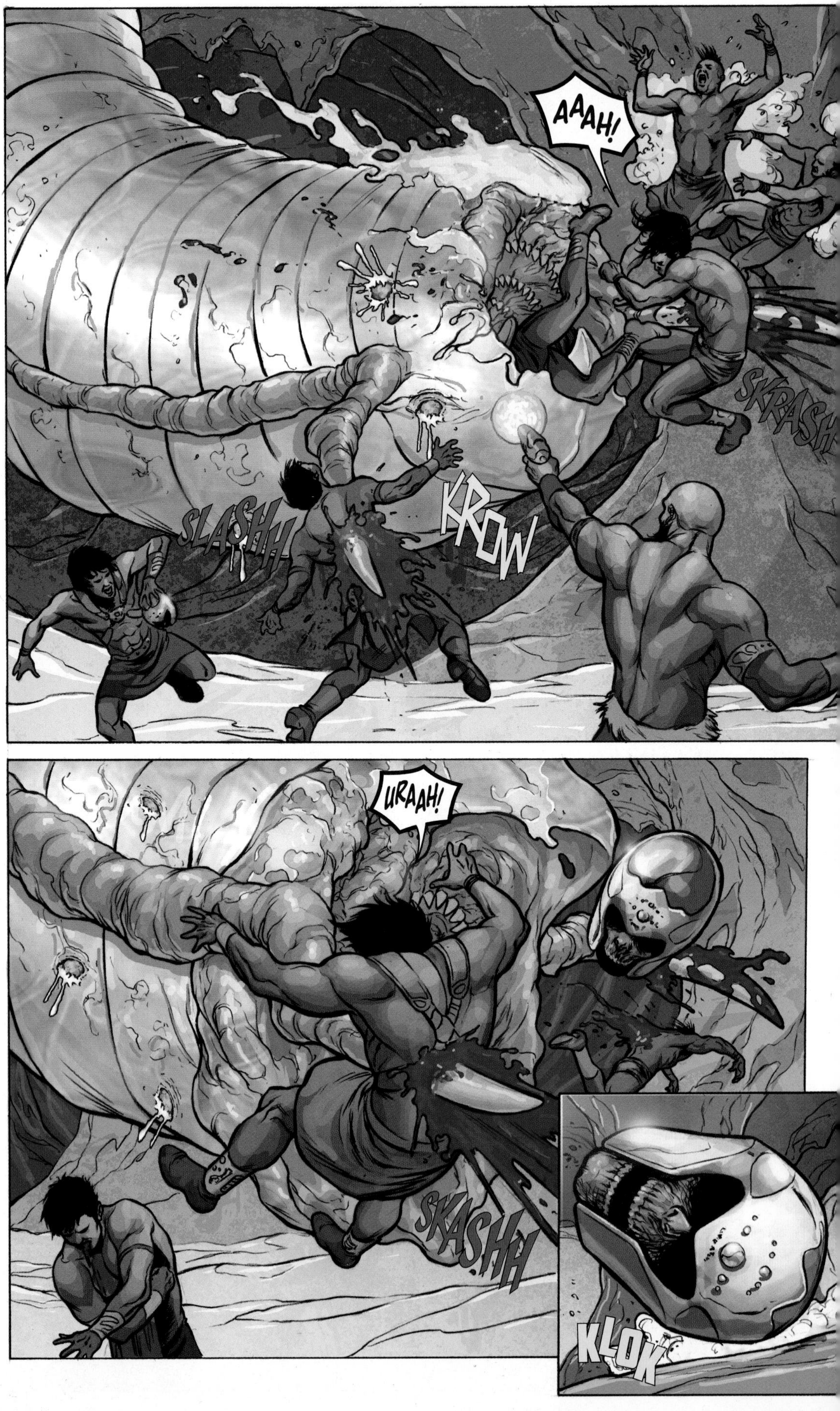
AAAH!
SKRASH
SLASHH
KROW
URAAH!
SKASHH
KLOK

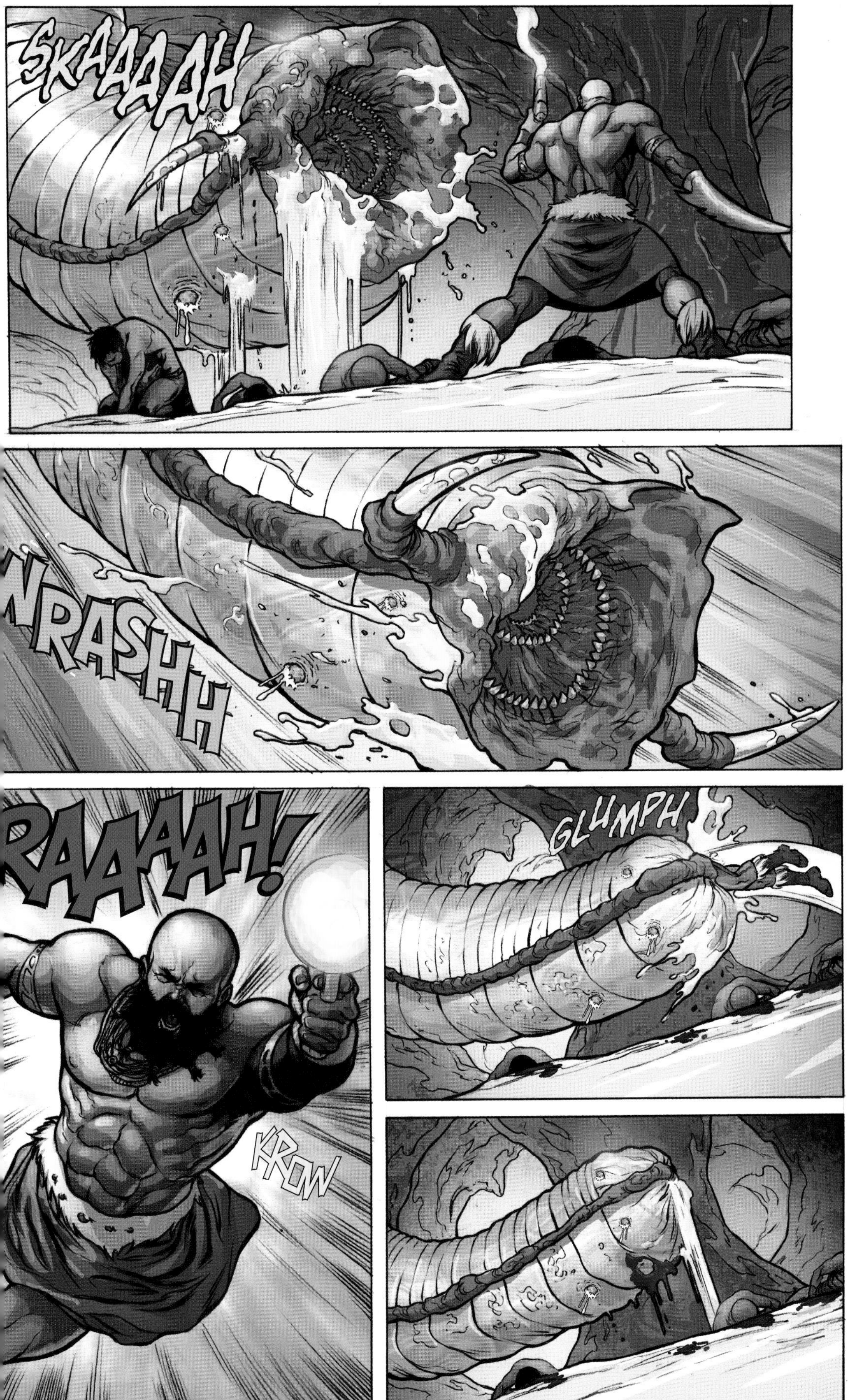
SKAAAAH
WRASHH
RAAAAH!
KROW
GLUMPH

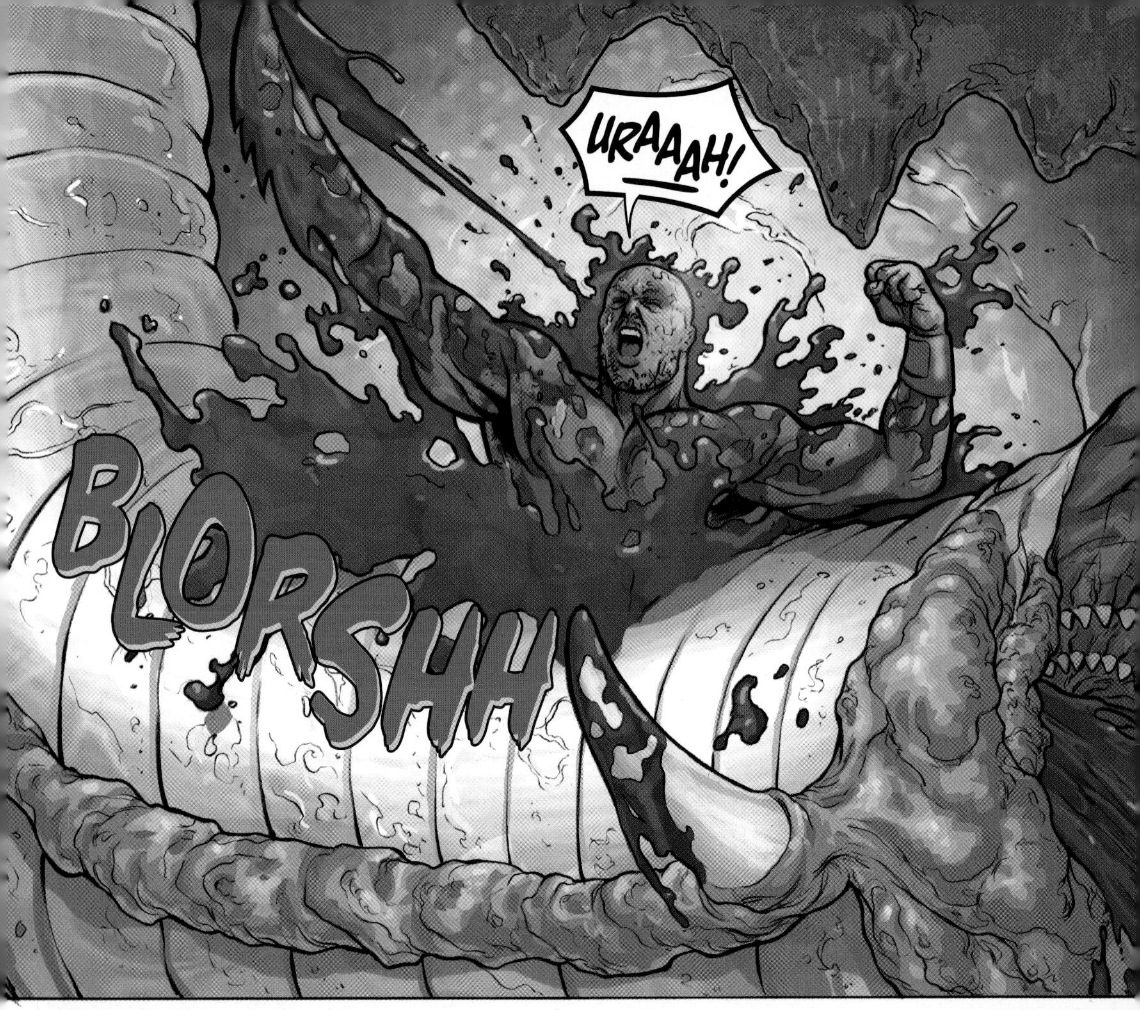
URAAAH!
BLORSHH
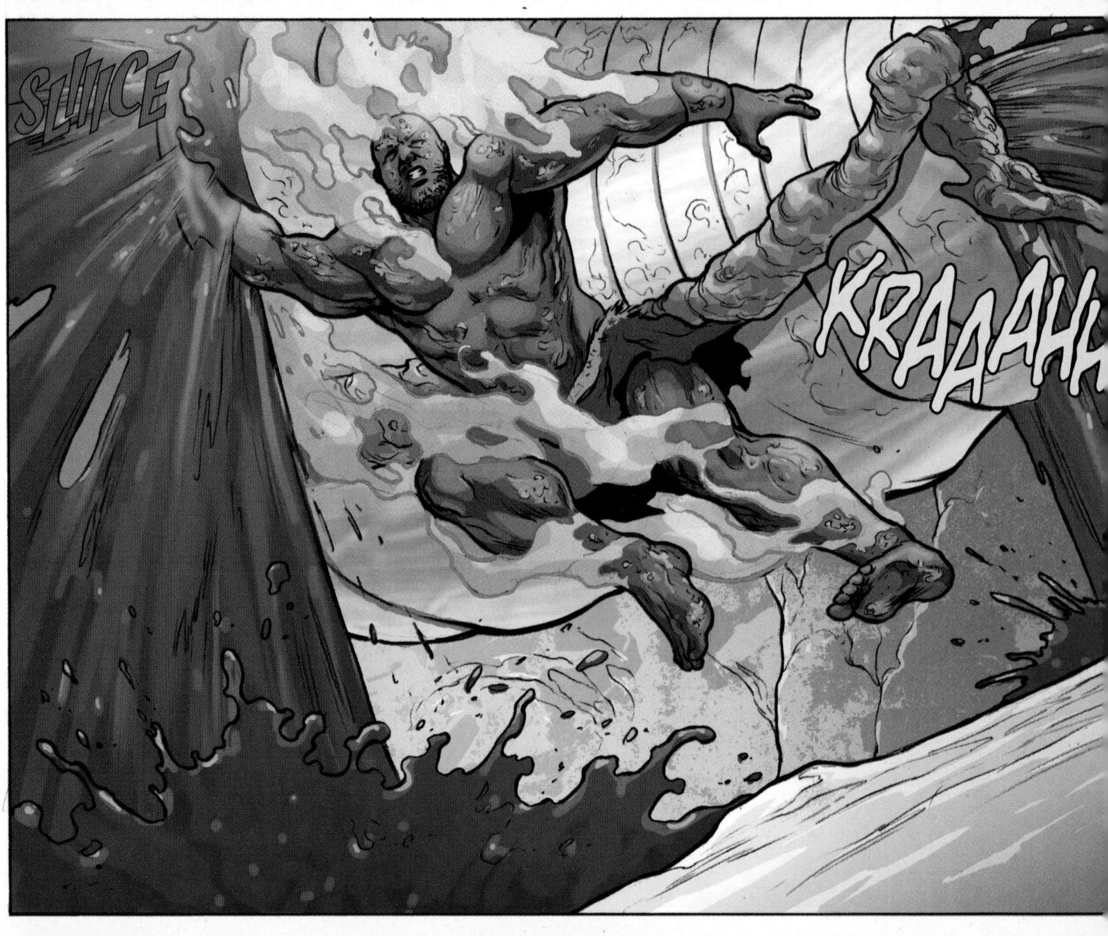
SLIIICE
KRAAAHH

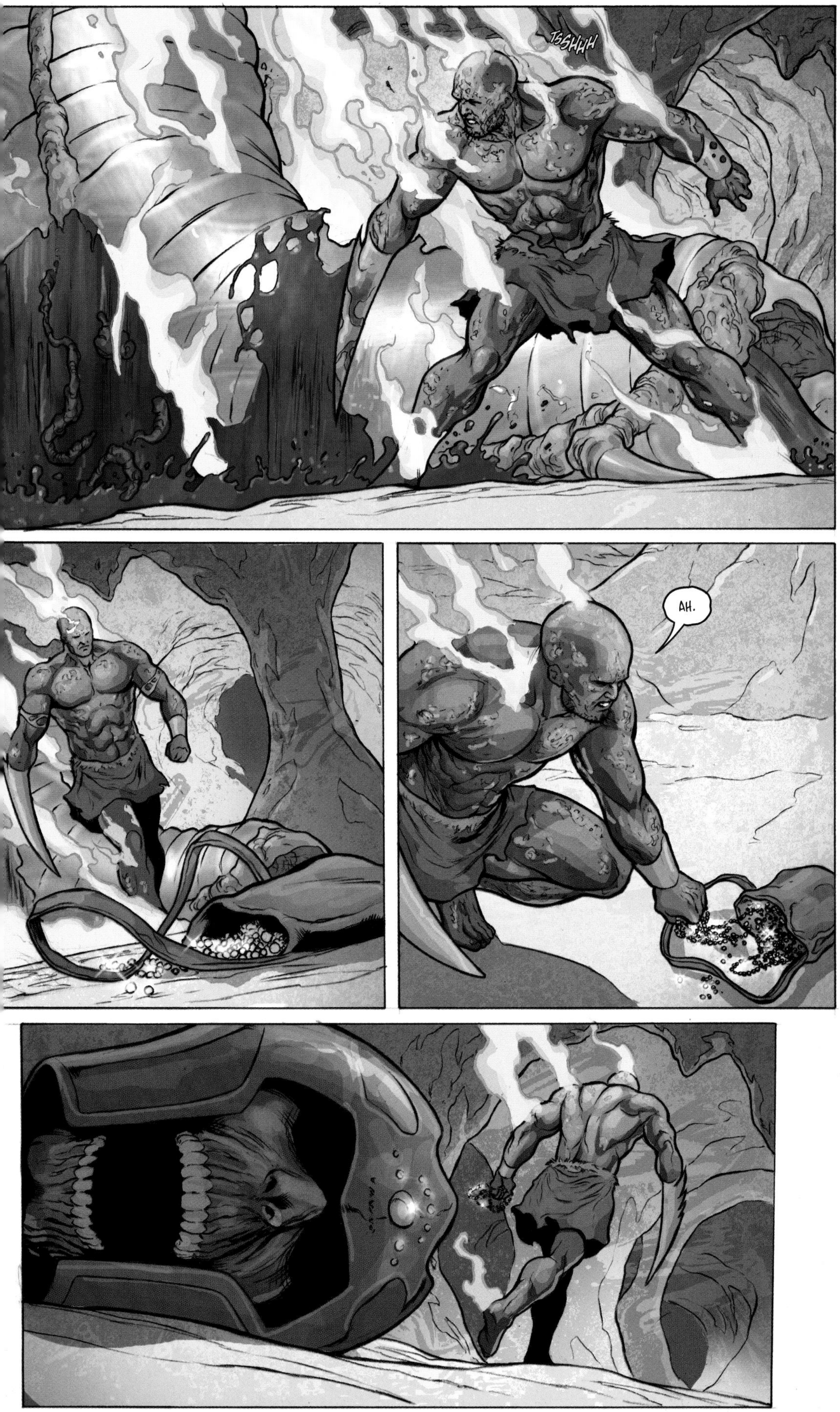
TSSHHH
AH.

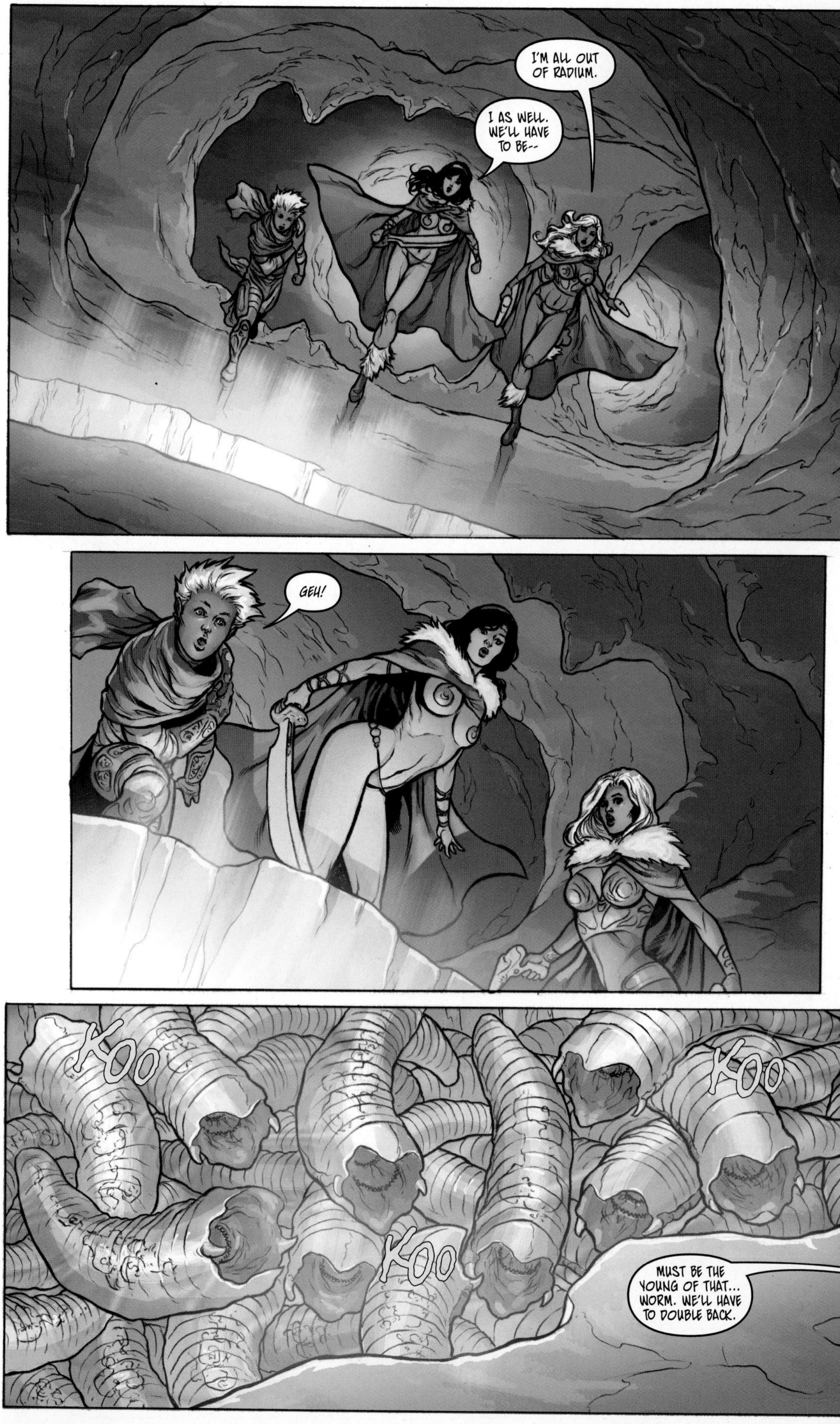

I'M ALL OUT OF RADIUM.
I AS WELL. WE'LL HAVE TO BE--
GEH!
KOO
KOO
KOO
MUST BE THE YOUNG OF THAT... WORM. WE'LL HAVE TO DOUBLE BACK.

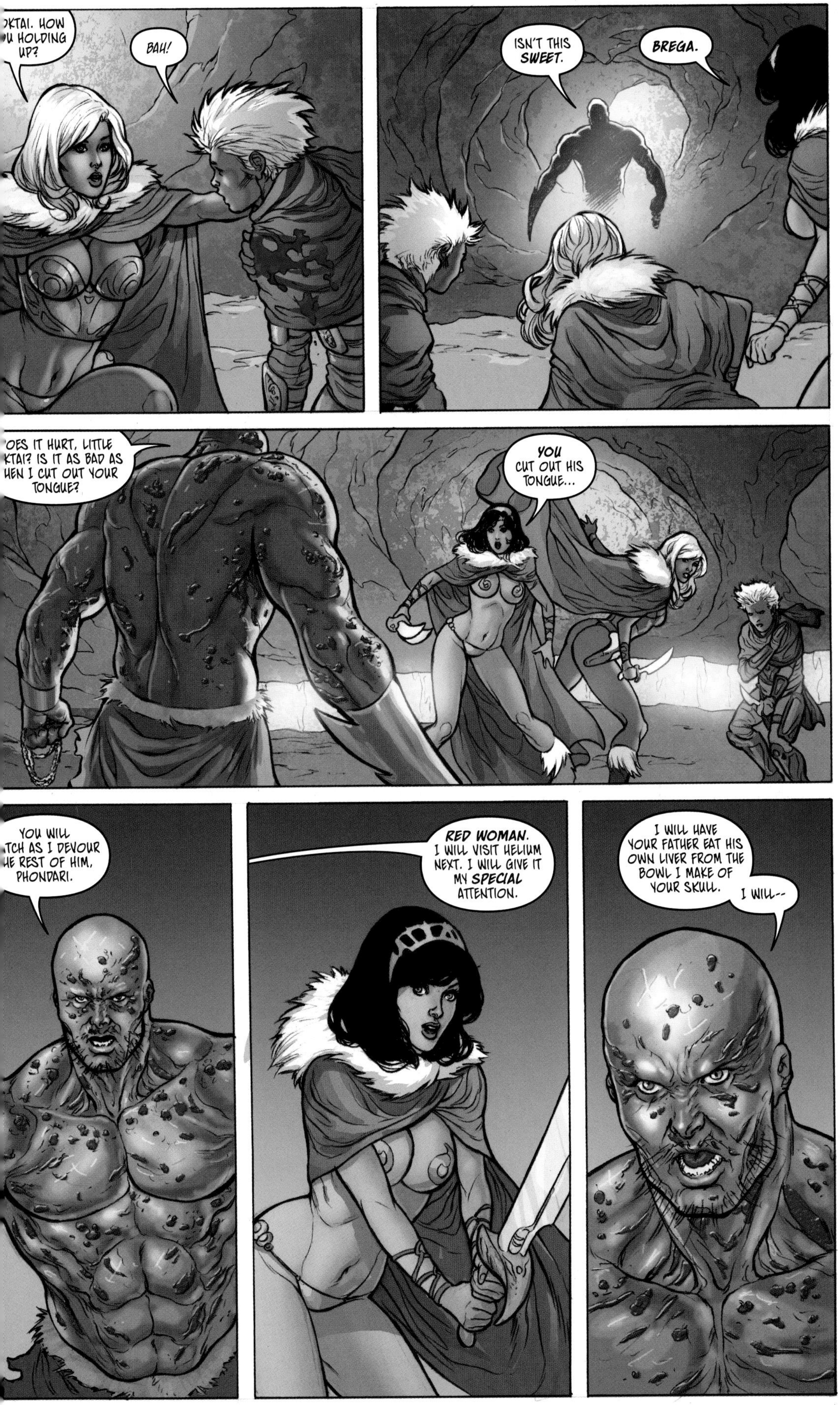

OKTAI. HOW YOU HOLDING UP?
BAH!
ISN'T THIS SWEET.
BREGA.
OES IT HURT, LITTLE KTAI? IS IT AS BAD AS HEN I CUT OUT YOUR TONGUE?
YOU CUT OUT HIS TONGUE...
YOU WILL TCH AS I DEVOUR HE REST OF HIM, PHONDARI.
RED WOMAN. I WILL VISIT HELIUM NEXT. I WILL GIVE IT MY SPECIAL ATTENTION.
I WILL HAVE YOUR FATHER EAT HIS OWN LIVER FROM THE BOWL I MAKE OF YOUR SKULL.
I WILL--

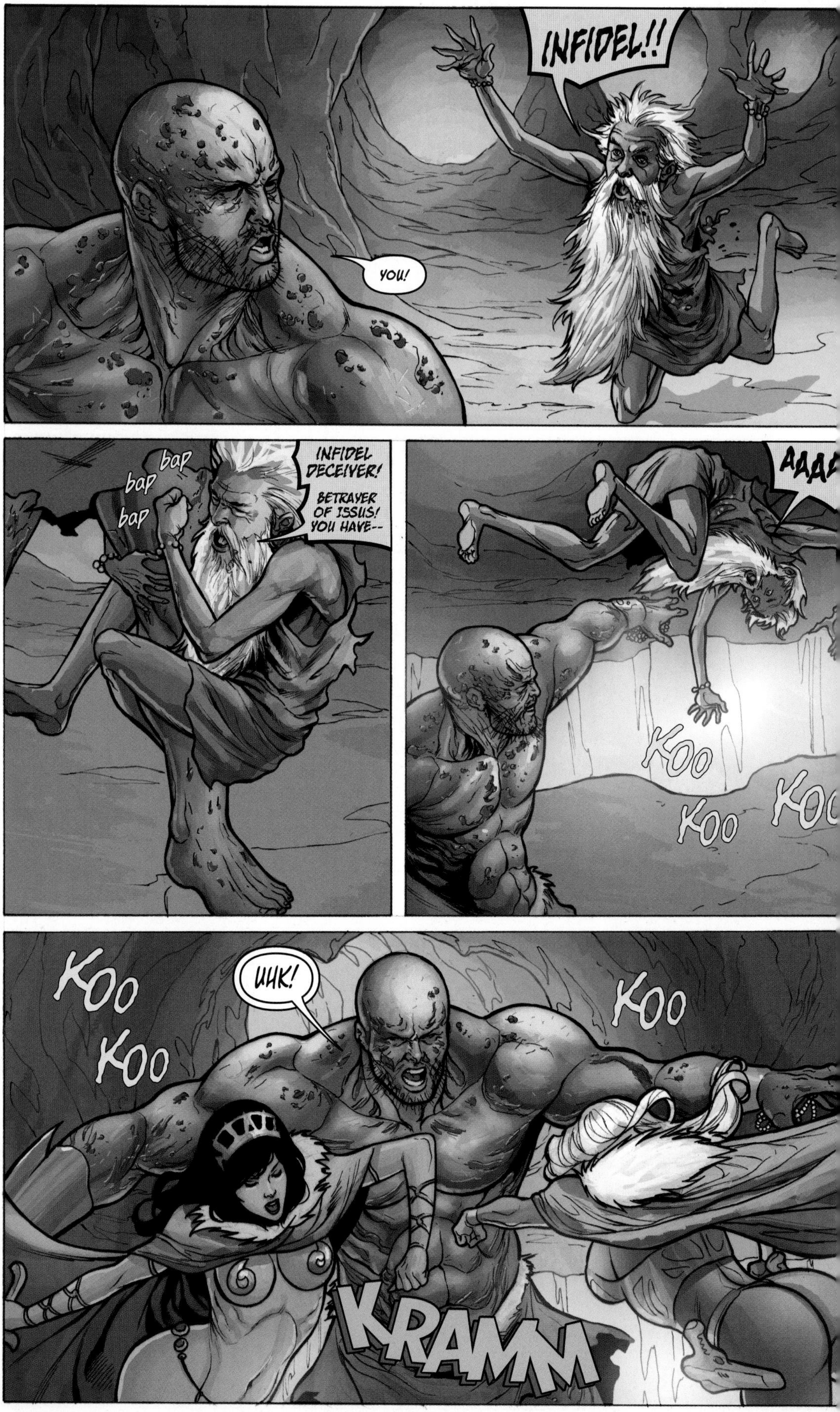
INFIDEL!!
YOU!
bap
bap
bap
INFIDEL DECEIVER!
BETRAYER OF ISSUS! YOU HAVE--
KOO
KOO
KOO
KOO
KOO
UHK!
KOO
KRAMM

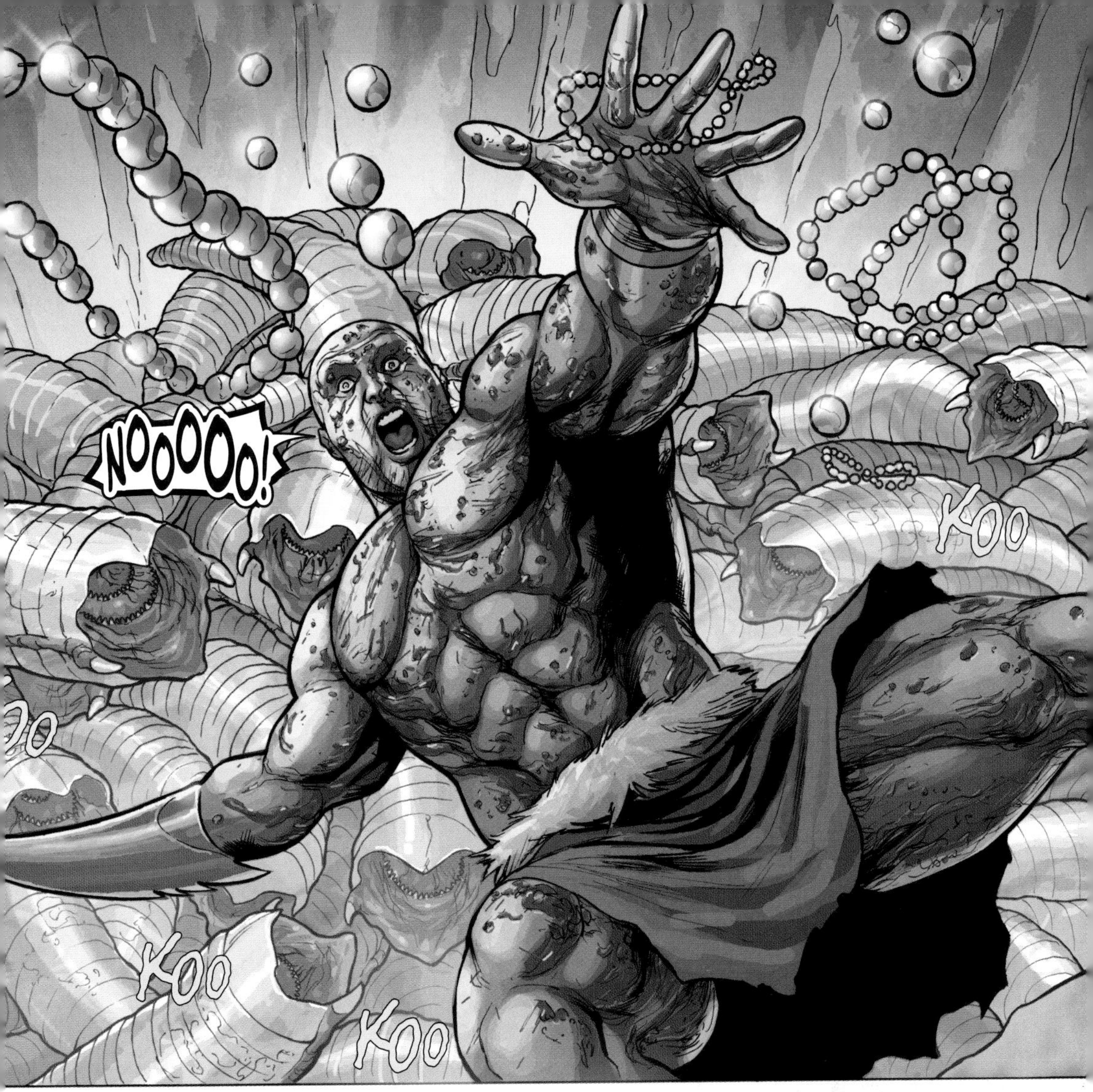
NOOOOO!
KOO
OO
KOO
KOO
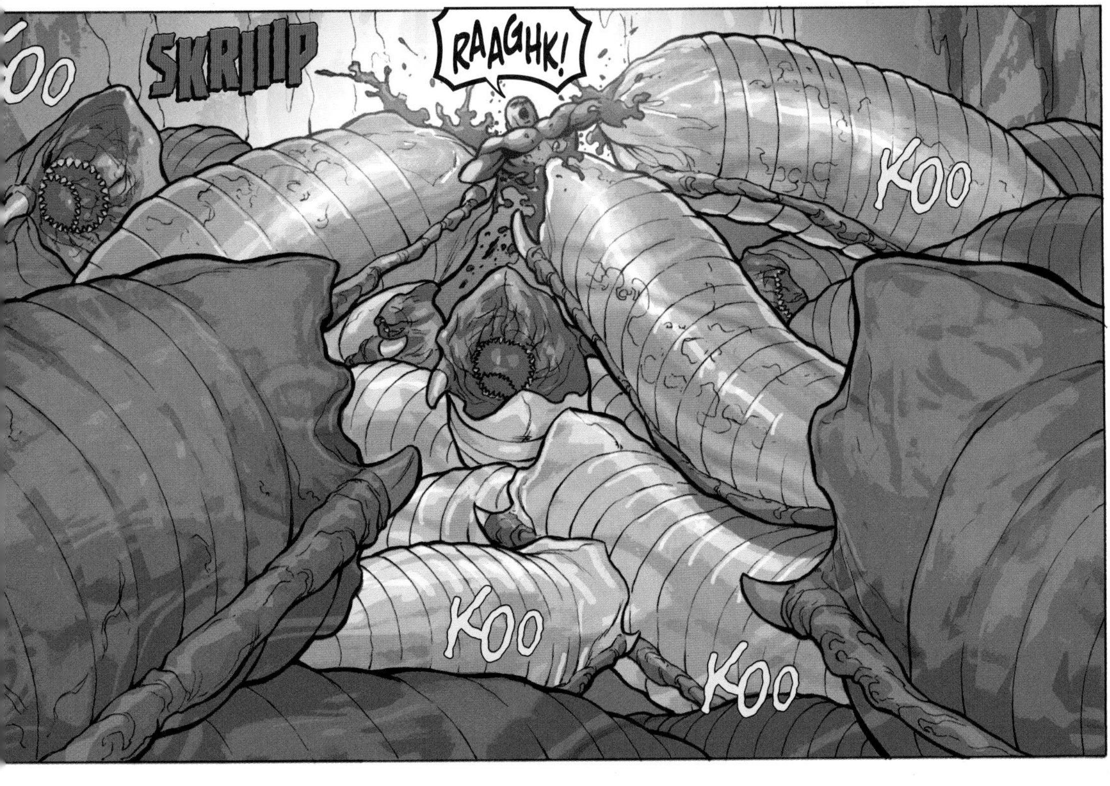
OO
SKRIIIP
RAAGHK!
KOO
KOO
KOO

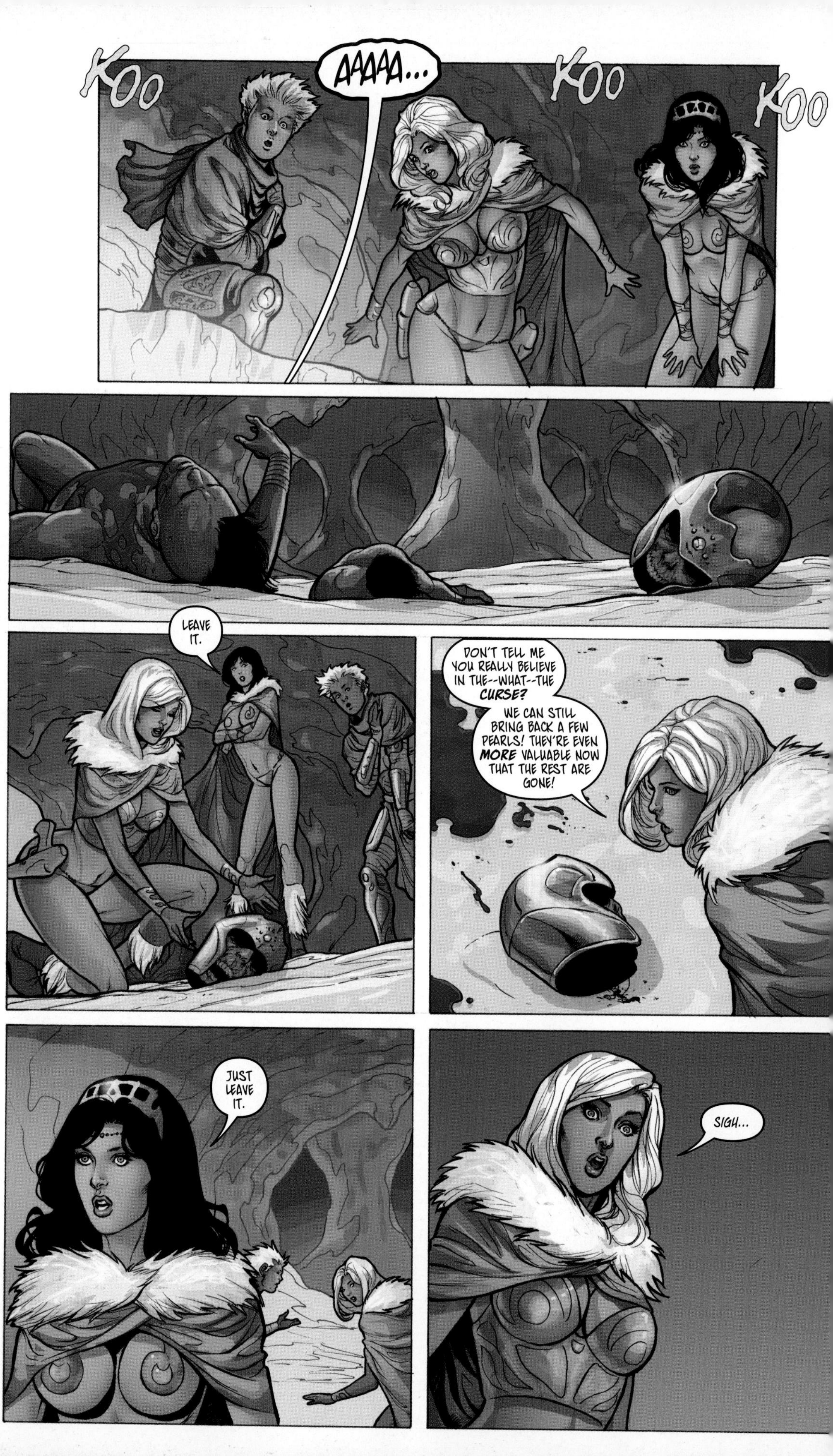
KOO
AAAAA...
KOO
KOO
LEAVE IT.
DON'T TELL ME YOU REALLY BELIEVE IN THE--WHAT--THE **CURSE?**
WE CAN STILL BRING BACK A FEW PEARLS! THEY'RE EVEN **MORE** VALUABLE NOW THAT THE REST ARE GONE!
JUST LEAVE IT.
SIGH...

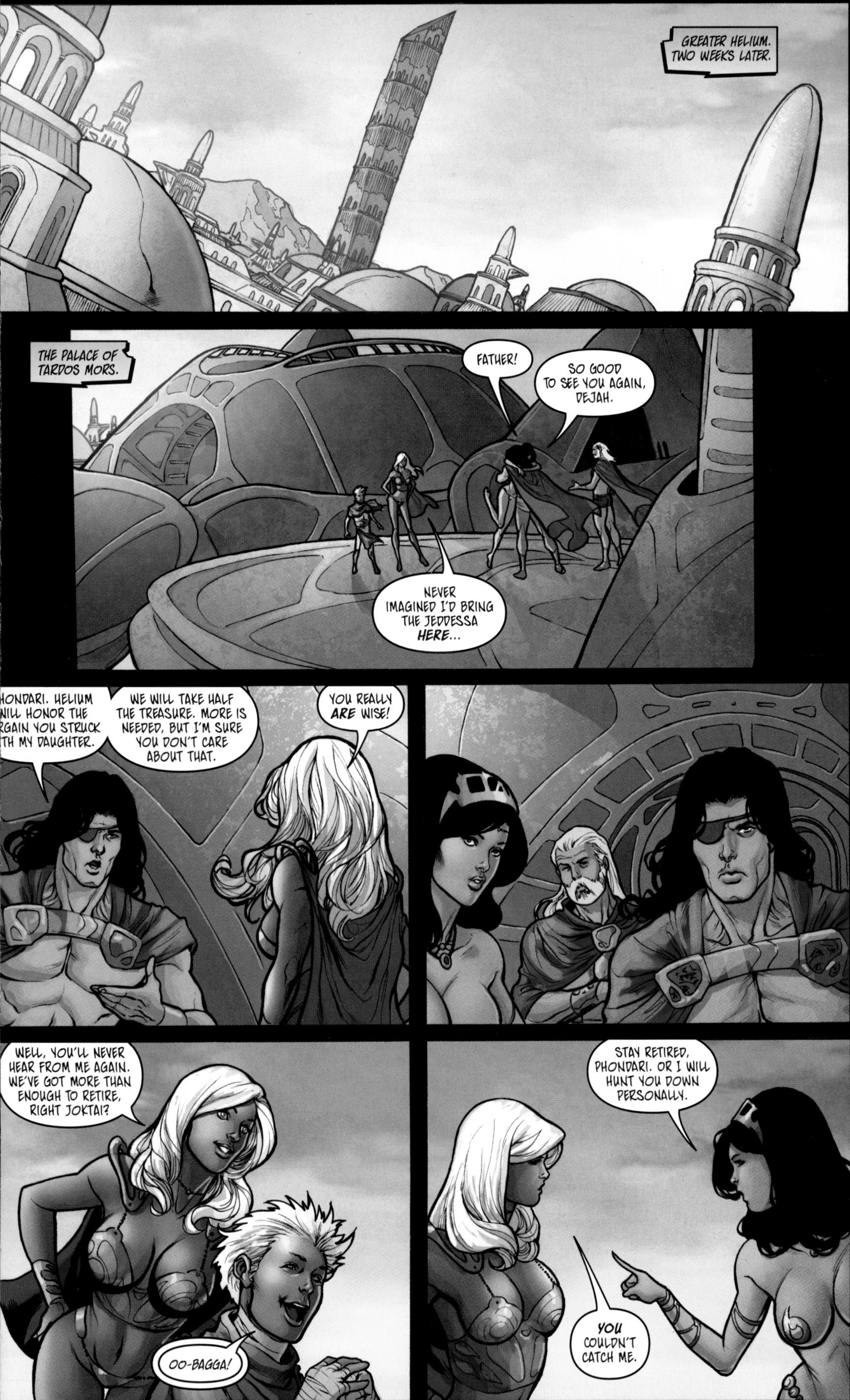
GREATER HELIUM. TWO WEEKS LATER.
THE PALACE OF TARDOS MORS.
FATHER!
SO GOOD TO SEE YOU AGAIN, DEJAH.
NEVER IMAGINED I'D BRING THE JEDDESSA HERE...
HONDARI. HELIUM WILL HONOR THE RGAIN YOU STRUCK TH MY DAUGHTER.
WE WILL TAKE HALF THE TREASURE. MORE IS NEEDED, BUT I'M SURE YOU DON'T CARE ABOUT THAT.
YOU REALLY ARE WISE!
WELL, YOU'LL NEVER HEAR FROM ME AGAIN. WE'VE GOT MORE THAN ENOUGH TO RETIRE, RIGHT JOKTAI?
OO-BAGGA!
STAY RETIRED, PHONDARI. OR I WILL HUNT YOU DOWN PERSONALLY.
YOU COULDN'T CATCH ME.

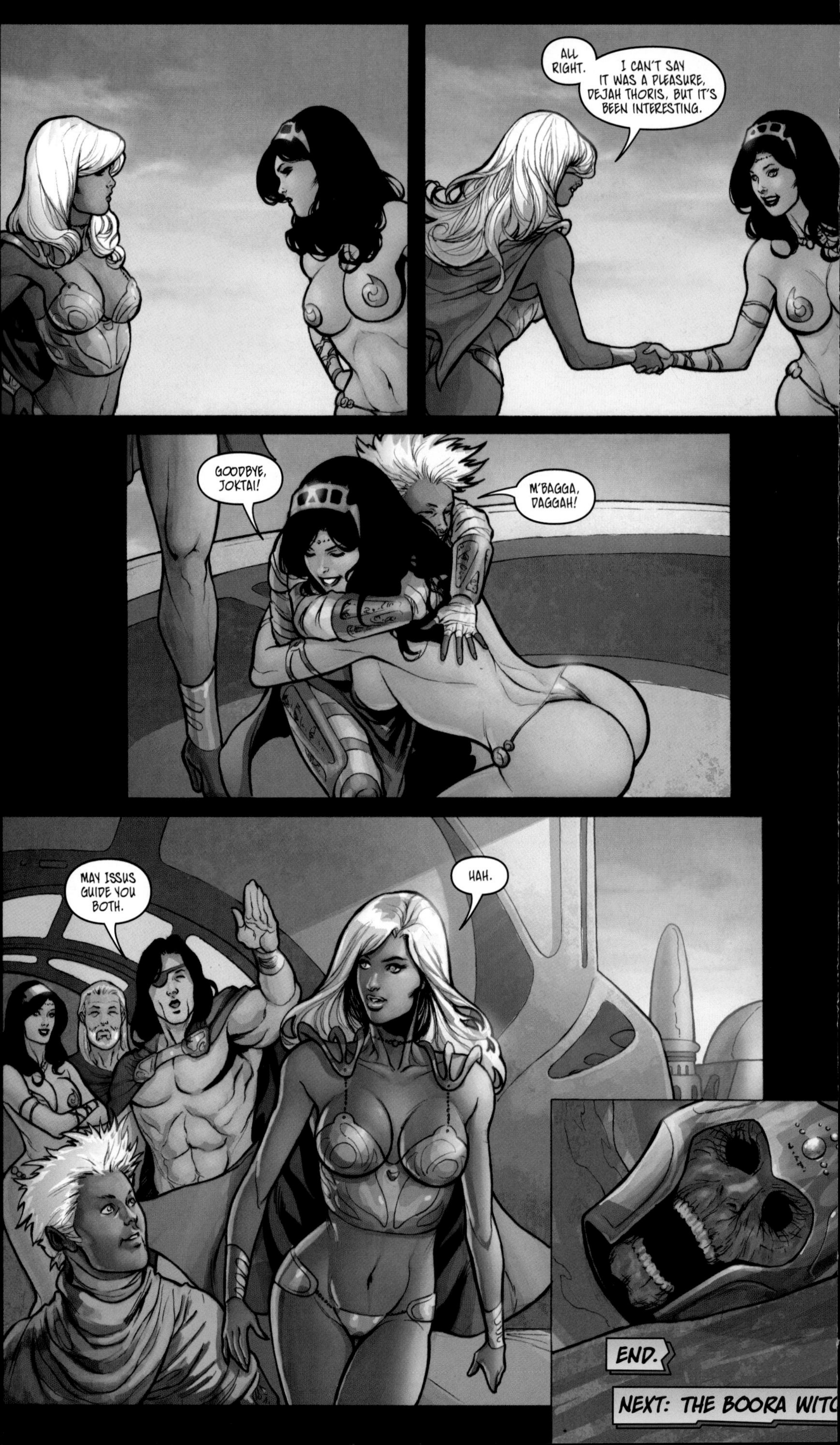
ALL RIGHT.
I CAN'T SAY IT WAS A PLEASURE, DEJAH THORIS, BUT IT'S BEEN INTERESTING.
GOODBYE, JOKTAI!
M'BAGGA, DAGGAH!
MAY ISSUS GUIDE YOU BOTH.
HAH.
END.
NEXT: THE BOORA WITC

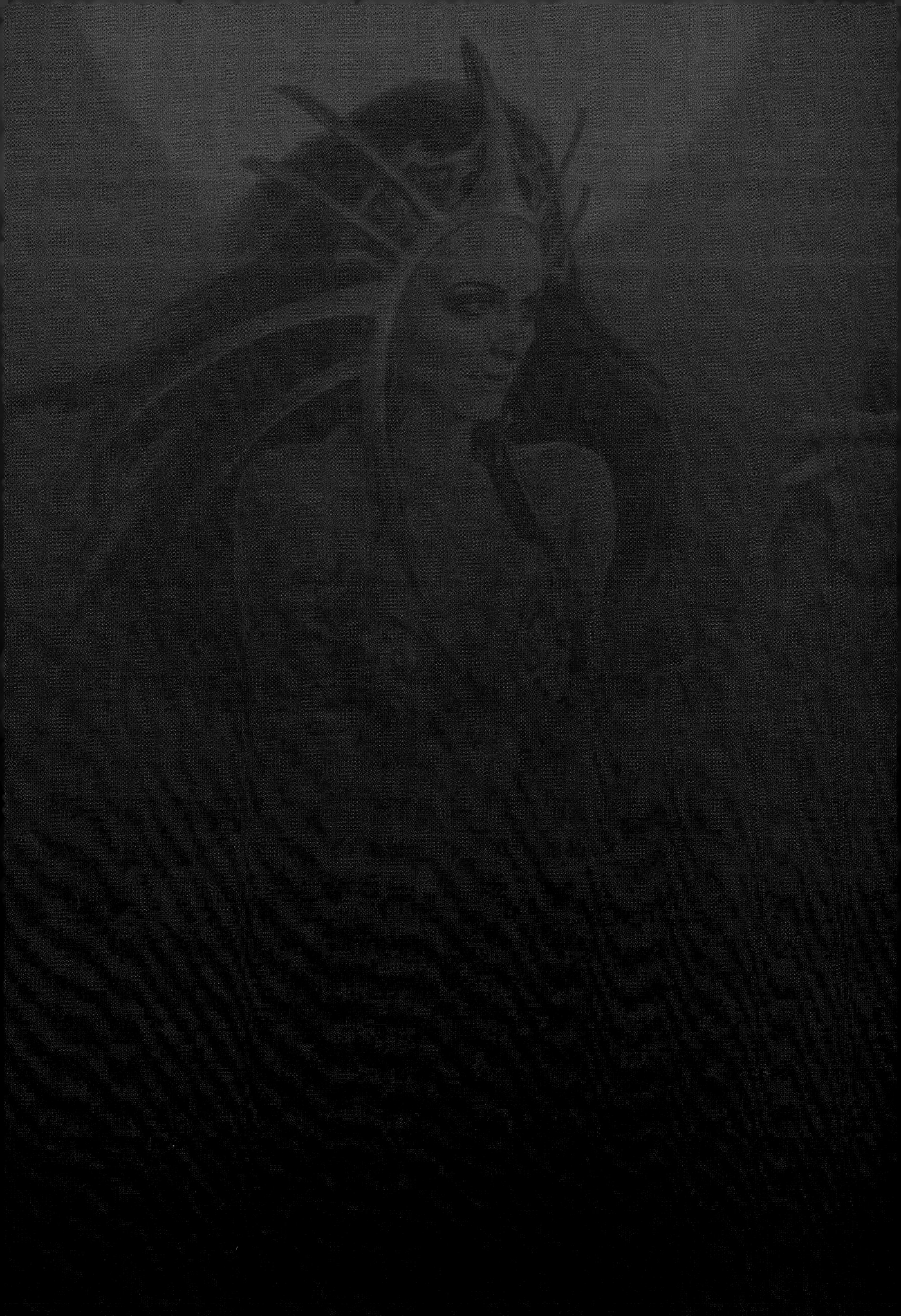

# BONUS MATERIALS

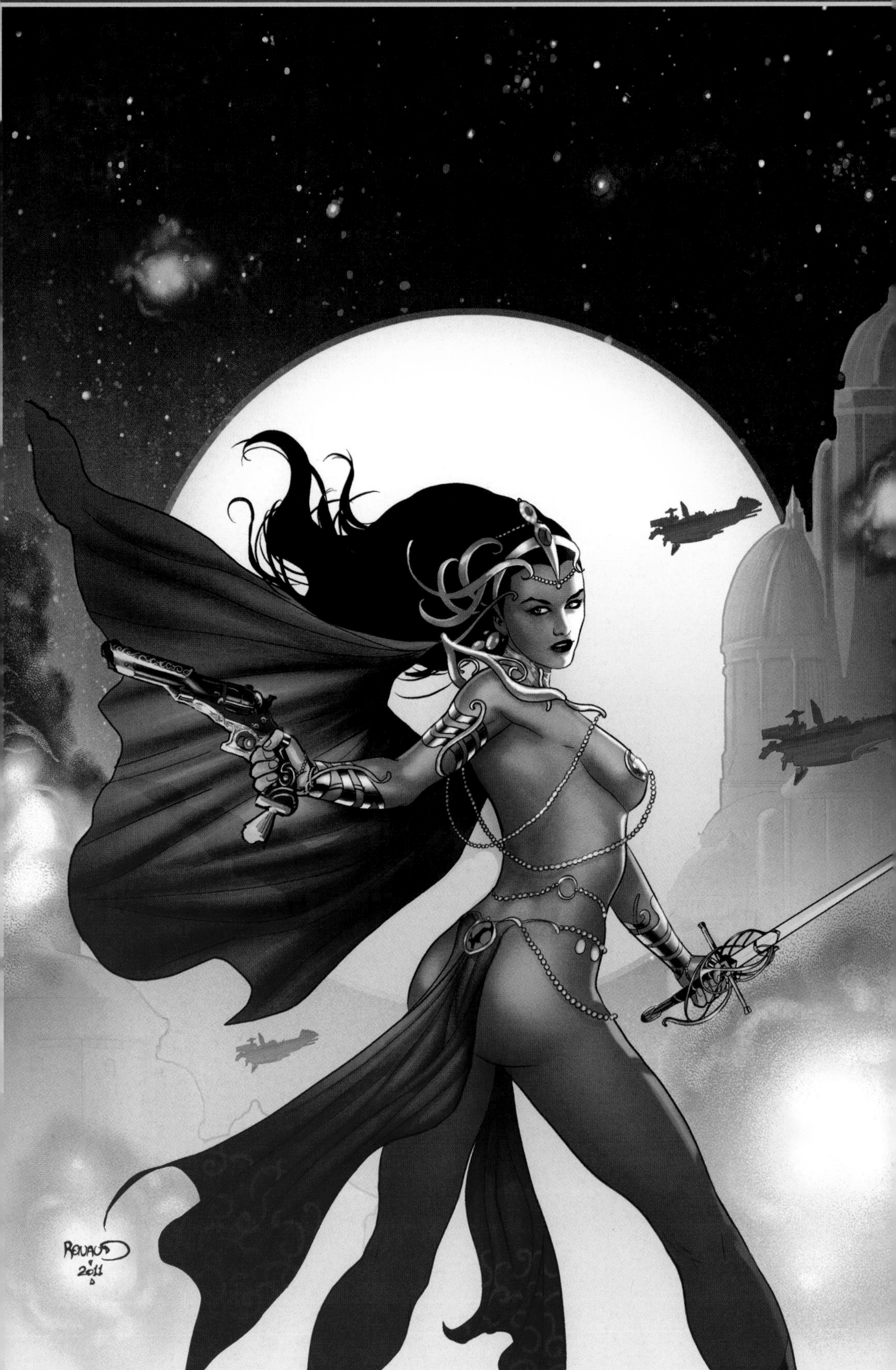
RENAUD
2011

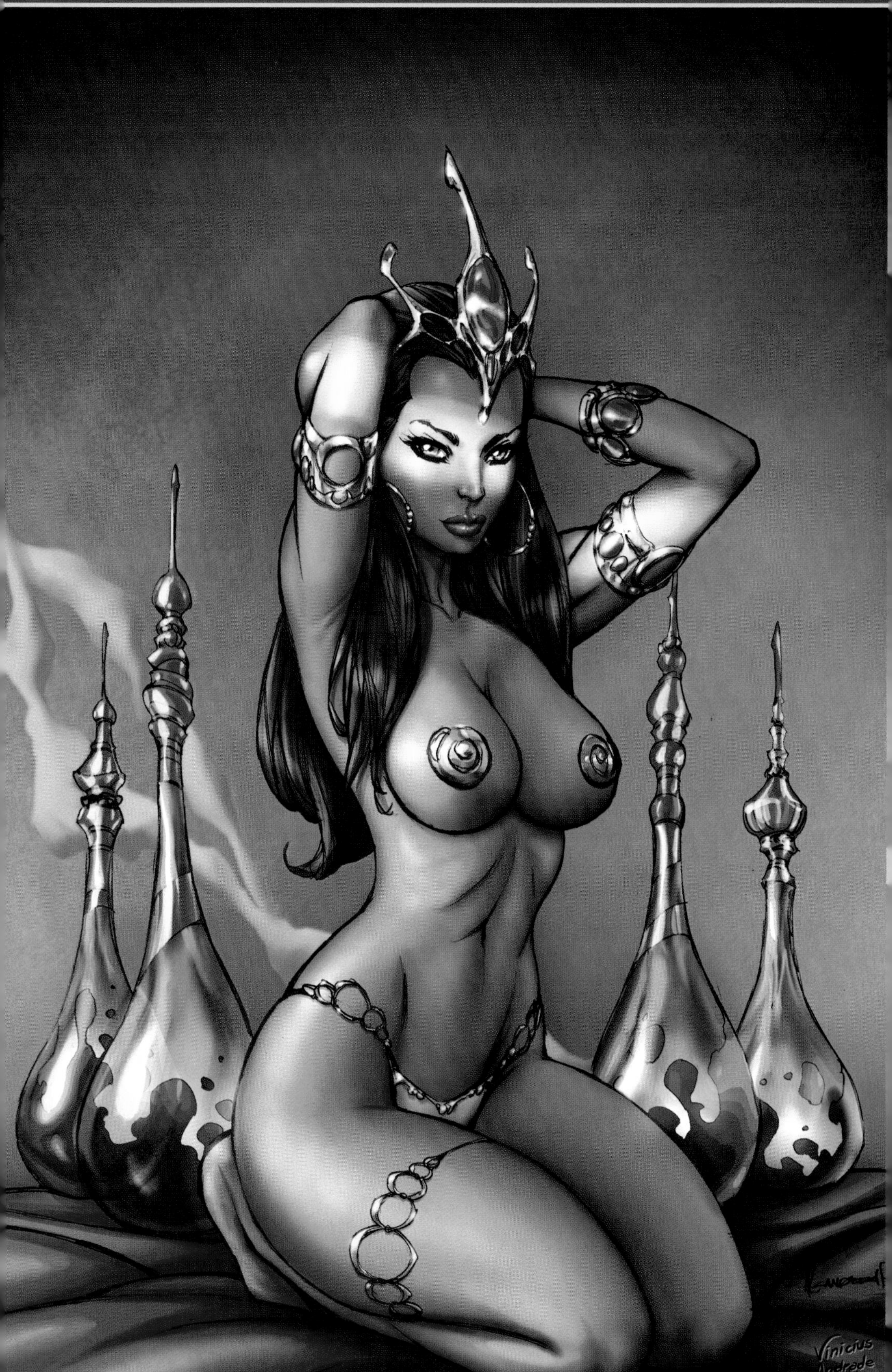
Vinicius Andrade

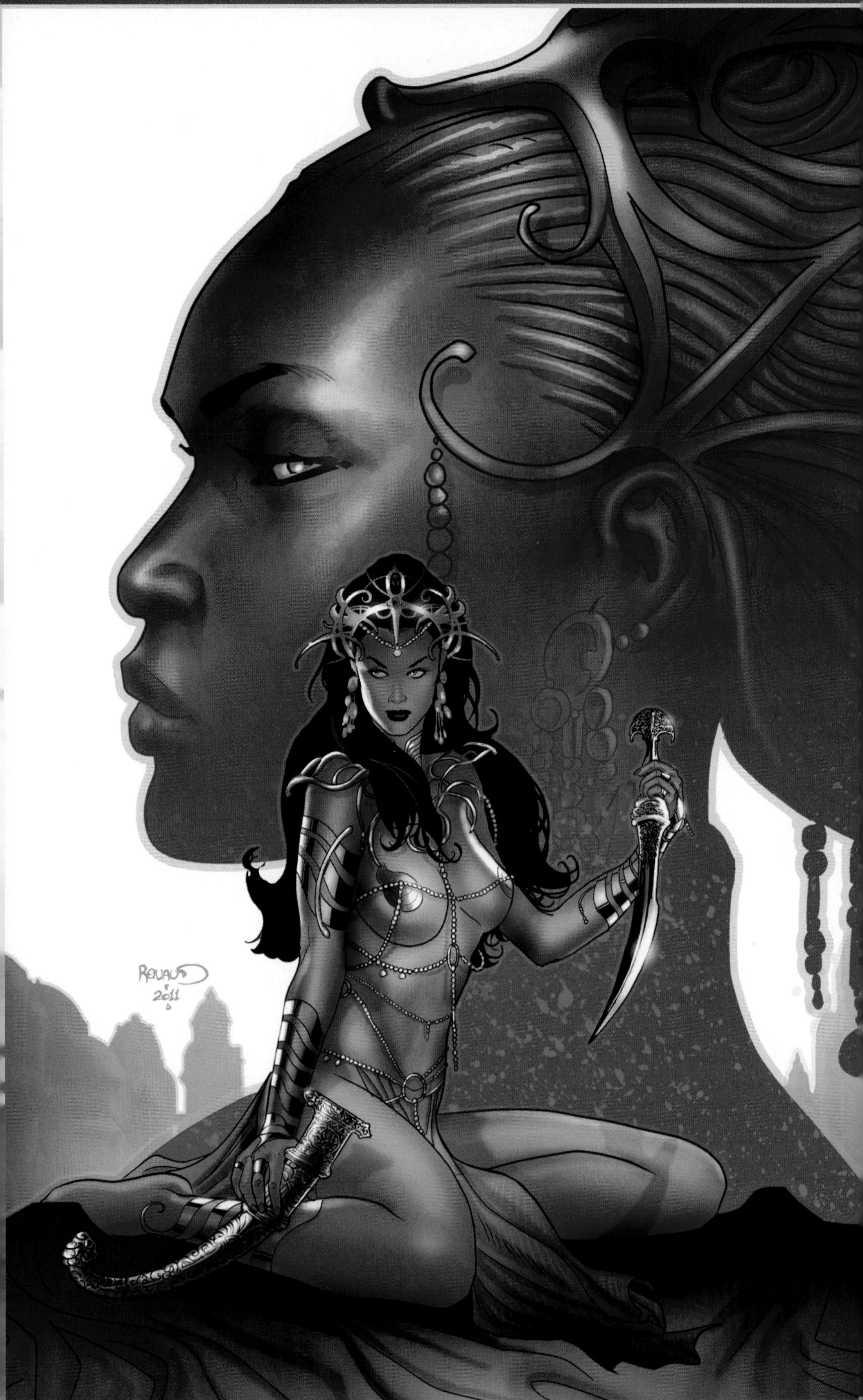

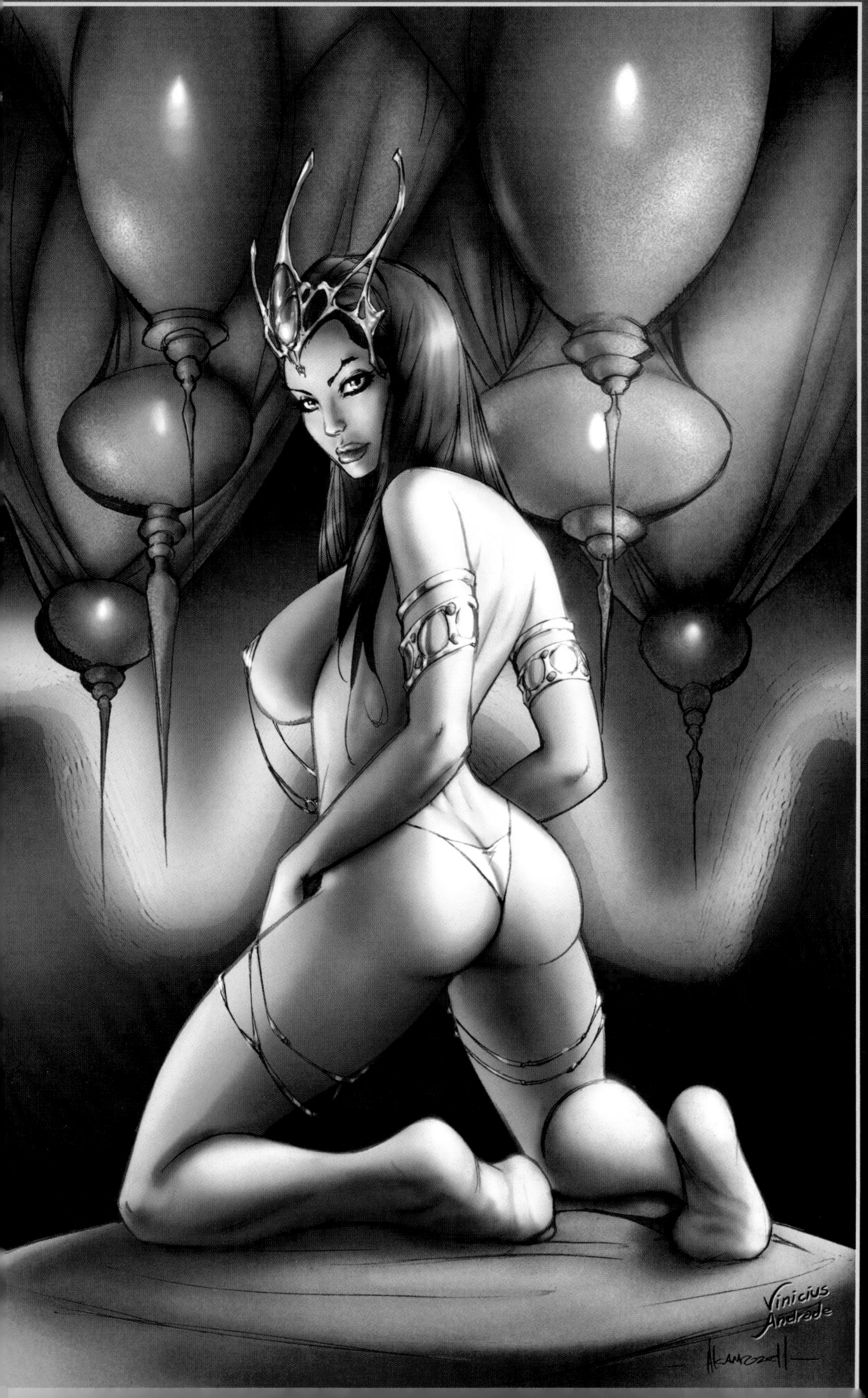
Vinicius
Andrade

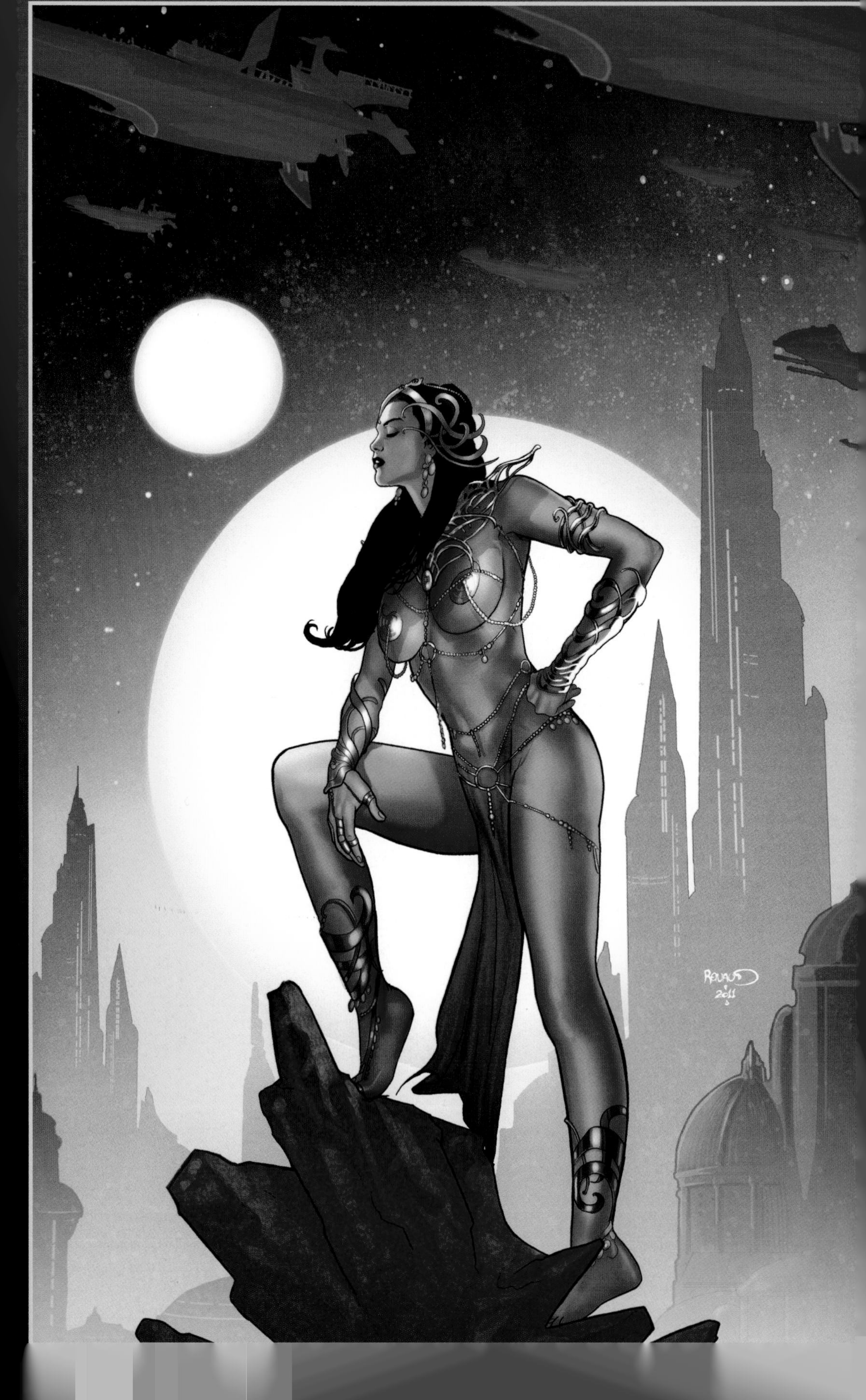
RENAUD
2011

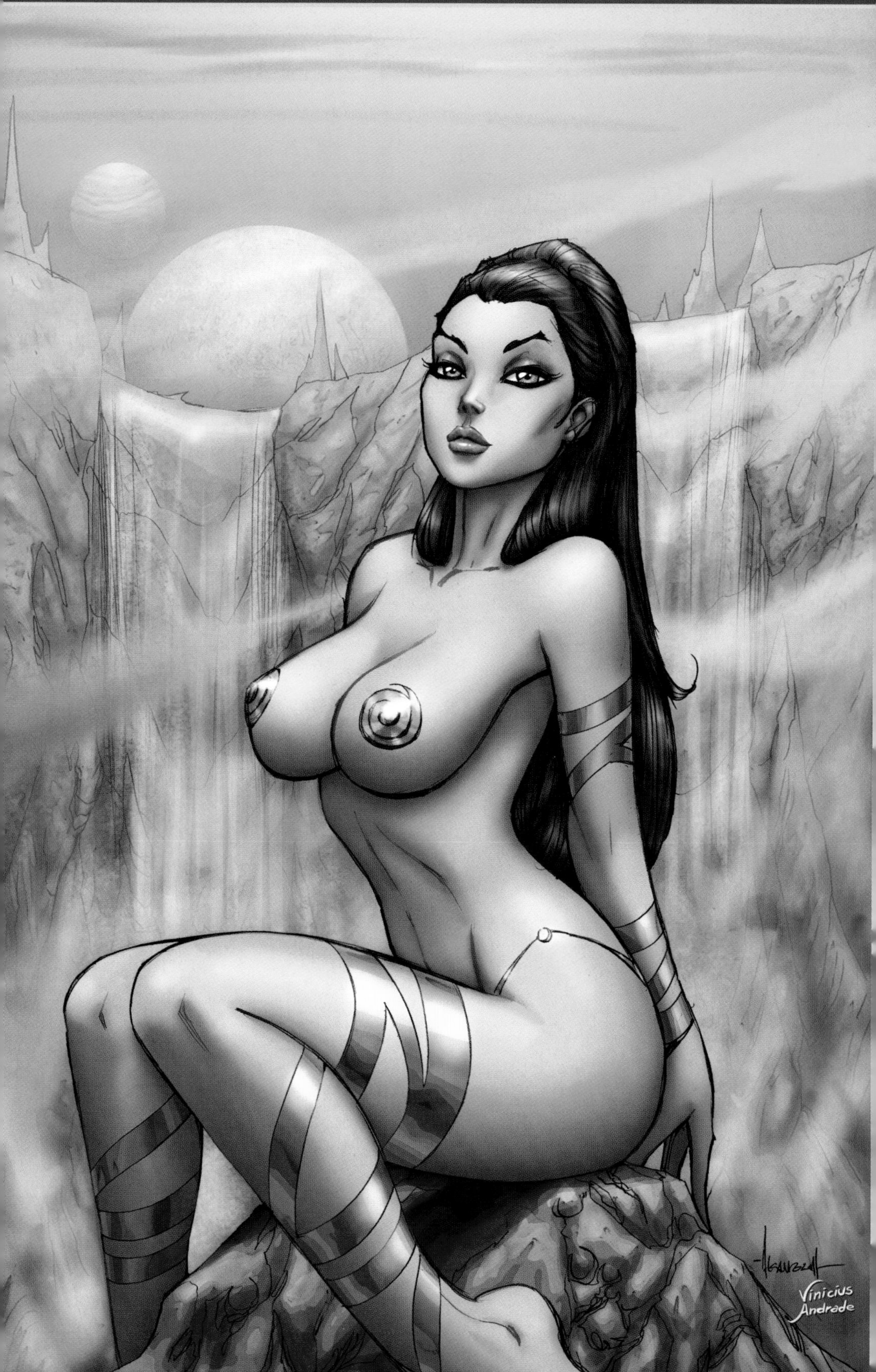
Vinicius
Andrade

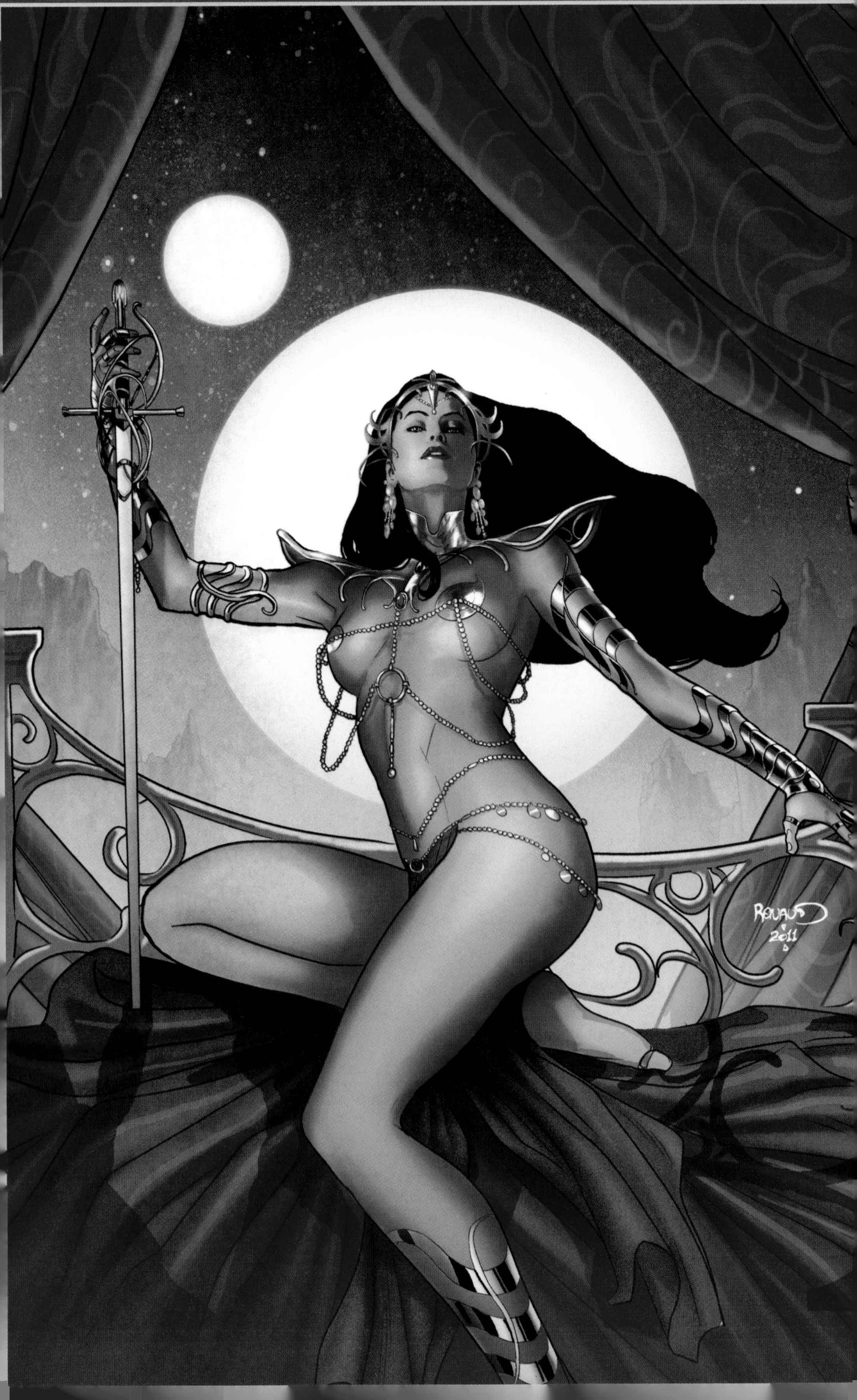
RENAUD
2011

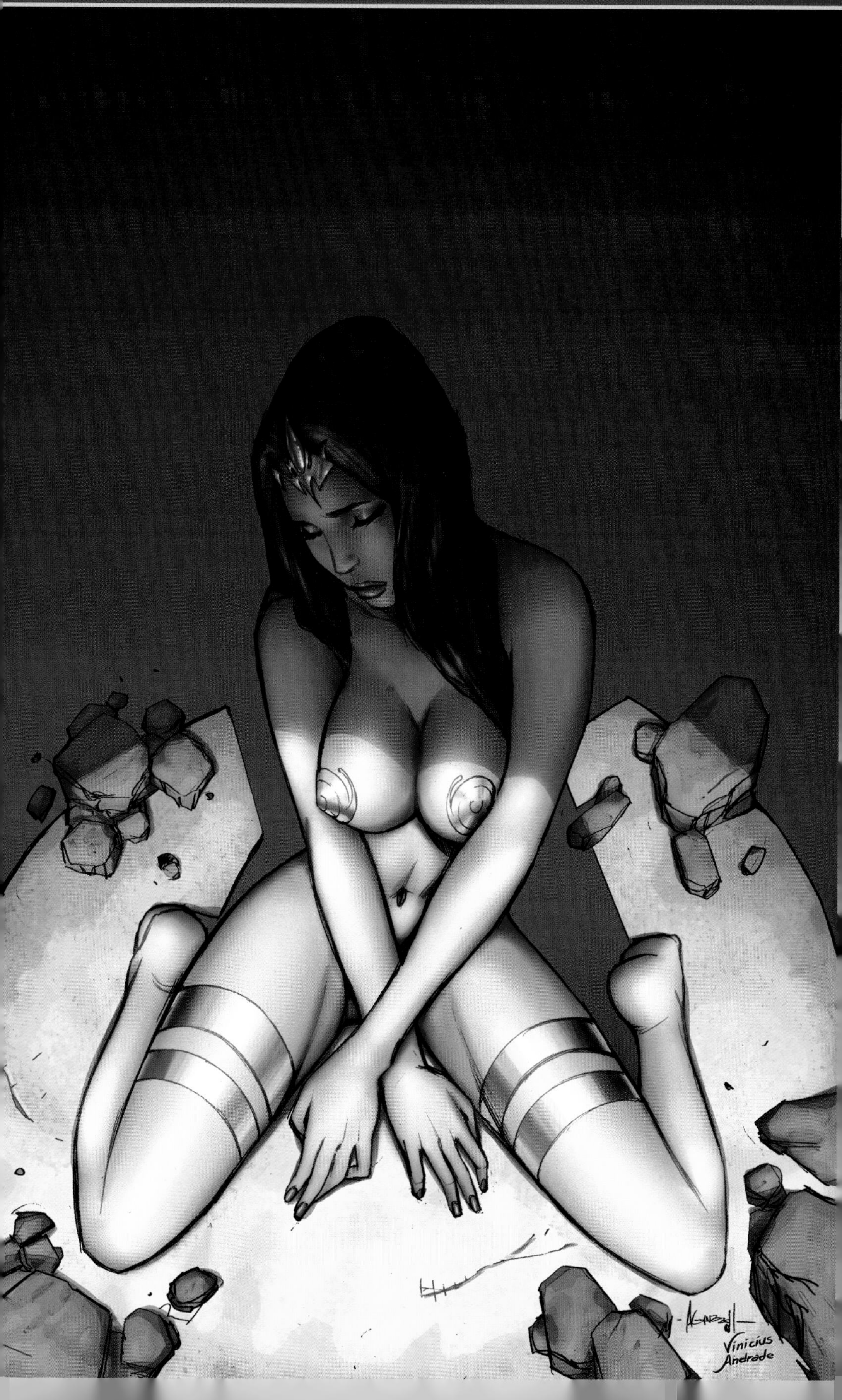
Vinicius
Andrade

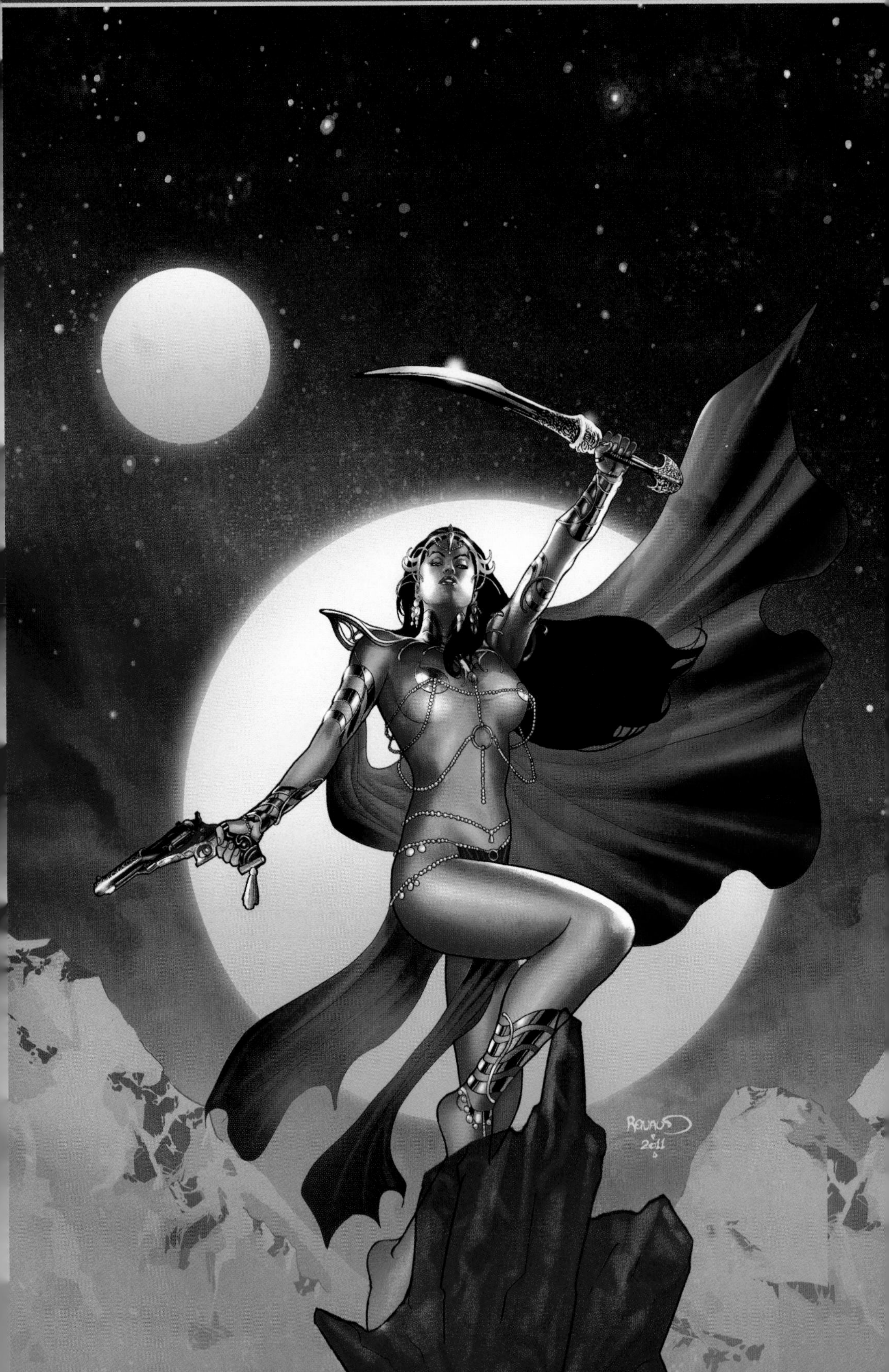
RENAUD
2011

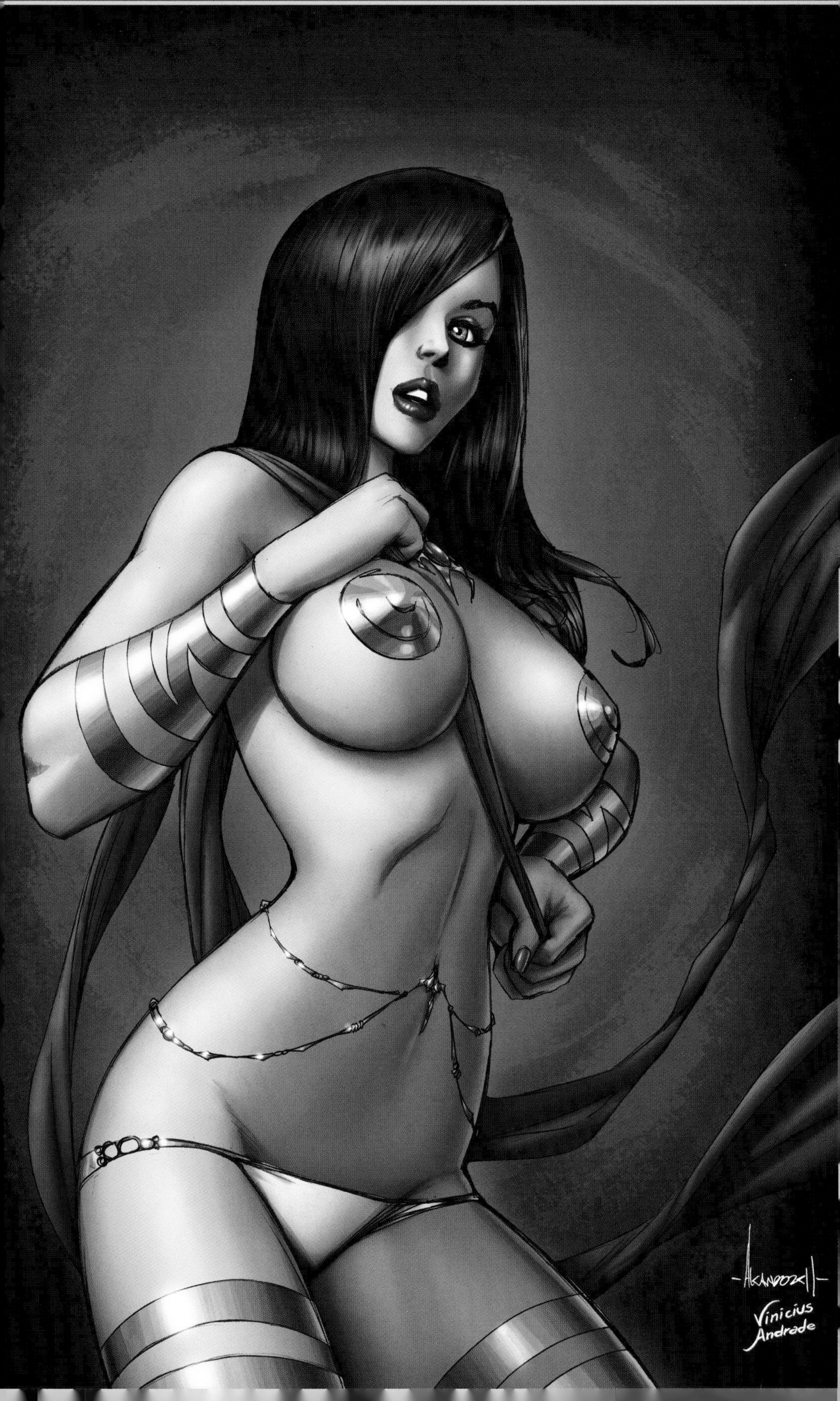
Vinicius
Andrade

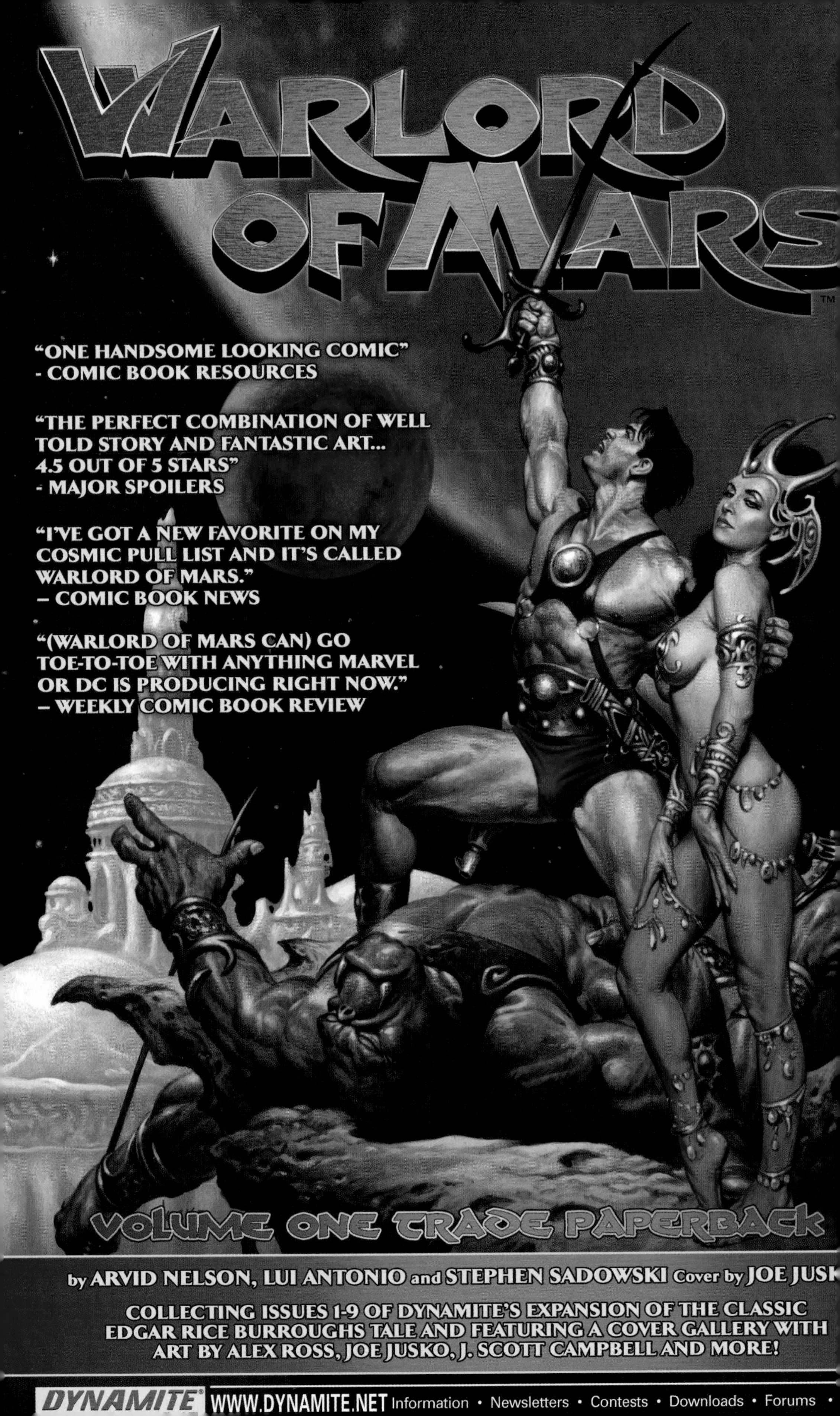
WARLORD OF MARS™
"ONE HANDSOME LOOKING COMIC" - COMIC BOOK RESOURCES
"THE PERFECT COMBINATION OF WELL TOLD STORY AND FANTASTIC ART... 4.5 OUT OF 5 STARS" - MAJOR SPOILERS
"I'VE GOT A NEW FAVORITE ON MY COSMIC PULL LIST AND IT'S CALLED WARLORD OF MARS." – COMIC BOOK NEWS
"(WARLORD OF MARS CAN) GO TOE-TO-TOE WITH ANYTHING MARVEL OR DC IS PRODUCING RIGHT NOW." – WEEKLY COMIC BOOK REVIEW
VOLUME ONE TRADE PAPERBACK
by ARVID NELSON, LUI ANTONIO and STEPHEN SADOWSKI Cover by JOE JUSK
COLLECTING ISSUES 1-9 OF DYNAMITE'S EXPANSION OF THE CLASSIC EDGAR RICE BURROUGHS TALE AND FEATURING A COVER GALLERY WITH ART BY ALEX ROSS, JOE JUSKO, J. SCOTT CAMPBELL AND MORE!
DYNAMITE®
WWW.DYNAMITE.NET Information • Newsletters • Contests • Downloads • Forums •

# WARLORD OF MARS
## FALL OF BARSOOM
### TRADE PAPERBACK

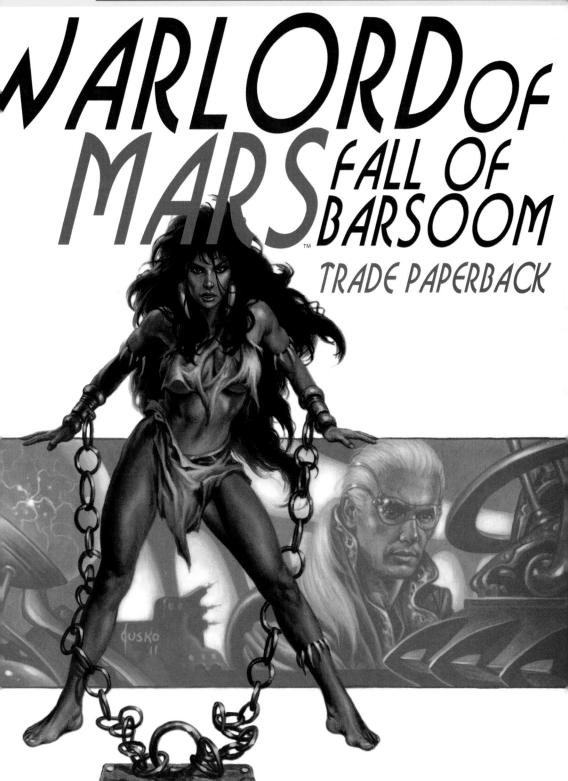

written by ROBERT PLACE NAPTON  art by ROBERTO CASTRO
collects issues 1-5 of the hit mini-series features all of the series
covers by JOE JUSKO and FRANCESCO FRANCAVILLA

DYNAMITE
ENTERTAINMENT

WWW.DYNAMITE.NET Information • Newsletters • Contests • Downloads • Forums • More

# CURRENTLY AVAILABLE AND UPCOMING COLLECTIONS FROM DYNAMITE
## For a complete list, visit us online at www.dynamite.net

### ARMY OF DARKNESS:

**Army of Darkness: Movie Adaptation**
Raimi, Raimi, Bolton

**Army of Darkness: Ashes to Ashes**
Hartnell, Bradshaw

**Army of Darkness: Shop 'Till You Drop Dead**
Kuhoric, Bradshaw, Greene

**Army of Darkness vs. Re-Animator**
Kuhoric, Bradshaw, Greene

**Army of Darkness: Old School & More**
Kuhoric, Sharpe

**Army of Darkness: Ash vs. The Classic Monsters**
Kuhoric, Sharpe, Blanco

**Army of Darkness: From The Ashes**
Kuhoric, Blanco

**Army of Darkness: The Long Road Home**
Kuhoric, Raicht, Blanco

**Army of Darkness: Home Sweet Hell**
Kuhoric, Raicht, Perez

**Army of Darkness: Hellbillies & Deadnecks**
Kuhoric, Raicht, Cohn

**Army of Darkness: League of Light Assemble!**
Raicht, Cohn

**Army of Darkness Omnibus Vol. 1**
Hartnell, Kuhoric, Kirkman, more

**Army of Darkness Omnibus Vol. 2**
Kuhoric, Raicht, Perez, more

**Army of Darkness: Ash Saves Obama**
Serrano, Padilla

**Army of Darkness vs. Xena Vol. 1: Why Not?**
Layman, Jerwa, Montenegro

**Xena vs. Army of Darkness Vol. 2: What...Again?!**
Jerwa, Serrano, Montenegro

**Darkman vs. Army of Darkness**
Busiek, Stern, Fry

### BATTLESTAR GALACTICA

**New Battlestar Galactica Vol. 1**
Pak, Raynor

**New Battlestar Galactica Vol. 2**
Pak, Raynor

**New Battlestar Galactica Vol. 3**
Pak, Raynor, Lau

**New Battlestar Galactica Complete Omnibus V1**
Pak, Raynor, Jerwa, Lau

**New Battlestar Galactica: Zarek**
Jerwa, Batista

**New Battlestar Galactica: Season Zero Vol. 1**
Jerwa, Herbert

**New Battlestar Galactica: Season Zero Vol. 2**
Jerwa, Herbert

**New Battlestar Galactica Origins: Baltar**
Fahey, Lau

**New Battlestar Galactica Origins: Adama**
Napton, Lau

**New Battlestar Galactica Origins: Starbuck & Helo**
Fahey, Lau

**New Battlestar Galactica: Ghosts**
Jerwa, Lau

**New Battlestar Galactica: Cylon War**
Ortega, Nylund, Raynor

**New Battlestar Galactica: The Final Five**
Fahey, Reed, Raynor

**Classic Battlestar Galactica Vol. 1**
Remender, Rafael

**Classic Battlestar Galactica Vol. 2: Cylon Apocalypse**
Grillo-Marxuach, Rafael

**GALACTICA 1980**
Guggenheim, Razek

### THE BOYS

**The Boys Vol. 1 The Name of the Game**
Ennis, Robertson

**The Boys Vol. 2 Get Some**
Ennis, Robertson, Snejbjerg

**The Boys Vol. 3 Good For The Soul**
Ennis, Robertson

**The Boys Vol. 4 We Gotta Go Now**
Ennis, Robertson

**The Boys Vol. 5 Herogasm**
Ennis, McCrea

**The Boys Vol. 6 The Self-Preservation Society**
Ennis, Robertson, Ezquerra

**The Boys Vol. 7 The Innocents**
Ennis, Robertson, Braun

**The Boys Vol. 8 Highland Laddie**
Ennis, McCrea

**The Boys Vol. 9 The Big Ride**
Ennis, Braun

**The Boys Vol. 10: Butcher, Baker, Candlestickmaker**
Ennis, Robertson

**The Boys Definitive Edition Vol. 1**
Ennis, Robertson

**The Boys Definitive Edition Vol. 2**
Ennis, Robertson

**The Boys Definitive Edition Vol. 3**
Ennis, Robertson, McCrea, more

### THE GREEN HORNET

**Kevin Smith's Green Hornet Vol. 1 Sins of the Father**
Smith, Hester, Lau

**Kevin Smith's Green Hornet Vol. 2 Wearing 'o the Green**
Smith, Hester, Lau

**Green Hornet Vol. 3 Idols**
Hester, Lau

**Green Hornet Vol. 4 Red Hand**
Hester, Smith, Vitorino, more

**Kevin Smith's Kato Vol. 1 Not My Father's Daughter**
Parks, Garza, Bernard

**Kevin Smith's Kato Vol. 2 Living in America**
Parks, Bernard

**Green Hornet: Blood Ties**
Parks, Desjardins

**The Green Hornet: Year One Vol. 1 The Sting of Justice**
Wagner, Campbell, Francavilla

**The Green Hornet: Year One Vol. 2 The Biggest of All Game**
Wagner, Campbell

**Kato Origins Vol. 1 Way of the Ninja**
Nitz, Worley

**Kato Origins Vol. 2 The Hellfire Club**
Nitz, Worley

**The Green Hornet: Parallel Lives**
Nitz, Raynor

**The Green Hornet Golden Age Re-Mastered**
Various

### PROJECT SUPERPOWERS

**Project Superpowers Chapter 1**
Ross, Krueger, Paul, Sadowski

**Project Superpowers Chapter 2 Vol. 1**
Ross, Krueger, Salazar

**Project Superpowers Chapter 2 Vol. 2**
Ross, Krueger, Salazar

**Project Superpowers: Meet The Bad Guys**
Ross, Casey, Lilly, Lau, Paul, Herbert

**Black Terror Vol. 1**
Ross, Krueger, Lilly

**Black Terror Vol. 2**
Ross, Hester, Lau

**Black Terror Vol. 3 Inhuman Remains**
Ross, Hester, Reis, Herbert

**Death-Defying 'Devil Vol 1**
Ross, Casey, Salazar

**Masquerade Vol. 2**
Ross, Hester, Laul

### RED SONJA

**Adventures of Red Sonja Vol. 1**
Thomas, Thorne, More

**Adventures of Red Sonja Vol. 2**
Thomas, Thorne, More

**Adventures of Red Sonja Vol. 3**
Thomas, Thorne, More

**Queen Sonja Vol. 1**
Ortega, Rubi

**Queen Sonja Vol. 2 The Red Queen**
Nelson, Herbert

**Red Sonja She-Devil With a Sword Vol. 1**
Oeming, Carey, Rubi

**Red Sonja She-Devil With a Sword Vol. 2: Arrowsmiths**
Oeming, Rubi, more

**Red Sonja She-Devil With a Sword Vol. 3: The Rise of Kulan Gath**
Oeming, Rubi, more

**Red Sonja She-Devil With a Sword Vol. 4: Animals & More**
Oeming, Homs, more

**Red Sonja She-Devil With a Sword Vol. 5: World On Fire**
Oeming, Reed, Homs

**Red Sonja She-Devil With a Sword Vol. 6: Death**
Marz, Ortega, Reed, more

**Red Sonja She-Devil With a Sword Vol. 7: Born Again**
Reed, Geovani

**Red Sonja She-Devil With a Sword Vol. 8: Blood Dynasty**
Reed, Geovani

**Red Sonja She-Devil With a Sword Vol. 9: War Season**
Trautmann, Geovani, Berkenkotter

**Red Sonja She-Devil With a Sword Omnibus Vol. 1**
Oeming, Carey, Rubi, more

**Red Sonja vs. Thulsa Doom Vol. 1**
David, Lieberman, Conrad

**Savage Red Sonja: Queen of the Frozen Wastes**
Cho, Murray, Homs

**Red Sonja: Travels**
Marz, Ortega, Thomas, more

**Sword of Red Sonja: Doom of the Gods (Red Sonja vs. Thulsa Doom 2)**
Lieberman, Antonio

**Red Sonja: Wrath of the Gods**
Lieberman, Geovani

**Red Sonja: Revenge of the Gods**
Lieberman, Sampere

**Savage Tales of Red Sonja**
Marz, Gage, Ortega, more

### VAMPIRELLA

**Vampirella Masters Series V Grant Morrison & Mark Mill**
Morrison, Millar, more

**Vampirella Masters Series V Warren Ellis**
Ellis, Conner Palmiotti, more

**Vampirella Masters Series V Mark Millar**
Millar, Mayhew

**Vampirella Masters Series V Visionaries**
Moore, Busiek, Loeb, more

**Vampirella Masters Series V Kurt Busiek**
Busiek, Sniegoski, LaChanc, mo

**Vampirella Masters Series V James Robinson**
Robinson, Jusko, more

**Vampirella Archives Vol 1**
Various

**Vampirella Archives Vol 2**
Various

**Vampirella Archives Vol 3**
Various

**Vampirella Archives Vol 4**
Various

**Vampirella Vol. 1 Crown of Worms**
Trautman, Reis, Geovani

**Vampirella Vol. 2 A Murder of Crows**
Trautman, Jerwa, Neves, more

**Vampirella And The Scarlet Legion**
Harris, Malaga

### MORE FROM GARTH ENNIS

**Dan Dare Omnibus**
Ennis, Erskine

**Garth Ennis' Battlefields Vol. 1: The Night Witches**
Ennis, Braun

**Garth Ennis' Battlefields Vol. 2: Dear Billy**
Ennis, Snejbjerg

**Garth Ennis' Battlefields Vol. 3: The Tankies**
Ennis, Ezquerra

**Garth Ennis' The Complete Battlefields Vol. 1**
Ennis, Braun, Snejbjerg, Ezquer

**Garth Ennis' Battlefields Vol. 4: Happy Valley**
Ennis, Holden

**Garth Ennis' Battlefields Vol.5: The Firefly and His Majesty**
Ennis, Ezquerra

**Garth Ennis' Battlefields Vol.6: Motherland**
Ennis, Braun

**Garth Ennis' The Complete Battlefields Vol. 2**
Ennis, Braun, Holden, Ezquerra

**Jennifer Blood Vol. 1: A Woman's Work Is Never Don**
Ennis, Batista, Baal, more

**Just A Pilgrim**
Ennis, Ezquerra

**Seven Brothers Omnibus**
Ennis, Woo, Kang, more

### ART BOOKS

**The Art of Howard Chaykin**

**The Art of Red Sonja**

**The Art of Vampirella**

**The Dynamite Art of Alex R**

**George Pérez, Storyteller**

**The Romita Legacy**